MW01279921

To:

_____

From:

_____

Date:

_____

Visit Christian Art Gifts website at www.christianartgifts.com.

Whispers of Hope

© 2013 Christian Art Gifts, RSA
        Christian Art Gifts Inc., IL, USA

First edition 2023

Devotions written by Stephan Joubert

Designed by Alyssa Montalto

Images used under license from Shutterstock.com

Scripture quotations marked NIV are taken from the Holy Bible,
New International Version® NIV®. Copyright © 1973, 1978, 1984,
2011 by Biblica, Inc.® Used by permission of Zondervan.
All rights reserved worldwide.

Scripture quotations marked (NLT) are taken from the *Holy Bible*,
New Living Translation, copyright ©1996, 2004, 2015 by Tyndale House
Foundation. Used by permission of Tyndale House Publishers,
Carol Stream, Illinois 60188. All rights reserved.

Scripture quotations marked THE MESSAGE are taken from *The Message*.
Copyright © 1993, 2002, 2018 by Eugene H. Peterson. Used by permission
of NavPress. All rights reserved. Represented by Tyndale House Publishers.

© All rights reserved. No part of this book may be reproduced
in any form without permission in writing from the publisher,
except in the case of brief quotations in critical articles or reviews.

ISBN 978-1-64272-925-2

Printed in China

28 27 26 25 24 23
10 9 8 7 6 5 4 3 2 1

WHISPERS
OF
Hope

January

New Year's Resolutions

There is a time for everything, and a
season for every activity under the heavens.
— ECCLESIASTES 3:1 NIV —

Once again, New Year's resolutions are being made everywhere. Well, I also have a couple of resolutions for the year that lies ahead, like making more time for silence in my life. God doesn't compete with all the noise in and around me. I realize that I have to hear Him on His terms, not mine in the New Year. That's why I actively plan to be still and quiet more often in the New Year in God's presence. I absolutely need to get to know the Lord better.

Another resolution: I don't want to send or answer any nasty e-mails or text messages this year. It's an unnecessary waste of energy to argue with those who believe that they know better or with those who are always the only correct ones. This year I also don't want to fret about frenzied drivers racing to save minutes of time while enduing hours of higher blood pressure.

Finally, I want to live this new year in front of me at "to-day-speed"—one day at a time for a full 365 days. I reckon that's just about fast enough.

A High Price

Bless—that's your job, to bless.
You'll be a blessing and also get a blessing.
— 1 PETER 3:9 THE MESSAGE —

Maybe you've heard of Maximilian Kolbe. He was a Franciscan priest who ended up in Auschwitz, the notorious German concentration camp, during World War II. One day a fellow prisoner from his block escaped. Now when someone escaped from Auschwitz, it was standard protocol that ten prisoners be chosen at random to be gruesomely killed. In short, you knew that if you escaped ten others would die in your place.

When Kolbe heard that one of the men who was randomly chosen to die had a wife and children, he immediately offered to take the man's place. Following two brutal weeks of torture, Kolbe finally died after being injected with a deadly acid. Kolbe's sacrifice always reminds me of Jesus' words that there's no greater love than when someone sacrifices his own life for his friends!

What do we ever sacrifice for each other? Which of the people around us have fuller and richer lives because of us? Who knows, maybe our faith is way too safe and boring. Maybe we are too much of a burden instead of a 24/7 blessing to others.

A Life of Their Own

May these words of my mouth and this meditation
of my heart be pleasing in your sight, Lord.

— PSALM 19:14 NIV —

Our words are alive. Just consider how powerful a run-of-the-mill phrase like "thank you" can be. Or a short sentence, like "I love you!" In the same way, sharp words can be very hurtful. Hard, loveless words are like gunshots. They wound people.

That's why the Bible instructs us to count our words before we let them loose on the world. By the way, this isn't merely good advice. God created us to be able to form second opinions. Our emotions are our first opinion formers. Researchers are of the opinion that our emotions are as much as a million times faster than our thoughts, which are our second opinion formers. When we literally count to three, we allow our thoughts to kick in. They can then eliminate the words that our emotions want to let loose prematurely.

We must think about our words before they leave our lips in the direction of other people's ears. Words that have already been spoken have a life of their own. The damage they inflict cannot be easily undone. Ask the Lord to dip your words in gold before they escape your mouth. Ask Him to turn your words into good medicine. Speak words of life and see what happens!

Put It Down

*Carry each other's burdens, and in this
way you will fulfill the law of Christ.*

— GALATIANS 6:2 NIV —

I once read a tale of two monks who went on a journey. At a river they encountered a woman who couldn't cross the fast-flowing water without help. The first monk refused to help her, since it was against their order's rules to touch a woman. The other monk immediately offered to help by carrying her on his shoulders across the river. Afterward, the rule-abiding monk went on for hours about his "shocking" breach of conduct. "I don't understand your unhappiness," the helpful monk eventually answered. "I put that woman down hours ago, but you're still carrying her around." How true! We don't get other people off our shoulders easily, especially not those who breach our own religious rules.

Stop your prejudiced opinions about others. You can't make your unasked-for religious views applicable to them. Only when you have the courage to establish an authentic relationship with them do you earn the right to talk to them about the Lord. Maybe today is the right time to put down your opinions about other people. Even better, place it on the shoulders of One stronger, Christ! Then you'll be able to carry the burdens of others much more easily.

Too Much Weight

Blessed are those who trust in the LORD,
and have made the LORD their hope and confidence.
— JEREMIAH 17:7 NLT —

"People say..." Isn't it remarkable how often you hear this? The opinions of "others" far too often determine what "we" or "I" think. Far too many churches and businesses are managed because of the opinions of others. Comments like "what would the church members say?" or "the opinions of our customers count the most!" are well-known expressions in these circles. People have to be kept happy at all costs otherwise they might withdraw their loyalty from us. But wait, do you really want to be a lifelong victim of other people's opinions? Do "they" have to keep you hostage? Is that really what the Lord expects of you? Should you work hard to win the favor of others, like some Christians think, or should you trust God to confirm your integrity in front of others in His own way?

If you constantly live for the approval of others, you're a victim. There's a better alternative. Strive only for God's approval. Put His kingdom first. Ensure that His approval motivates you. Try to receive the best compliment ever from the Lord one day: "Well done, good and faithful servant." Then you'll be free of "their opinions."

Disconnected from Christ

*Start children off on the way they should go,
and even when they are old they will not turn from it.*
— PROVERBS 22:6 NIV —

We're all accustomed to the stereotypes some people use when talking about the younger generation. I'm referring to expressions like, "the youth of today has completely lost their way." Older people far too easily accept that today's younger generation is a "lost generation." That's why a young guy recently caught me off-guard. After a youth service where I spoke, he told me that he's deeply concerned about older people.

I couldn't believe my ears. Normally these statements work the other way around. "What is it about older people that concerns you?" I asked. "I think their religion doesn't really bring peace to their hearts. They're disgruntled with their lives and blame it on others," he replied. "Be careful not to generalize," I said. "I know many elderly people whose lives are flooded with wisdom." In any case, it's wonderful that young people are also concerned about the older generation. Young and old people alike are branded as "difficult" far too easily, but it's not automatically true. Age is not the problem, discontented and disconnected people are. Every day we must choose to be a blessing to others. Otherwise we're living one day at a time in discontent. That's really not how God wants us to go through life.

The Speed of Light

*Teach us to number our days,
that we may gain a heart of wisdom.*
— PSALM 90:12 NIV —

Time is money. There's no time for lounging around and doing nothing. No wonder we have phrases like "time management" or "effective use of time." Nowadays we even need to learn how to save time to be effective! There you have it: We're time addicts! We constantly run around at the speed of light to every new demand in the hope that we'll save two or three minutes somewhere. If we do, we immediately forget about the "saved time" when we arrive anxious and tired at our destination.

No, we don't really save time. We just drive up our heart rate and heap loads of stress on our shoulders through our hectic daily pace of life. This is because we're chasing after wind and dust storms. The Lord doesn't intend for us to live like this. It's not part of His plan that we live at the speed of light every day. We were made for relationships. And we need time for these—time to stand still and time to take hands.

Well, do you ever have time for that? Do you have the courage to reduce your speed-of-light lifestyle to walking pace? Then you'll start experiencing God and others again.

Sensitivity

So be careful how you live. Don't live like fools,
but like those who are wise.
Make the most of every opportunity.
— EPHESIANS 5:15-16 NLT —

Sometimes I'm left dumbfounded at people's utter lack of sensitivity. Not long ago, a woman told me about a colleague whose brother had died at a young age. Then, someone too-holy-for-words sent him a text message to "comfort" him with the words of Proverbs 10:27 that says, "the years of the wicked are cut short." Proverbs does indeed say that, but it's not directly applicable, one-to-one, to each and every person who dies prematurely. Similarly, not every person who attains a ripe old age is enjoying God's favor (as some readers of the Ten Commandments might deduce!). We don't have any right to summarily condemn people who die young.

Indeed, the book of Proverbs was written to teach people how to discern between wisdom and folly. Proverbs definitely wasn't intended to be used by spiritual bullies intent on increasing other people's pain and suffering further through thoughtless text messages and other forms of Bible bashing. It's also not for people who say they need an instant answer for every possible crisis or heartache. Let's learn to handle God's Word with respect and care. Let's serve one another rather than injuring others with our knowledge of the Bible.

Ambassadors for Christ

*"Let your good deeds shine out for all to see,
so that everyone will praise your heavenly Father."*

— MATTHEW 5:16 NLT —

A church leader once shared how he and his wife showed up at a restaurant late one evening, a couple of minutes before closing time. The owner didn't want to serve them because the kitchen was about to close. The church leader caused a big ruckus and expressed his unhappiness with the poor service. The next morning his phone rang. It was the restaurant owner's wife. "Were you maybe at our restaurant last night?" she inquired. Then she added, "My husband, who doesn't attend church at all, keenly watches your messages on television. He says it looked like you at the restaurant last night, but he couldn't believe that you'd be so rude. I'm phoning just to make sure."

The church leader had to admit that it was indeed he who visited the restaurant. He apologized, but the restaurant owner said that he was now finished with Christianity for good. This story caused me to reflect deeply on my own behavior. I know I'm often an embarrassment to the Lord and to others rather than an effective ambassador. Sometimes I speak without thinking, and other times I'm abrupt, even unfriendly.

How about you? Are you a dependable ambassador?

Chasing Fear Away

"Have I not commanded you? Be strong and courageous.
Do not be terrified; do not be discouraged, for the
LORD your God will be with you wherever you go."

— JOSHUA 1:9 NIV —

Elie Wiesel, a Romanian-born Jewish American, Holocaust survivor, author of fifty-seven books, and Nobel Peace Prize winner, tells the story of his visit to a Jewish community during the reign of the old communistic regime in Moscow. During a religious feast, some of them openly danced in the streets. When asked why they were dancing, a woman answered: "All year I live in fear. But once a year, on this day, I refuse to be afraid. Then I'm a Jew and I dance in the streets!"

We should also learn how to dance. We live in times where fear is one of the dominant emotions for many of us. Tragic, or what!

Did you know that we're born with only two basic fears? The fear of loud noises and the fear of falling. Still, many adults now have hundreds of fears. That's why we need to learn anew how to celebrate, not just once a year but every day. Our identity is anchored in the Lord, who is infinitely bigger than the biggest of our fears. Jesus is our Lord. Thus, we can dance and sing, even with tears on our cheeks. We can be glad and call the bluff of every old or new fear that threatens us.

Promotion

"Do not store up for yourselves treasures on earth, where moths and vermin destroy, and where thieves break in and steal. But store up for yourselves treasures in heaven."

— MATTHEW 6:19–20 NIV —

For many people promotion means only one thing—*more stuff*! *More* money, *more* tangible benefits, *more* houses, *more* cars, *more* vacations, *more* status. For followers of Jesus, the word "promotion" should mean something completely different. It can't equate to more tangible things. Promotion should rather mean to grab every opportunity that the Lord offers you, sacrificing your valuable time and energy in His service.

The right type of promotion in God's service is to cast aside all the construction plans for your own little earthly kingdom and to exchange them for the privilege of being a daily blessing to other people. True promotion is to be part of the lifelong adventure of building God's kingdom. This yields dividends that have eternal value. Promotion in God's kingdom becomes visible when you spend *more* time at the Lord's feet; when you make *more* time for the poor and the lonely; when you do *more* kind things for others; and also when you worry *less* about yourself and your own temporary needs.

The Difference

*The LORD your God will bless you in all your
harvest and in all the work of your hands,
and your joy will be complete.*

— DEUTERONOMY 16:15 NIV —

There's a big difference between dreamers and doers. Doers live out their dreams, while dreamers constantly talk about how they will one day change the world. But it never gets beyond idle talk. The problem with most dreamers is their desire for control, predictability, and security. The Roman philosopher Tacitus said the desire for safety always stands in the way of the good intentions of those who merely dream of changing the world.

Doers are very different from dreamers. Doers never sleep through their dreams. They constantly search for the fastest and most effective routes between the vision that God placed in their hearts, and their hands and feet. Doers give body to their dreams. Their calling is to take God's people forward and closer to the manifestation of His vision. Therefore, doers are brave individuals who don't allow believers to fall into spiritual comfort zones. They're not interested in winning any spiritual popularity contests or in being the center of attention.

No, they fulfill their calling by empowering others to give wings to the vision that God placed in their hearts through His Spirit. So then, are you a dreamer or a doer?

Built for Relationships

Do nothing out of selfish ambition or vain conceit.
Rather, in humility value others above yourselves.

— PHILIPPIANS 2:3 NIV —

Genesis 2 tells us that there was trouble in the Garden of Eden, of all places. The reason: Adam was home alone and relationship hungry! He couldn't find a soul mate. God said this was not good, since man was not made to be alone.

All these "Rambo" figures that take on the world alone might be Hollywood's idea of success, but it's false. No human is an island. We're built for relationships. We long for God and other people. We want to cherish and love. Our hearts remain restless until we find rest in the arms of God.

From His side, God also yearns for a living relationship with everyone bearing His signature. We are His artwork— His personal property. We are the highlight of His beautiful creation. That's why He sent His Son to look for us when we were lost in the dark. When we wandered the farthest from Him, Jesus came, caught up with us, and accompanied us back to the Garden. By the way, there's still some space left in Paradise. Move back there immediately—back into the relationship where you belong!

Sharing

John answered them all, "I baptize you with water.
But One who is more powerful than I will come,
the straps of whose sandals I am not worthy to untie.
He will baptize you with the Holy Spirit and fire."

— LUKE 3:16 NIV —

John the Baptist's words to the soldiers, tax collectors, and poor—who asked him what they should do to live in right relationship with God—touches my heart immensely (Luke 3). No, he doesn't offer them some quick escape route to heaven. Neither does he offer them a safe bomb shelter to protect them from life's assaults. On the contrary, John brought heaven down to earth by saying that he who has two sets of clothing should give one set away to those who have less. Soldiers needed to learn to be happy with their pay, and tax collectors needed to stop making unfair profits.

John doesn't teach people who suffer to passively wait for help from elsewhere else. Even the poorest of the poor have something to share. This is an important biblical principle that we often overlook. The poor widow who gives her last couple of cents to God in Luke 21 is a good example of this. At that very moment when she gave everything she had, she became the latest spiritual millionaire. Our faith shines the brightest through the money and stuff we give away. Even the poorest among us can share something of ourselves with others.

In Remembrance

*"Truly I tell you, wherever the gospel is
preached throughout the world, what she has
done will also be told, in memory of her."*

— MARK 14:9 NIV —

This is how Jesus responded to the remarkable woman who poured a bottle of very expensive perfume over His head at a dinner in Bethany. It was more than a year's income for the average person in Palestine that she "wasted" on Jesus. But it was exactly the right kind of wasting! It was the right thing to do since Jesus was the recipient.

To pour out your life before the Lord—by giving your money, talents, time, and energy to Him in an overly generous way—might seem like a useless waste in the eyes of those around you. However, that's not the case when the Lord is the Recipient.

Learn from this woman that the wasting of earthly things is in order sometimes. Learn from the Lord's contemporary heroes who are doing such wasting in the proper way. Go and practice the art of over-the-top wastefulness in such a way that heaven and earth will start noticing. It's not too late.

Living Generously

You should remember the words of the Lord Jesus:
"It is more blessed to give than to receive."

— ACTS 20:35 NLT —

Paul's farewell speech to the church in Ephesus in Acts 20 on the island of Milete touches my heart over and over again. It should be one of the more well-known and popular texts in the church. Especially precious are the apostle's words that he worked hard to always have something to give to the poor. This verse belongs in the same category as John 3:16, the Lord's Prayer, and Psalm 23. Why? It's the heart of God, pure and simply expressed.

In these deep words of Paul, we encounter the true heart of the gospel in a nutshell, namely that we must always live generously. That's what the gospel is all about—giving, not receiving. And not storing up things just for ourselves. We don't work only for our own retirement package or the next luxury item on our never-ending shopping list. No, we also work hard to be able to care for those who are suffering. Our biggest investment in God's kingdom is to reach out every time we encounter someone who is less privileged than ourselves. So, how about a fresh re-appreciation of Acts 20:35 today, here and now?

Spiritual Finesse

*Start with GOD—the first step in learning
is bowing down to GOD; only fools thumb
their noses at such wisdom and learning.*

— PROVERBS 1:7 THE MESSAGE —

Some have it, others don't. I'm speaking about spiritual finesse. In the book of Proverbs it's called wisdom. Wisdom, the type that starts with reverence for God according to Proverbs 1:7, touches your daily life dramatically. This kind of wisdom is to know when to say your say and when to keep your mouth closed. It's to never storm blindly into any situation with an artificial quick fix. Wisdom makes you dare to do God's will but also mindful of the traps of folly.

Spiritual finesse is to know the difference between wisdom and folly and to apply that knowledge wisely. Where do you find this type of finesse? Listen afresh to Proverbs where it's taught that it all starts with a life of dedication to God. Wisdom is equal to full-time, day in and day out respect for the Lord. This type of wisdom is the reason why you can't help but treat other people with respect. Respect for God continually flows over into respect for other people.

Such a life filled to the brim with spiritual finesse causes you to read the "handle with care!" sticker on others every time and to respect it!

Danger

"My grace is enough; it's all you need."
— 2 CORINTHIANS 12:9 THE MESSAGE —

Experts say that one of the biggest dangers staring modern society in the face is our endless consumer mentality. Too many people are like bottomless pits who need to satisfy one desire after the other, here and now. Tomorrow is way too late because tomorrow there's already a new CD, cell phone, car, or set of clothes that must be acquired. How true was this in the festive season just passed? It was barely over and people descended on every possible sale like vultures. Our closets are taking strain. Our houses are stacked, and still the end is not in sight!

How tragic that the abundance of possessions has become the yardstick for measuring success in our day. But the question still remains: When is enough finally enough? One can walk around in only one set of clothes at a time and drive around in only one car at a time. Are the lives of consumers truly filled with peace when they have all the right things to their name? No, because I suspect they are still drinking at the wrong well. Living water is found elsewhere—at Jesus' well of life. Only His water gives life eternally.

Junk In, Junk Out!

Guard your heart above all else,
for it determines the course of your life.

— PROVERBS 4:23 NLT —

You are what you watch! Watching television isn't always just an innocent time killer. It forms your thoughts. It shapes your humanity without you even realizing it. No wonder television addiction is highlighted by social researchers as one of the biggest inhibitors of our psychological health and relational adaptability. It changes far too many good people into lazy couch potatoes and robs them of their creative thoughts and active participation in the rest of life. TV time is often wasted time.

Choose carefully what you watch. Watch with discernment. No, you don't have to be against everything and everyone on the tube. It definitely won't help to throw out the baby with the bathwater. There are still valuable lessons to be learned from movies, stories, and other programs. Let your faith in Jesus Christ be the filter through which you watch television. Let your core values of respect, caring, and integrity take new lessons from everything you watch. Share this with others. Use the lessons you learn as conversation points to teach people to watch differently, to think differently, and to live differently. Let television work for you rather than the other way around.

Being Thankful

*Since we are receiving a kingdom that is unshakable,
let us be thankful and please God by
worshiping Him with holy fear and awe.*

— HEBREWS 12:28 NLT —

You're not a victim of your emotions. You can be thankful every day. You can have an "attitude of gratitude" lifestyle. How? Here are a few pointers:

Choose to live every day proactively in the Lord's name, never merely reactively. Refuse to react to everyone and everything. You don't have to have an opinion about everything under the sun.

Don't get attached to strangers in a dysfunctional manner. Don't allow bad drivers or criminals to fill you with anger. Detach yourself emotionally from negative people. Don't allow them to pull you down. Don't seek revenge. God has freed you from "an eye for an eye" and "a tooth for a tooth" games long ago. Don't play along.

Show thankfulness in little ways to every person you encounter today. Be quick to thank them. Give suitable compliments often. Pray with someone regularly.

Count the blessings in your life today and thank God willfully for these. Live today's portion of life in a rhythm of thankfulness, not a "shuffle of critique."

From Chaos to Calm

God is our refuge and strength,
an ever-present help in trouble.
— PSALM 46:1 NIV —

In one moment, even the stormiest seas can become calm. In the blink of an eye, huge storms can abate. The same can also happen in your life. Chaos can instantaneously make room for peace. Noise can be replaced by soft silence in an instant. Unrest can be chased away by heavenly peace. How? Just realize afresh that the Lord is God. He alone! Believe the Word that the Lord is with you right there in the storm. Believe the Word that He is the only hiding place in time of danger.

Subside. Calm down. Come to rest. Let your heart become still and calm. Let your turbulent mood find a hiding place at the Lord's feet. Look up. Notice the Lord, high over nations and far above the dead gods of this world. See Him in faith. Bow gently before Him in the name of Jesus. Kneel in worship.

Know that the Lord is the Almighty. He has all power in His hands. He alone is Lord, only He. He is your only hope, your only Savior. Notice Him, and come to rest in His presence. Look up to Him and experience His heavenly peace.

God's Dreams

"Before I formed you in the womb I knew you."
— JEREMIAH 1:5 NIV —

God dreams, and He dreams big. He dreams about a new world, where His will prevails. He dreams about a society where hate comes second and injustice loses. He dreams about the poor having enough food to eat and about lonely people being cared for. He dreams about people who live together safely and who love one another. He dreams about His kingdom spreading across the earth like a runaway bushfire and billions of people bowing before Jesus. He dreams of people who discover His treasure in the field, as Jesus tells us in Matthew 13, and then surrender everything to get hold of it.

God dreams new dreams. Here's the good news: you have a pertinent place in God's dreams. He noticed you when He dreamed big about people and His creation. He wants to use you to make His dreams a reality. You should report for duty at once. He'll take care of the rest. The Lord will cause streams of living water to flow through you. He'll use you to touch the lives of those around you. He will give His dreams wings in and through your life. So, what are you waiting for?

Unconditional Love

What marvelous love the Father has extended to us! Just look at it—we're called children of God!

— 1 JOHN 3:1 THE MESSAGE —

I'm sold out on Philip Yancey's definition of grace. In his book *What's So Amazing about Grace?* he says there is nothing we can do to make God love us less, and there is nothing we can do to make God love us more. He loves us regardless. God loves us on Christ's behalf. He loves us despite ourselves, not because of who and what we are. God's amazing love is not performance driven; it is always relationship based. Listen again: He doesn't look at who does the most for Him and then loves those people more. He doesn't love us more when we are obedient and less when we fail.

God is our Father. That's why His love for us is a constant reality. It comes without a performance clause that's flourishing everywhere in the business world. Grace is nothing more than God's free care for us. Grace is a godly verb. It says that Jesus is on our heels with a handful of fresh goodness. That's why grace is also a rest word for you and me. Now then, stop running. Go and rest in God's arms. He'll do the rest. He loves you.

A New Identity

You are all one in Christ Jesus.
— GALATIANS 3:28 NLT —

Someone I know bought a new house a couple of years ago. While he was working in his new garden, a neighbor came over with some tea. She asked, "Is the master of the house here?" He naughtily replied that the master would only be home that evening. She inquired at the front door again that evening. When he opened the door, she said, "Oh, I see you are the butler, too!" After he corrected her in a friendly way, they became really good neighbors.

Unfortunately, such misunderstandings and faulty perceptions are daily realities. Luckily, Paul teaches in Ephesians 2 that Christ permanently demolished the wall of separation between Jew and non-Jew. There is now a new generation of people who follow Jesus and who are blind to man-defined differences such as nationality, ethnicity, gender, or social status. The apostle reiterates this point in Galatians 3:28. As followers of Jesus, we don't need to erect "safety barriers" around us to protect our identity. Our identity is seated in Christ.

Our lives are now all about Him in whom we find our safety and peace—only about Him! That's why the differences between ourselves and others need not threaten us at all.

Life in Abundance

Don't copy the behavior and customs of this world,
but let God transform you into a new person by changing
the way you think. Then you will learn to know God's
will for you, which is good and pleasing and perfect.

— ROMANS 12:2 NLT —

Live abundantly! Live generously. For a change, live on "abundance hill" instead of in "shortage valley." How? Give away, that's how! Give generously, give excessively, and give constantly. What should you give away? No, the question is not what, but who. Give yourself. As a rule, don't primarily give away your money or your valuable time. Give of yourself. The Lord asks your whole life. He asks all your commitment, time, and energy. Give yourself generously and profusely to Him. Let your life be God's full-time temple! Don't hold back.

Also give yourself to others. Be present with your whole heart to everyone in whose presence you find yourself each day, and not only with your head. Also not with a few crumbles of leftover time that you found somewhere deep in your schedule. Give your heart to every person that the Lord wants you to serve today. Then you're living abundantly. Then your heart is truly free. Then you realize how the treasure chambers of heaven open up.

Opinions

Your words are my joy and my heart's delight.
— JEREMIAH 15:16 NLT —

"Everyone is entitled to an opinion," someone says. "And to their own idea of the truth," he adds. "Yes, surely, but does that mean that all opinions are equal?" I wanted to know. Danger lights start flashing when every thinkable opinion is considered to be valid. Of course we can look at life in many different ways, but there is also right and wrong. This applies to everything from traffic rules to the most basic questions about God and life.

My compass for truth is the Bible. It is the life book for everyone who wants to live in tune with God's will. No, the Bible is not a book to hurt others with. Nor is it a book of verses from which a few favorite texts can be drawn arbitrarily and the rest forgotten. It is also not a scientific handbook by which today's scientists need to be proven right or wrong.

When the Bible is read correctly, it becomes medicine. The Bible is a compass pointing directly to Christ. When I read it book by book and correctly understand the context within which it was written, the Bible shapes my conscience and points my heart in the right direction.

Honesty

An honest witness tells the truth.

— PROVERBS 12:17 NLT —

I wonder if people also crack jokes in the company of dietitians, like "Now we must be careful what we eat, because there's a dietitian present"? Strangely, some people feel that they need to make funny remarks in the presence of spiritual leaders, such as, "We should watch what we say now, because the pastor is here." Masters of ceremony at weddings often fall into this trap.

Once at a wedding the MC even came and apologized to me after he let loose some rough jokes on the crowd. "You are at the wrong address," I answered him. "I think you need the Lord's forgiveness more than mine right now."

That's all I could think of saying at that moment. Tactful? Maybe not quite. However, for a while now I don't sing in that choir of religious folks who are burdened by other people's behavior in secret and don't do anything about it in public. I don't want to be as tactful as some people who don't do anything about what's wrong except be worried about it. That's why I opt for honesty, even though it sometimes can be costly.

A Grandfather in Heaven

*I am convinced that neither death nor life,
neither angels nor demons, neither the
present nor the future, nor any powers, neither
height nor depth, nor anything else in all creation,
will be able to separate us from the love of God.*

— ROMANS 8:38–39 NIV —

In his phenomenal book *The Problem of Pain,* the well-known theologian and Christian thinker, C. S. Lewis, asks if the world really wants a father in heaven. He thinks many people rather want a heavenly grandfather. They want a forgetful figure who lost touch with reality and whose only desire is for everyone to have a good time here on earth. These words of Lewis give expression to many people's naïve idea of a universal deity that plays heavenly nanny and constantly needs to fulfill our requirements and all our desires. For the rest, it is better that He stays out of humanity's way. Obviously, this is not a reliable, biblical view of God.

God is not the one who needs to ensure that my life is a constant ball. Sometimes, pain and suffering is exactly the megaphone the Lord uses to reach a deaf world, as C. S. Lewis puts it. God's presence is definitely not equal to the absence of hurt and hardship. That's humanity's big mistake about God. Even clergy fall into this trap. That's why rediscovering the words of Romans 8 is so important today—God is always near, even in prosperity and in pain.

While We Are Sleeping

In peace I will lie down and sleep,
*for you alone, L**ORD**, make me dwell in safety.*
— PSALM 4:8 NIV —

Your faith does not only happen when you're awake. Put differently, your trust in God ought to have a direct influence on how you sleep every night. The psalmist tells us in Psalm 3 that he lies down in peace and falls asleep instantly, even when a thousand people are storming toward him. He knows his life is permanently in God's hands, even when he closes his eyes at night. He knows God does not sleep, as Psalm 121 tells us. God is never off duty—never! He is awake 24/7 and 365 days of the year.

When you and I are in dreamland, God is wide awake. That's why we can trust Him with our lives and those of our loved ones when we close our tired eyes at night. Even our dreams should bring us closer to God, says the well-known Christian song.

We are always in the hands of the living Lord. Therefore, we can lie down in peace, even though the land is on fire. We can even trust God, in the words of Psalm 127:3, to give us what we need while we are sleeping every single night!

God Is in Control

We know that God causes everything to work together for the good of those who love God and are called according to His purpose for them.

— ROMANS 8:28 NLT —

A few years ago, Lloyd's Bank of London tried to determine what happens to all the paperclips in their bank. Of the approximate 100,000 in use, close to 25,000 ended up in vacuum cleaners or were thrown away; 14,163 were broken from excessive bending during telephone conversations; 4,434 were used for scratching ears or cleaning teeth; and only 20,286 were used as paperclips. In short, even the simplest of items—like paperclips invented by Samuel B. Fay in 1867—are used in ways other than intended.

It seems to me that if we can't even control the use of paperclips, we will be far less likely to be able to control each other or the flow of life. Maybe it was never our calling to do so. The secret of life is simply to love God and each other. And to find daily joy in simplicity, as Ecclesiastes teaches us. That's why God's invitation to us is to eat our food with pleasure and create joy before God with daily portions of simplicity. When we stop trying to control everyone and start trusting God to provide for us in His way, we make joy a welcome expectation in our lives.

Ingredients of Life

We know that God causes everything to work together for the good of those who love God.

ROMANS 8:28 NLT

Have you ever eaten raw flour? What about uncooked eggs? I'm sure you've had a taste of pure sugar before. On their own, these foods are almost impossible to eat, let alone stomach. Yet in combination with other ingredients, in the correct amount, and in the proper order, they come together to make cake—something so enjoyable that it is a centerpiece of most major celebrations.

In your life, God will give you experiences that you will not be able to stomach. On their own, they will be hard to swallow and may even make you feel sick. Even the thought of having to experience them will make your mouth dry and gut churn. But as this passage says, God causes everything to work together for your good. In their right time, correct amount, and mixed together, the raw ingredients of your life will produce something beautiful that will be worthy of praise to God. In Christ, no difficult thing in your life is wasted. God will use it all. Let this be a new reason to celebrate God today!

February

Grace and Forgiveness

Make a clean break with all cutting, backbiting,
profane talk. Be gentle with one another,
sensitive. Forgive one another as quickly and
thoroughly as God in Christ forgave you.

— EPHESIANS 4:31-32 THE MESSAGE —

The guilty party in an illegal money-making scheme was caught and thrown into jail. Everyone in the local community, where this fraudster was also a well-respected leading figure, was deeply shocked. Many of them lost their life savings by investing in this man's money-making scheme. Shortly afterward, the local priest preached a sermon where he praised God that justice was done and that this man was behind bars. He seriously prayed that the church members would be repaid their losses.

When a congregation member who also lost everything suggested that they all visit the fraudster in jail and pray for him, everyone was shocked. "We are not ready for such action yet. Our people got hurt too badly," was the official reply. The man decided to go alone. In jail, he knelt next to the fraudster who had robbed him. Together they prayed for grace and forgiveness. That day the Lord's grace was visible in the jail. Christ showed up there as Savior. Thereafter, these two started a wonderful prison ministry. And the religious townspeople? Well, they remained bitter.

Machine Versus Organism

You must grow in the grace and knowledge
of our Lord and Savior Jesus Christ.
All glory to Him, both now and forever! Amen.

— 2 PETER 3:18 NLT —

There's a very important difference between a machine and a living organism. Machines are impressive, but machines can't grow. Machines become more powerful but never more alive. Machines are clones of one another. They work exactly the same. Unfortunately, some people think and live like machines, even in the church. You soon realize when someone has a machine-like approach, they stack everyone in the same boring boxes. They expect everyone to talk, think, and act the same.

We need to rediscover a sense of the beautiful and unique ways in which God deals with each of us. We are not living machines. Each of us is precious, growing, and constantly changing. The Lord is busy—at his own tempo and with endless heavenly wisdom—shaping everyone who believes in Christ into His image. Let's refuse to go through life in a clinical way, without emotion—like machines. Let's take up our places in the Lord's large earthly vineyard where a unique grace-spot is reserved for each of us. With Him there's more than enough space, grace, food, and water for everyone. He offers exactly the right type of growth-power for every one of us.

Jesus—The New Hobby?

Humility is the fear of the LORD;
its wages are riches and honor and life.

— PROVERBS 22:4 NIV —

Jesus has become a hobby for far too many people. Whenever they show up at His "place" on Sundays, He must entertain them with good sermons and good worship music. Sadly, Jesus must make people feel good all the time. That is His job description according to many. Apparently He is there to serve the selfish needs of people. Well, Jesus is not for sale, like a toy on the shelf of any store. You do not play around with Him and decide at your own leisure when and how you will allow Him into your life. He is the Son of God. He is the Messiah, not little Jesus, the meek and mild toy for those bored, selfish, egotistic, me-myself-and-I "Christian" types.

Read the stern warnings in Jesus' own words before you decide to walk with Him: death, rejection, disappointment, a cross, far more questions than answers, suffering, joy, a strange happiness, true service—these experiences will become your companions on the road with Jesus. He will lead you on new routes. He will also let you discover old and new treasures in his Father's house that will fill you with a strange new joy but on His terms alone.

Giving

But when He, the Spirit of truth, comes,
He will guide you into all the truth.

— JOHN 16:13 NIV —

"I give to my church." Have you ever said these words to beggars or those people who collect money on the street for welfare organizations? May I ask an uncomfortable question? Is your responsibility suddenly dealt with because you make a monthly contribution at your congregation? Is the reach of your calling inside God's kingdom only as far as the boundaries of your local church? Does your monthly contribution set you free from the responsibility to help people that appear unexpectedly on your radar?

Have you ever considered that the first and last line of relief is not only your local church but also you yourself? Did you forget that helping the poor is like making a loan to God, as the book of Proverbs teaches? You are a full-time, daily representative of Christ. That's why it is not right to say you only make contributions at your local church. Open yourself to be where God asks you to be. Be His full-time 911 relief number. No, you can't help everyone. But be sensitive to the guidance of the Spirit. Give extravagantly when He calls on you! Give as a sacrifice!

Dissatisfaction

*May these words of my mouth and this
meditation of my heart be pleasing in your sight, Lord.*
— PSALM 19:14 NIV —

People's nerves are at breaking point nowadays. At least, so it seems to me. Recently, when cash registers at a certain shop were not functioning, and that on the first Saturday of the month, there were many unhappy faces. The poor personnel got much attention from some sharp tongues. When my wife remarked to the lady behind the cash register that it can't be nice to constantly be spoken to in such a harsh way, she was in tears on the spot.

I know I am the last one to speak, but we seriously need to stop finding fault with everything and constantly complain about bad service. We criticize way too much and too easily. Our faith needs to be felt in the way that we drive our cars, treat our housekeepers, or speak to cashiers.

Our smallest deeds tell way more about ourselves than we will ever realize. And also about our relationship with God! Coincidentally, it is in these simple matters that the sincerity of our faith is truly tested. What does it help that we are faithful in all the big things but are found wanting in the smaller matters?

Unremarkable

The LORD has done it this very day;
let us rejoice today and be glad.

— PSALM 118:24 NIV —

"My life is completely unremarkable," someone told me recently. "Bleak days, bleak clothes, bleak happenings— that's more or less the story of my life," she concluded. Ouch! I felt so sorry for her. She sounded so discouraged and helpless. How many bleak days are slipping lifelessly through the fingers of thousands of people every single day? Maybe that is why Shirley Valentine says in the great movie of the same name: "I got lost in unused time." Don't let this happen to you.

Do what Paul suggests to the Ephesians: Buy out the time! Take the best out of every day. Let every day count. After all, you only have one day to live at a time.

Declare today a feast and invite a friend to celebrate it with you. Serve a feast to someone less privileged. Carry the burden of someone who's struggling for an extra mile. Memorize your favorite chapter of the Bible, and go and tell it cheerfully to someone else. Don't get caught up in the unremarkable. Not today. It's going to steal your soul. It's going to break you down. It's your choice!

Bigger and Better

Cast your cares on the LORD
and He will sustain you.

— PSALM 55:22 NIV —

In *Prince Caspian*, the fourth book in the popular Narnia series of the larger-than-life Christian author, C. S. Lewis, there is an encounter between Aslan the Lion (who resembles Christ) and one of the little girls. After seeing him again, she tells him that he is bigger. To this Aslan replies, "That is because you are older, little one." "But aren't you bigger?" she asks him. Then he replies, "I am not. But every year you grow, you will find me bigger."

That is precisely what happens on the Lord's journey. He grows bigger and bigger in our eyes as we begin to grow in our faith. Of course He is the Almighty God, the One who transcends time and eternity. He *is* big. He *is* the Lord, whether people grasp that or not. God is not dependent on our recognition, knowledge, or acceptance.

Still, the more we learn to walk close to Christ, the more we see the Lord's glory. Then our problems and worries shrink. Do you know something of this reversed growth journey? The bigger the Lord grows in your life, the more all your cares dissipate.

Integrity

"When you pray, go into your room, close the door and pray to your Father, who is unseen. Then your Father, who sees what is done in secret, will reward you."

— MATTHEW 6:6 NIV —

Integrity is a verb; it happens. Integrity is not automatically the same as religious deeds. In Matthew 6:1-18, Jesus says that religion can easily be practiced without integrity. Deeds like prayer, fasting, and helping the poor can be misused to earn respect in the eyes of others. Therefore, followers of Jesus should deliberately choose not to do things merely to be seen by others. God's approval matters most to them. They choose to live outside of the spotlight, not on the *stage* of life.

Integrity happens, even if no one else knows about it. You don't have to give big testimonies or enjoy favor in the eyes of everyone before you start having integrity. Integrity is first and foremost about your deep, enduring love for the Lord. Integrity shows in your genuineness and character in the eyes of the living God. Integrity also happens in all those critical choices that you make daily that no one knows about. Choices like whether you will look at filth on the Internet, whether you will help a poor person without making a scene about it, or whether you will pack away your prejudices about others that irritate you again and again. The choices you make in such instances reveal whether you have integrity or not.

Prayer

Rejoice always, pray continually,
give thanks in all circumstances;
for this is God's will for you in Christ Jesus.

— 1 THESSALONIANS 5:16-18 NIV —

Father of all grace and goodness,
In the name of Christ I rest at Your feet
In still reverence I look up at You
Your greatness is far too big for me to comprehend
Your goodness is too overwhelming to understand
But the little that I do grasp of You makes me joyful
It causes me to leave myself and my loved ones
in Your care today
Holy God, Your approval really counts most of all
Your love is all that matters
That's why Your praise is all that's on my lips today
And why my life wants to sing Your praise
Teach me to serve You well
Lord please be merciful; Lord be close
Let Your light shine everywhere
Let Your wisdom be our wisdom
In Jesus' name,

Amen.

Life in CAPITAL LETTERS

*Live a life filled with love, following the example
of Christ. He loved us and offered Himself
as a sacrifice for us, a pleasing aroma to God.*

— EPHESIANS 5:2 NLT —

Martin Luther King Jr. once said that even if you have a lowly job, you should do it with the same commitment and enthusiasm that Michelangelo relied on when he was sculpting his great works or that Mozart used in composing his genial music. That's also what Paul meant when he wrote in Colossians 3 that everything we do and say should glorify God. Put another way, the Lord's name should preside in CAPITAL LETTERS over every word we speak and everything we do. Like a flashing billboard, our lives should reflect God's splendor and importance.

How do you live your life in the right CAPITAL LETTERS? Well, you invite God humbly to be the Guest of Honor in your life every day. Ensure that He's the Guest of Honor in every conversation you have. Then all your words will be carefully chosen, tasteful, and uplifting. Ensure that the Lord is the witness to everything you do. Then your work will be done for His glory alone and not primarily for your boss or company. Then you'll do your work with pride, thoroughness, and commitment. Your light will shine for Christ in new ways.

Trust God

Trust in the LORD with all your heart; do not depend
on your own understanding. Seek His will in all
you do, and He will show you which path to take.

— PROVERBS 3:5-6 NLT —

It's not uncommon for us to be overly protective of those who are close to us. As parents we want to protect our kids from the rough edges of life. We also like to go the extra mile for our close family and friends. However, we can't always be physically there for each other. And it's surely not always the wisest thing on earth to try and keep our loved ones away from the adventures of life, even though life is full of dangers, challenges, and surprises. Sadly, life doesn't happen on some cloud, but right here in the real world fraught with danger. This side of the grave, life isn't perfect.

Maybe our calling is to pray for those we love while they are living in the danger zones of life, rather than to keep them hidden. We should rather keep their names in front of our heavenly Father.

We should trust God with their lives and pray that He keeps them safe and on the right path. We need to trust God to guide us and our loved ones in life *and* death.

Depreciating with Age

Therefore we do not lose heart.
Though outwardly we are wasting away,
yet inwardly we are being renewed day by day.

— 2 CORINTHIANS 4:16 NIV —

Depreciation is a problem that affects most items in our homes. At some time or another, the value of all earthly possessions decreases—sometimes so much that they become completely worthless. Take something like a new car. The moment you drive out of the dealer's showroom, its value plummets by thousands of dollars! Equally sad is that people are also the victims of depreciation. The older we get, the less consumer value we have to society around us.

The same does not apply to God. The Bible teaches us that the exact opposite happens in His presence. Paul says in 2 Corinthians that even as our bodies are wasting away, inwardly we are being renewed day by day. Followers of Jesus are on an upward-sloping growth curve. Because God is busy with an appreciation exercise in us, our value and quality increases continually. Day by day we grow substantially in wisdom and spiritual knowledge. Above all, we move closer to our wonderful, final destination. Therefore, we can and must live with joy. Even when we feel lonely or rejected, we are valuable in the hands of God. Our worth increases before Him. Appreciation is our new password.

Living with Purpose

I have fought the good fight,
I have finished the race,
and I have remained faithful.

— 2 TIMOTHY 4:7 NLT —

Many years ago, good friends of mine involved their elderly friend Ernie in the youth ministry of their church. Ernie stayed involved until his death in his nineties. Ernie's work at the youth ministry was to pack the dishwasher every Wednesday evening after they served a great feast to the youngsters.

One day Ernie told my friends that he asked the Lord the previous night to take him home. At this stage he was deaf in both ears and could no longer bear the deep longing for his late wife. But then he thought of all the young people that he served and wondered who would pack and unpack the dishwasher after they spent time together each week. Right there Ernie chose to carry on living with a new vigor. He did exactly that until the end of his life. Ernie knew that once the race was over, Jesus would be waiting for him with the crown of righteousness in His hand (vv. 7-8). That's why he couldn't stop living or stop running before the race was over. Just like Ernie, we are called by God to live with purpose, no matter how old or young we are.

The Hairs on Your Head

*"Even the very hairs of
your head are all numbered."*

— MATTHEW 10:30 NIV —

Those guys who shave their heads, and those of us whose hair is getting less and less by the day, are making things easy for God. There's far less hair left on our heads to count! On a more serious note, Jesus says in Matthew that God is so close to us that He even numbers the hairs on our heads. He knows how many of those hairs fall out every day. If I can remember correctly, I read somewhere that a normal person loses on average about 125 per day. None of them escapes heaven's attention.

Why do we receive such special attention? The answer's simple: As followers of Jesus, we are God's most precious earthly assets. We are His handiwork. We are His permanent property. That's why the Lord carries us around in His hand every day, as Jesus tells us in John 10:28-30. Absolutely nothing that happens in our lives ever escapes His attention. He hears every prayer that passes from our lips in the name of His Son. He knows of every step that we take. He is in attendance at every conversation that we have. The Lord is involved in the detail of all that we do. He that numbers the hairs on our heads is in our vicinity again today.

Memory Loss

The LORD is compassionate and merciful,
slow to get angry and filled with unfailing love.
— PSALM 103:8 NLT —

Do you ever close that little black book in which you carefully record other people's mistakes and shortcomings? Do you go to bed angry night after night? Well, here's a newsflash if you struggle with amnesia regarding other people's misdemeanors: God chooses not to remember. He gladly forgets people's sins, shortcomings, failures, wrong deeds, defects, and factory faults. He doesn't hold His children's wrongs against them; He doesn't remember them anymore. Even better, He forgets every time, over and over again. For whom does He do this? Well, for everyone that knocks on His door in the name of Jesus.

God is forgetful when it comes to those things that people bring to Him in remorse. The reason? The cross of Calvary is the permanent heavenly eraser in His hand. Grace says in five life-changing letters that God is on our side. It says that He fully loves us no matter how deep and far we have fallen. Grace says that God starts over time and again in our lives. He forgives and forgets. He closes old books forever.

A Spectator Sport

"I have come that they may have life,
and have it to the full."

— JOHN 10:10 NIV —

Bleachers are wonderful places. From there, you can shout anything from praise to criticism. You can encourage the players on the field, or you can write them off. But best of all—after the match, you can go home untouched. All that your loyalty costs is a tired voice and a glad or not-so-glad heart, depending on the outcome.

Spectators are normally friendly, as long as their team is winning. But, when their team is losing, they become critical. Therefore, the only guys making a real difference are the players on the field. For them, the match is far more than a time killer for a few hours every week. They make huge sacrifices. They give their hearts and bodies for their sport.

We must decide once and for all whether we're players or spectators on the playing field of faith. God doesn't want us to consider our faith as a spectator sport. The Lord asks that we turn our playing field into His territory. We don't know whether we'll get another playing opportunity tomorrow. But, at least we've received today as a gift from heaven. Therefore, we can't dare to be spectators on some church bleachers. Let's play with full commitment on the Lord's playing field, according to His instructions.

No Safe Bid

*God called you to do good, even if it means suffering,
just as Christ suffered for you. He is your example,
and you must follow in His steps.*

— 1 PETER 2:21 NLT —

Just listen to those wishes we express at the beginning of the new year or on someone's birthday. Such wishes are normally "safe." They teem with words like happiness, health, and prosperity. It's fine to express a wish that good things will happen to another person on their journey, but are these the only good things in life? Is it only in prosperity that your faith grows? Is life only about green pastures and still waters? Or isn't the deep, dark valley of Psalm 23 maybe one of God's favorite places of growth?

What about a daring challenge today? One like provocateur and author Erwin McManus signs in his books: "Risk everything!" Isn't that exactly what we need sometimes in our faith? Even more, is faith as such not a constant challenge? Isn't it the chance of a lifetime to walk with the living God? Faith asks for courage in the midst of disbelief, selfishness and opposition. As Paul tells us in Romans 8, faith asks that we must carry on hoping despite all hopelessness. It asks for boldness to walk on God's heels when you'd rather be going off in your own direction.

Unfashionable

*We are being transformed into
His image with ever-increasing glory,
which comes from the Lord, who is the Spirit.*

— 2 CORINTHIANS 3:18 NIV —

"You have to take me just as I am," a difficult church member told me once. "Why?" I asked. "Well, that's just how it is since I'm not the one that's going to change," he replied. "No, you're wrong," I said. Second Corinthians 3:18 teaches us that God's Spirit transforms us into the likeness of Christ with ever-increasing glory. We are definitely not lifelong victims of ourselves, our education, or circumstances. We don't have the luxury of staying as we are for the rest of our lives. Christ gives us the grace *and* the privilege to change and grow.

Too many people around us are victims of this member's "I can't change" syndrome. That's why negative issues such as our deep-rooted prejudices toward each other still run strong, despite our "deep religiosity." Does this happen because we believe we have the right to think like we always did? Does it happen because in church we often only speak about faith or moral sins while dodging questions about how we need to treat each other across cultural and racial divides? Or maybe because we ourselves are such bad examples of true transformation in this area? Listen, we can change. No. God can change us, and He will!

Danger Zone

"I have told you these things, so that in Me you
may have peace. In this world you will have trouble.
But take heart! I have overcome the world."

— JOHN 16:33 NIV —

Some believers are caught up between the church and the world. They prefer to spend more time in what they consider God's exclusive terrain, the world of the church. There they feel safe. There God's Word resounds, and there He is praised. The "real world" outside the church is dangerous and unpredictable for those who prefer the safety and predictability of religious bomb shelters. No wonder they keenly use texts such as 2 Corinthians 6:14-7:1 as their motivation to stay clear of the "sinful world."

Does Paul mean that we should build the walls of our religious shelters thicker and wider when bad things happen around us? Should we see the world as a place of enmity where "we" take a stand against "them"? Should we withdraw ourselves from the world and only be busy with "spiritual" things? Should others first become exactly like us before we make space for them in our midst? I don't think so. Paul didn't mean that we as followers of Jesus should flee or withdraw to religious bomb shelters. What he meant in 2 Corinthians 6 is that our lifestyle should be radically different.

The Harbor or the Storm?

*I know the LORD is always with me. I will
not be shaken, for He is right beside me.*
— PSALM 16:8 NLT —

Think with me about the following question: Where do you discern God's will the clearest—in the harbor or in the storm? Let me explain: with the harbor I mean the well-known, religious terrain among fellow believers in church or Bible studies. The storm represents the everyday world with its unpredictability, dangers, unbelievers, and challenges. Listen to that question again: Where do you discern God's will the clearest—in the harbor or in the storm?

Let me make it easier. Think about Jesus' behavior on earth. Now, where did He spend most of His time—in religious harbors, or in dangerous storms? Was Jesus more often among the religious or more often among the doubters, sinners, outcast, strangers, and losers? I think you know the answer—obviously Jesus spent more time amongst the non-religious! Why? Because He came specifically for those people, as He says in Mark 1.

If it's true that Jesus spent more time in the storms than in the "safe harbors," where should we then spend most of our time? In the storm, of course. Now why are we always trying to discern God's will in spiritual harbors? Let's all get back to stormy waters.

Hindering God's Work

Be strong and do not give up,
for your work will be rewarded.

— 2 CHRONICLES 15:7 NIV —

I often think of a pastor who once told me that God works when we get out of the way. That's why he spends his time practicing how to get out of God's way. Wise words! I know that I sometimes stand squarely in the way of the Lord's work. I often speak without being asked for my opinion. At other times, there are no brakes to my eagerness to work. Mistake!

It seems like the best way to get out of the way is to discover God's heavenly rhythms. Sometimes He's in a hurry. Then we don't have the luxury of sitting still and waiting, like when Lot and his family had to flee to escape the destruction of Sodom.

At other times, God seems to have years of patience. Just ask Abraham. At the age of seventy-five, God asked him to move. But God only fulfilled His promise of a child twenty-five years later (Gen. 12-17). The required method for Lot and Abraham, and their families, was to know at what speed they were journeying with God. Sadly, they failed. Lot's wife looked back and paid a dear price. Sarah and Abraham twice laughed at the Lord. Learn from them and set your pace to God's!

Teaching Stones to Talk

*This hope will not lead to disappointment. For we
know how dearly God loves us, because He has given
us the Holy Spirit to fill our hearts with His love.*

— ROMANS 5:5 NLT —

Can stones talk? Yes. When? When humanity starts silencing God. That's what Jesus says when the religious leaders try to silence those who are welcoming Him to Jerusalem. Maybe we should start listening to the stones around us.

Humanity is trying to kill God's voice by silencing it, shouting louder, and looking straight past it. No wonder that we are currently experiencing what a friend of mine once called "a God-eclipse"! With our technologically advanced fire-extinguishers, we think we can extinguish God's burning bush. With our clever theories about the Bible, we think we have the power and authority to do a so-called "post-mortem" on the Scriptures. And then we wonder why the world is in such chaos and why we feel so alone.

Luckily, God's not the prisoner of our radical unbelief, anger, bitterness, and arrogance. He doesn't stop being Himself when we stop being respectful, faithful, and humane. Even then He stands unchanged. Then He still allows Himself to be found by every seeker of grace. Then He removes every God-eclipse as His grace flows over and eradicates our darkness. That's why today is framed with hope.

The Best Wine

*Don't you realize that your body is the temple of the Holy
Spirit, who lives in you and was given to you by God?*

— 1 CORINTHIANS. 6:19 NLT —

I once knew a family who would have regular family
reunions over a large meal. They celebrated with good wine
and loaves of homemade bread. Over time, the beloved
grandfather of the family needed more and more help
eating, to the point that he was completely fed by someone
else. Whenever he would request a drink of the best wine,
a family member would have to tear a piece from one of the
many loaves, soak it in the wine, and once full of the best
wine, gently and carefully bring the wine-soaked bread to
their aging grandpa. The common bread, torn and ripped,
was treated with the same honor as the wine it was soaked
with.

You are full of the Holy Spirit. Because you put your faith
in Jesus, you are soaked up with the very Spirit of Christ. If
ever there was a time that someone could call you common,
it is no longer. God has bestowed you with the honor of
being soaked through with the wine of His Spirit. Out of
reverence to the Spirit within you, stop hating yourself.
Stop feeling bad about who you are. You are saturated with
the Spirit; you are no longer meant for shameful things but
honor!

Charging into the Storm

*Whether you turn to the right or to the
left, your ears will hear a voice behind
you, saying, "This is the way; walk in it."*

— ISAIAH 30:21 NIV —

Some people are wandering around aimlessly in the wind
and the weather. We should be there for them. We should
serve and love them in the name of Jesus without writing
them off. Why do we then spend more time sitting in
religious harbors than serving and helping out there on
the open sea? Is God's will not clearly audible, visible, and
tangible when we are among the poor, the lonely, and the
lost? Who knows, maybe that's the reason why so many
believers never find God's one and only will for their lives.
They're not at the right place often enough—out there in
the storm where Jesus is busy saving people who drown in
their own sins and shame!

How do you get into God's rhythm of navigating the
storms of life? Well, there are no quick recipes or shortcuts.
It's a lifelong journey of humility, obedience, reflection
on God's will, and carefully listening for the voice of His
Spirit. He'll teach you how to survive and thrive in the
storm. He'll help you over and over again on how to be the
hands and feet of Christ and how to touch the lives of those
in serious need of grace.

Whatever

> *"Though your sins are like scarlet, they*
> *shall be as white as snow; though they*
> *are red as crimson, they shall be like wool."*
> — ISAIAH 1:18 NIV —

Is the word "whatever" part of the vocabulary of Jesus? Perhaps. Often He criticized the religious people of His day, who were so busy obeying their strict religious laws they didn't have any time left to serve their neighbors.

Jesus observed how the religious professionals harshly judged others that didn't obey their laws to the very last letter. Then He shook His head in dismay and said, "Whatever!" Jesus saw how the religious people rigorously obeyed harsh Sabbath laws without caring a hoot for the sick or the poor. Then He shook His head in amazement and said, "Whatever!"

Religiosity doesn't bring people a single inch closer to God. It turns many of them into self-appointed saints. It creates an us (the saints) versus them (the sinners) distinction. No wonder religious people still don't mix with non-religious types. "If only they could change and become nice, religious people like us, then we would gladly accept them into our midst." Well, Jesus just weeps at this. No, He does more than this. He invites people like you and me to join Him in His undiluted love for sinners.

The Guest of Honor

Blessed are those who are generous,
because they feed the poor.

— PROVERBS 22:9 NLT —

Food is a concrete part of our faith. That's why most feasts in the Bible had to do with food and eating. Whenever the Israelites celebrated a feast in the presence of God, they ate. The "get-togethers" of the early Christians were also characterized by simple meals. Our communion is a faint representation of the early Church's festive meals. Food, joy, and faith go hand-in-hand. The first Christians recognized this as important. That's why they enjoyed eating together, despite the persecution and opposition they encountered. They invited the risen Lord as a Guest of Honor to every meal.

It's sad that we're still struggling to find the proper connection between our faith and food. Yes, I know that we are in a festive setting between Christmas and New Year. But, for the rest of the year, we seem to lose our festive mood. Could that be because food just isn't "spiritual" enough for most of us? Go and learn from the first Christians and from other believers, like the writer of Ecclesiastes who found joy in the simplicity of bread and wine. Eat your bread with joy every day. Declare every meal a feast.

False Perceptions

*Wisdom will multiply your
days and add years to your life.*
— PROVERBS 9:11 NLT —

Did you know that more people die annually across the globe as a result of falling coconuts than of shark attacks? Really! The shark researcher George Burgess found that around 150 people die annually as a result of falling coconuts. That's fifteen times more than all the people who die annually due to shark attacks. People get anxiety attacks when watching movies like *Jaws* and sit frozen in front of National Geographic's shark programs, but no one would take a movie like *The Killer Coconut Tree* seriously.

It's funny how faulty perceptions can be formed and how easily we drink them in like lemonade on a hot day. That's why we should be careful not to be taken in by the media, text messages, e-mails, and even some religious folk.

Proverbs teaches us to continuously think about life and to be cautious. We're not allowed to storm blindly into any situation or believe every new rumor that's doing the rounds. Don't believe every carrier of bad news. Don't lend your ears to people who say, "Have you heard what this or that church leader has done this time?" or similar stories. Protect your ears from false stories. Stop spreading rumors.

Duty!

*Whatever you do, work at it with all
your heart, as working for the Lord.*

— COLOSSIANS 3:23 NIV —

Traditional English culture was built on the principle of duty. Everyone in society had certain duties that they had to fulfill—an army officer towards his troops, a husband towards his wife, citizens toward governments, members toward their churches, etc. This duty thing found its way into our society. Many things were done purely out of a sense of duty and not necessarily from an inner conviction. People fulfilled their religious duty by attending church on Sundays, by making a small monthly contribution to the church, and so forth.

Then came the new digital era that brought an abrupt end to many of these duties. All of a sudden, everyone wondered where order and discipline evaporated to. Much of what people saw as order earlier was, however, just the consequences of an outward sense of duty that everyone formally adhered to. True transformation always happens inside people. When you do the things you do for the Lord and others out of love instead of duty, you're doing them correctly. Duty is only fulfilled when people are driven by authoritarian figures or feelings of guilt. Conversely, love always comes from the heart.

Be motivated by the words of Colossians 3.

The Salt of the Earth

"You are the salt of the earth. But what good is salt
if it has lost its flavor? Can you make it salty again?
It will be thrown out and trampled underfoot as worthless."

— MATTHEW 5:13 NLT —

In some places today, salt is used to repair and improve roads. Namibia is such an example: unsaturated salt from salt pans north of Swakopmund was used to improve the condition of the roads along the coast. Salt is also used in cooler climates like Canada and the U.S. to de-ice roads in winter. So it was in Jesus' day—roads were covered with salt. It appeared to be genuine salt, but it had lost its saltiness.

In today's Scripture verse, Jesus says that we are the salt of the earth. Elsewhere, He instructs believers to be "salt and light" in society. Salt is used to season and preserve food, and in the past people even used it to flavor their tea. Salt was highly esteemed by the Romans, and at one time its army was even paid in salt.

What the world desperately needs today is Christians who are willing to be the salt and light in their families, schools, churches, and communities. Our mandate is to make a difference in a dark and dying world.

On this earth, we are Jesus' hands and feet. Where do we start? By showing His love and light one smile, one thought, one gesture, and one act of kindness at a time.

March

Protecting Others

*If you need wisdom, ask our generous God, and He
will give it to you. He will not rebuke you for asking.*
— JAMES 1:5 NLT —

Always protect the integrity of other people. It's your full-time calling as a follower of Christ to first believe the very best of other people, like 1 Corinthians 13 teaches. Read it and make this valuable spiritual lesson your own. The Lord expects you to honor, serve, and respect fellow believers and all other people. Don't summarily believe unproven stories or general perceptions about them. What help does your faith give you if you play along with the rest of the world's game of gossip, suspicion spreading, and backstabbing others? Don't live with a critical heart—it'll make you spiritually sick. Rather become a thinking, careful believer that lives with God's wisdom.

Ask the Lord to give you some of His wisdom today. Read James 1 where the author says that the Lord gives wisdom to anyone who asks for it. But then we should accept and embrace it without doubting God's readiness to give. Also read portions from the book of Proverbs this week and learn a few new wisdom principles. Thank God for His flooding grace.

Pray for the heavenly wisdom that will help you discover the difference between duty and love. Pray for a society that's love driven instead of duty driven.

Invisible

Always give yourselves fully to the
work of the Lord, because you know that
your labor in the Lord is not in vain.

— 1 CORINTHIANS 15:58 NIV —

I once read an interview with the well-known South African boxing referee, Stanley Christodoulou. When asked about the greatest compliment he received as a referee, he referred to a world title fight that he handled somewhere in the USA. After the fight, he relaxed at the hotel's restaurant. Someone with whom he struck up a conversation asked whether he watched the fight earlier that evening. For Stanley it was the best compliment imaginable that he as referee was so "invisible" in the ring that the spectator didn't even recognize him.

I think as followers of Christ we must become just as invisible. We sometimes stand in the way of others seeing the Lord. Our church infighting, theological debates that's front page news, and our inability to love each other is blocking our sight. Let's get out of the way. Won't it be a wonderful spiritual practice to just get out of the way and allow God to do what only He can do through His Holy Spirit? How?

Well, by (a) expecting no recognition for what we do for the Lord, (b) expecting no "thank you" when we do good for someone, (c) staying out of religious and other arguments, and (d) loving God quietly, but intimately, every day.

Happiness

> *There is nothing better than to be happy*
> *and enjoy ourselves as long as we can.*
> — ECCLESIASTES 3:12 NLT —

Followers of Jesus aren't automatically the happiest people in the world. The same applies to those of other religions. The happiest people on earth are apparently those of Costa Rica, followed closely by Denmark (*World Database of Happiness*, 2000-2009). According to the research among 149 of the world's nations, the unhappiest people are those in Togo, followed by the citizens of Tanzania.

Happiness has to do with quality of life for most people. The problem with this understanding of happiness is that it will disappear like an early-morning mist as soon as external circumstances change. Just observe what happened in many first-world countries after the economic collapse that started in 2008. Many people's happiness was blown away in an instant.

Happiness that doesn't come from the heart is temporary. It's paper thin. Find your happiness in your relationship with God. His presence is neither dependent on your circumstances nor on that of your country. Listen again. *The Lord's grace is not measured by your circumstances!* The Bible is filled with wisdom that teaches how God allows Himself to be found in special ways during hard times.

Your Last Move

*Real wisdom, God's wisdom, begins with a holy life and
is characterized by getting along with others. It is gentle
and reasonable, overflowing with mercy and blessings,
not hot one day and cold the next, not two-faced.*

— JAMES 3:17 THE MESSAGE —

You're only as good as your last move on the chess board
of life. Football players are assessed on Mondays based on
their game the previous Saturday. Preachers are evaluated
based on their last sermon. A writer's most-recent book
determines his success. Ditto for an actor's performance in
his latest movie. This is not the way things should be. We
should give each other more chances than just the last thing
we did or, for that matter, didn't do. The latest controversy
should never overshadow all the good things that a person
has done, especially not between friends.

We can't live with short-term memories when the
integrity of others is at stake. We shouldn't dare write each
other off based on something that didn't impress us. The
Lord's love causes us to always start over and afresh with
each other. We should believe and expect the best of each
other as 1 Corinthians 13 teaches. Our last move is never the
only move in the eyes of our friends and fellow believers. It's
about a whole lifetime of integrity before God and others.

Caring for Creation

The earth is the Lord's, and everything in it.
— PSALM 24:1 NIV —

A 2007 study by British television Channel 4, about what the average Briton's "life footprint" looks like, pointed out that the average person in his or her lifetime uses 3.5 washing machines, drives eight cars, goes through 15 computers, receives 628 Christmas presents, uses 36,000 gallons of fuel, knows 1,700 people, produces 750 tons of CO_2, reads 532 books, reads 2,455 papers (equivalent to 24 trees), and cries 61 liters of tears!

What does your life footprint look like? What are you spending most of your time and energy on? What role do possessions play in your life? Do your footprints during the week leave a trail leading to those who are in need? Are the friends of Jesus—the poor, the outcast, and the lost—your friends too? Does your faith cause your footprint to look any different than what it previously did?

Talking about footprints—what does your carbon footprint look like? We can't allow God's creation to be destroyed right under our noses. Drive less. Use less electricity. Every kilowatt-hour of electricity you save is equal to one kilogram less CO_2 in our air. The creation is God's gift to us. We should take better care of it in His name.

Living Humbly

*It is a good thing to receive wealth from God and
the good health to enjoy it. To enjoy your work and
accept your lot in life—this is indeed a gift from God.*

— ECCLESIASTES 5:19 NLT —

King Hezekiah got a second chance. When the prophet
Isaiah gave him the bad news that he would soon die
(Isa. 38), he fell down and begged God for mercy. God heard
his cry for help. Right there, the king got a handful of extra
life—a full 15 years. Instead of allowing God's mercy to
make him humble, he later openly bragged about his wealth
and power to a foreign delegation. He even took them on a
sight-seeing tour, showing off his weapons and his palace
to make them understand just how large and glorious his
kingdom was.

Hezekiah's arrogant behavior upset the Lord to the extent
that He announced that his rule would come to an end and
that his sons would not rule in his place. Then followed
Hezekiah's shocking reaction: "As long as it doesn't happen
in my lifetime." Talk about selfishness! Let others suffer as
long as I'm excluded! Don't be like Hezekiah. Make room
for others and for the generation that follows. Don't keep
the best part for yourself. Don't live arrogantly. Everything
you have is a gift of grace from the hand of the living God.

Not Like "Everyone"

*For we are God's workmanship,
created in Christ Jesus.*

— EPHESIANS 2:10 NIV —

"You made my day," the shop attendant told me. A wide smile spread across his face. I was stunned. "What did I do?" I asked, surprised. "You called me sir!" he answered. Then he told me that people often treated him with disrespect. He wanted to know why I called him "sir." All I could think of was that God's Word teaches me to treat other people with respect, and this is how I try to live.

After driving away from the shop, I realized anew how easy it really is to do small things in the name of the Lord, like treating others with respect. How sad that we don't succeed in constantly walking the extra mile for everyone who crosses our path. Just as I shared this story with another person, someone told me that I don't live in the *real world* where *everyone* is bad.

Well, I don't have the luxury of generalizing. I don't know "everyone." I also don't know what the aim of everyone is. But Jesus teaches me in Matthew 5-7 that I don't have the luxury to live and think like everyone. I know that each person is not everyone, but a unique creation of God.

A Prayerful Life

Are any of you suffering hardships? You should pray.
Are any of you happy? You should sing praises.
— JAMES 5:13 NLT —

"We just need to pray more. Then God will bless our country," someone said. Everyone agreed. "How do you know that?" another person asked. While everyone just sat there, one answered, "The Bible says so." "Yes," the rest agreed. "Where in the Bible do you read that prayer's primary function is to ensure safer circumstances for everyone?" this person continued. Again there was silence. Someone said, "It's written somewhere that you should 'pray and you shall receive.'"

"Yes, but does that mean that everything will suddenly be better if we send larger volumes of prayer heavenwards?" the questioner wanted to know. "Do you really think that there's a prayer meter that measures how long each of us prays and how many people pray for a particular matter and then these matters get a higher priority from God?"

He carried on, "Prayer is not a quick fix. It is primarily about God and His glory. If there is someone who needs to be changed by prayer, then it is primarily the one who prays himself." Then everyone started talking at the same time. Some agreed, some not. I walked away with some new perspectives on prayer.

The Fate of Millions

"My Father! If it is possible, let this cup of suffering be taken away from Me. Yet I want Your will to be done, not Mine."

— MATTHEW 26:39 NLT —

That Thursday evening in Gethsemane was a time of blood-sweat for Jesus. One last time, He stood there before the choice of moving forward or backward. It was forward to the cross or back to heavenly security. Jesus could now leave the life-threatening playing field and return to his Father's home.

In between the olive trees and a few sleeping disciples, Jesus' options were suddenly very limited. But He made exactly the right choice. In those dark moments God's will was His only route indicator. That's why Jesus spoke some of His best-known words during His greatest anxiety: "Father, let this bitter cup pass Me by, but if not, let Your will be done!" Gethsemane finally sealed the course of Jesus. To turn away here, short of the goal line, was never even an option. There was always only one choice for Jesus. He knew very well that He would have left us exposed to our own mercy for eternity if He deviated from His calling.

The fate of millions carried the path of Jesus past Gethsemane to Calvary. We are the reason He braved that course through darkness. But it's precisely this choice on that dark night in Gethsemane that swung the door to God's mercy wide open for us.

The Sun Stands Still

The Sun of Righteousness will
rise with healing in His wings.
— MALACHI 4:2 NLT —

Our sun is slowly but surely burning out while it provides light and life to all here on the planet. What a strange live-and-let-die rhythm! This fireball will be burned out completely in another few million years. Something similar also happened with the Sun/Son of Righteousness on the cross of Calvary. On that day, Jesus hung on Jerusalem's most dangerous and deadly piece of wood. There He was, the dying Light for a pitch-dark world.

While Jesus' own life-light was being extinguished, a new heavenly light was switched on in a dark world. Death in exchange for life—this is the new life-rhythm of Calvary. There on the cross Jesus stood in God's way on behalf of all, in order for us to be able to walk away freely. Unearned and absolutely free—that's the fresh language of Calvary. The cross speaks prominently about the eternal Sun/Son being switched off for three days. It tells about the death of One who's equal to life for all who embrace His sacrifice in faith. Calvary tells that God switched off the "Sun of Righteousness" for a short while so that His light and life can shine through us forever. That's why we can't but stand in awe in front of the Man of the cross.

The Hardest Heart

"I will give you a new heart and put a new spirit in you; I will remove from you your heart of stone and give you a heart of flesh."

— EZEKIEL 36:26 NIV —

Sometimes even the strongest among us discover grace in unexpected places. The Roman officer on duty at the cross when Jesus hung there on dark Good Friday had his life brought to an abrupt standstill when the sun went out. When Jesus breathed His last breath on that Friday afternoon, this officer said out loud that Jesus truly is the Son of God. A hardened soldier, whose work it was to ensure that convicted criminals died the cruelest death possible, encountered the One who can move heaven and earth.

Even in the tragic dying moments of Jesus, His true identity could not be hidden. This Roman officer never in his wildest dreams imagined he would encounter God's Child in real life, even less likely on a wooden cross in Jerusalem of all places. But that's exactly how God works. On a certain day, at a place where you don't expect it, He makes Himself known to you. Like a treasure in a field that someone discovers (Matt. 13), you discover God in the most unexpected places. Then the hardest heart crumbles as new words are confessed about God's Son.

The Empty Tomb

*"Be sure of this: I am with you always,
even to the end of the age."*

— MATTHEW 28:20 NLT —

The deceased leader of Christendom didn't lie somewhere forever entombed in Jerusalem while mourners walked hopelessly past. His grave is empty. Jesus is no longer to be found there. Death could not hold on to its most important victim. On the third day after His crucifixion, Jesus rose from the dead. The difference between hope and despair is the empty grave of Jesus. That's what the New Testament tells us over and over again. The resurrection of Jesus is the big difference between life and death. The empty grave is the answer to all the pain and insanity of this life. It shouts out loudly and visibly that another kind of life is possible, one filled with hope and meaning.

Now Jesus' place in heaven is filled again. He is the One before whom everyone in heaven and on earth will bow. The words of the angels at His empty grave on Good Sunday, after Jesus threw off the ties of death for good, echoes over all the earth: "He is not here. He has risen!" The last words of Jesus here on earth were that He would be with us always, until the last day (v. 20)! We are not religious orphans. He is here with us.

A New Song

Sing to the LORD a new song;
sing to the LORD, all the earth.
— PSALM 96:1 NIV —

Paul and Silas held a celebration in a jail in Philippi (Acts 16) one night. Do you remember how the two of them were cruelly assaulted and beaten to a pulp earlier that same day? Afterwards they were thrown into the maximum security cell of Philippi's stinking jail. At midnight, Paul decided to sing. It was not hate songs against their enemies. They did not ask for those who assaulted them to be punished by God. Nothing of the sort. All that was on the lips of Paul and Silas was praise for God.

With bloodied bodies and broken voices—how can you sing properly when your body is in shock?—they sent the purest sounds imaginable to God. Paul and Silas wouldn't have won an *Idols* competition that night, but their sincerity to bring God praise under the worst imaginable circumstances touched God's fatherly heart. That's why the earth suddenly started shaking.

It is about time that we as followers of Jesus started singing different songs. All too easily we join the choirs of the discouraged. We constantly listen to the most popular music where hateful songs and inflammatory lyrics have the upper hand. Let's learn from Paul that true hits are songs of praise to God.

Look Who's Walking

*He has shown you, O mortal, what is good. And
what does the LORD require of you? To act justly
and to love mercy and to walk humbly with your God.*

— MICAH 6:8 NIV —

Cleopas was upset after hearing that the grave of Jesus was empty on that Sunday after the crucifixion (Luke 24:1-35). Angry and disappointed, he and another disciple walked the eight miles back to their little town Emmaus in the hot desert sun. Then Jesus joined them—but they didn't recognize Him. Actually, Jesus should have been celebrating with His angels on that day. He should have been with His disciples to celebrate the victory feast. But He chose to spend the greatest Sunday in world history with two doubters, walking back to their insignificant little town. He chose to eat a simple meal with them that evening. Then their eyes were opened. After a full day in the presence of Jesus, these two disciples recognized Him when He shared a meal with them!

Jesus celebrates His victories very differently from how we do. He does it by lovingly walking with people who are angry at Him. He does it by breaking a piece of bread with those of little faith—and then allows God to open their eyes. Jesus is always on the cul-de-sac routes of life, where He is busy catching up with the bitter, lonely, and lost people. The feast of a lifetime is awaiting them!

Enough for Today

The steadfast love of the LORD never ceases; his mercies never come to an end; they are new every morning.

— LAMENTATIONS 3:22–23 ESV —

Are you ever tired of being tired? Whenever someone asks me how I'm doing, I always seem to respond the same way: "tired!" Wouldn't life be easier if God gave us all the strength, energy, and grace we need for a lifetime right now? Like a lump sum of grace? But that is not how God doles out strength.

God does not give us all the grace we need for a lifetime in a single moment; He gives us just the right amount of grace for today. Why? So that we learn to trust Him daily and not leave Him. Didn't the prodigal son leave after his father gave him his full inheritance and only return after he had lost it all (Luke 11:15–31)? Every day, God faithfully gives you just enough strength for each moment. So it's okay to feel weak and at your limit; that does not mean that God has forgotten you. In fact, He is very near, giving you just enough grace for right now. What sets Christians apart is not that they're indestructible, but that they resurrect. Trust God today for your daily grace!

MARCH 16

Fire on Your Tongue

Watch your words and hold your tongue;
you'll save yourself a lot of grief.
— PROVERBS 21:23 THE MESSAGE —

Language is alive. The book of Proverbs says that our words are like knife stabs. Or like fine silver. Just consider how powerfully a phrase like "I appreciate you" can influence the life of another. Or a sentence, like "you are special!" On the other hand, sharp words can deeply hurt others. Hard words are dangerous. That's why the Bible says that we must carefully weigh our words and calculate their weight before they finally leave our mouths. We need to ruminate on our words twice before they leave our mouths.

Once spoken, words take on a life of their own. Therefore, ask the Lord to dip your words in pure gold before they escape from your mouth. Ask Him to change your words into medicine instead of life-threatening weapons that bruise others. Ask Him to touch your tongue like He did Isaiah's. Do you remember that when Isaiah told God that his lips were unclean, there was a coal taken from the heavenly altar to touch his tongue? His mouth was immediately purified with heavenly fire. After that, Isaiah could speak God-honoring language and share words of hope and life with others.

Starting Over

If anyone is in Christ, the new creation has come:
The old has gone, the new is here!
— 2 CORINTHIANS 5:17 NIV —

Imagine you had the chance to start over—what would you do differently? Well, according to researchers, most people would want to be someone else if they could start over. How sad that the story of our lives, of which we are the main authors, often degenerates into chaos. Well, you do have a chance to start over on God's terms. You have at least the rest of today available to do just this.

Today is full of unused hours, minutes, and seconds. You have the choice between seizing them to make the best of them to the glory of God or just being your old self for the rest of today. Don't do that! Choose today to start over in the name of the Lord. Let His light shine. "How?" you ask. Well, I somewhere saw the ad of an American motor oil producer that might be applicable here. It said: "We don't want to change the world. We just want to change your oil!" You don't have to change the whole world. You just need to be a living blessing to one other person who crosses your path somewhere during the day. That's the right kind of starting over.

Light Versus Darkness

*You, Lord, are my lamp;
the Lord turns my darkness into light.*

— 2 SAMUEL 22:29 NIV —

Who wins when light and darkness meet? Well, the Pharisees believed that darkness wins. When holy and unholy was on the same terrain, they were of the opinion that the unclean walked away with the victory. That's why religious folk had to avoid sinners. Even today many churchgoers believe this. That's why they make so little impact for God. They're continually hiding in religious shelters and moaning about evil being on the increase.

Jesus differs radically from this hide-and-criticize mentality. He was not scared to be among the "unclean ones." Lepers and sinners could even touch Him. This upset the overly religious ones, but Jesus was not scared that sinners were "contagious." Too many believers are scared of people who do not believe like they do. Learn from Jesus that light is always stronger than darkness. Holiness is more contagious than unholiness. Those who are hiding in the dark are the ones who need to watch out. They might just bump into God's grace when they deal with God's children. The sad part is that many Christians don't believe this.

Forgiveness

*Be kind and compassionate to
one another, forgiving each other.*
— EPHESIANS 4:32 NIV —

In one of his books, the well-known writer Ernest Hemingway tells the story of Paco, who flees from his father after a disagreement and goes to live in Madrid. Later his father is so saddened by this that he posts an advertisement in the daily *El Liberal*: "Paco, all is forgiven. Meet me at Hotel Montana, noon Tuesday." That Tuesday, 800 boys named Paco showed up at the hotel.

It is easy to speak about forgiving—until you have someone to forgive, as C. S. Lewis says. It is easy to speak about forgiveness from pulpits. It is something completely different when you or your loved ones are the victims of injustice. Or when you are exploited by someone close to you. Well, here's a newsflash: you cannot forgive. You will never manage this yourself. But you know Someone who specializes in forgiveness. He's the best in the universe at it. His name? Christ! Only He can, through His Spirit, help you to close those books and find new joy in life. Here's the route: take your darkest feelings to Him today. Put your hurt and unforgiveness on His shoulders. Also, leave it right there. Repeat this exercise every time that bitterness starts welling up in you.

Be the Difference

Keep your eyes open, hold tight to
your convictions, give it all you've got,
be resolute, and love without stopping.
— 1 CORINTHIANS 16:13-14 THE MESSAGE —

Is it only my imagination or is selfishness presently the order of the day? Not to mention hate, suspicion, and fear. Have the headlines of the world now become the headlines of Christians as well? Are we following the example of the Pharisees to only do good to those who will return the favor and to hate our enemies? Do we follow Jesus just as long as it is comfortable? Let's break this vicious circle. Let's follow the advice of Romans 12 by showing kindness to our opponents. Let's make those that stand against us red with shame by repaying their anger with goodness. Let's pray that the Lord will teach us what it means to follow Him. Let's remember that God's route is not only the road to church on Sundays. Let's allow the Holy Spirit to free us from hate and suspicion.

We can bring joy to at least one other person today through a text message, a call, or a quick visit. Then our own life-cup will be filled automatically. We can allow Jesus to let His love flow through us like a stream of living water (John 7:38). We can break this stronghold of selfishness in the name of Jesus.

Victory Tomorrow

*"I have told you these things, so that in Me you
may have peace. In this world you will have
trouble. But take heart! I have overcome the world."*

— JOHN 16:33 NIV —

If tomorrow looks dark, today is cast in shadows. If the future feels uncertain, the present is a bad place to be. Unfortunately, many believers also feel like this about tomorrow. That's why they look just as despondent. They stare themselves blind against that future that the media, the economy, and politicians hold up in front of them—not to mention that never-ending choir of hopeless individuals who constantly share the latest round of bad news with everyone in range.

How about a piece of truly good news? Well, here it is: God has sorted out the future already. It is not classified information that the future belongs exclusively to the Lord. Just read what the final scoreboard says in Revelation 20-22: THE LORD WINS! Nothing and nobody can prevent Him from reaching His goal. God is full speed underway to let His new heaven and new earth dawn. *Know* every day afresh that the Lord will win.

Never forget that Christ awaits you at the end of your own journey with a heavenly crown of righteousness in His hand (2 Tim. 4:7-8).

Wisdom Wins

*Joyful is the person who finds wisdom,
the one who gains understanding.*
— PROVERBS 3:13-15 NLT —

The well-known composer Joseph Haydn's orchestral members were very tired. The duke for whom they worked promised them a vacation, but time and again he postponed it. Haydn then came forth with a clever plan. His solution was to write his well-known *Farewell* Symphony in 1792. As this piece of music unfolds, one instrument after another becomes quiet. Haydn arranged beforehand that every musician had a candle in front of him, which he would extinguish after he finished his part in the symphony. As the symphony progressed the stage became darker until finally it was pitch black. The duke got the message and allowed them to take their long-overdue vacation.

Haydn's behavior sounds like the wisdom found in the book of Proverbs. Proverbs teaches that there are sometimes better ways of getting things done than using words. Sometimes keeping quiet is better. At other times, a symbolic gesture or an unexpected soft answer is just the thing to defuse a difficult situation. Ask the Lord to flood you with His kind of wisdom—then you will know how to act appropriately in every situation.

Living Wisely in a Hurried World

*Wisdom is sweet to your soul. If you find it, you will have
a bright future, and your hopes will not be cut short.*

— PROVERBS 24:14 NLT —

We live in a super-fast, information-overloaded world.
Already in 1990 Octo Barnett found that if a medical professional read two new medical research papers every day
for one year, he or she would be about 800 years behind at
the end of that year. That's the telling tempo at which new
information appears in the medical world.

It is not only science that grows at the speed of light.
The digital realm is also exploding. For instance, during
February of 2010 Facebook grew from 373 to 394 million
active monthly users. Meanwhile, Twitter grew by 1,382
percent between February 2009 and February 2010.

Information overload is paralyzing us. It causes difficulty
in making decisions because we never feel we have enough
information. Well, here's a newsflash: You will never have
enough information at your disposal. Live with the light that
you have. Trust the Lord and make your decisions bravely.
Trust your intuition and not the constant flow of new data.
This time tomorrow, today's information is old news. Only
the grace and wisdom of God is timeless. It endures forever.

Ask and Receive

If you need wisdom, ask our generous God,
and He will give it to you.
He will not rebuke you for asking.

— JAMES 1:5 NLT —

How do you receive wisdom from God? It's simple, actually. James writes in chapter 1 that you just go ahead and ask for it. That's all. There's no secret. Just ask. Also believe that you will receive it. If you don't believe that you will receive the wisdom you prayed for, you are like an ocean wave being thrown back and forth at will. Then there's no solidity in your faith. That's why you need to believe that you will receive what you've asked for—in this case divine wisdom. You don't have to feel it. Wisdom is not a simple feeling—it is a way of living before God and others.

Follow the advice of James today. Pray for the necessary wisdom to live a godly life. Also receive it in faith, because James warns that we shouldn't pray as if God were absent. He gives His wisdom abundantly to those who don't doubt Him. He lavishly hands out His goodness to those who are not flung around like the waves on the ocean of doubt. Humbly ask for wisdom. Ask God to teach you to live a wise, humble, and considerate life.

The Purpose of Life

*Not even the wisest people discover
everything, no matter what they claim*

— ECCLESIASTES 8:17 NLT —

"When I finally discovered the purpose of life…someone else changed it," an author once wrote. It seems like we are all searching for purpose in life. We are searching for that one big answer that would make all our questions disappear.

The wise author of Ecclesiastes says that no one can discover everything God is doing under the sun. Not even the wisest people discover everything. He comments, "In my search for wisdom and in my observation of people's burdens here on earth, I discovered that there is ceaseless activity, day and night. I realized that no one can discover everything God is doing under the sun. Not even the wisest people discover everything, no matter what they claim." There you have it! You can only start understanding God and His works when you admit your inability to understand life around you.

Christ Is the Way

*Jesus said, "I am the Road, also the Truth, also
the Life. No one gets to the Father apart from Me."*

— JOHN 14:6 THE MESSAGE —

The author of the book of Ecclesiastes refuses to offer simple answers to the puzzles, questions, and problems of life. Our inability to understand this hard life of ours, where crime, disease, unemployment, and broken families are the order of the day, does not mean that God cannot be understood or that He is absent. To the contrary, God is near and knowable.

Jesus is the open door to His heart. He is the way! To bump into Jesus is to run into the arms of God. To find Jesus is the answer to life's big riddle. To rest in Him is to find that peace which surpasses understanding.

To find Christ does not mean that all your answers about life's riddles will disappear at once, as if by magic. But it does mean that you will get to know the ONE who is larger than life. It means that you know Him who will let you live for eternity on this and the other side of death. It means that you will find purpose and meaning in your life as you learn to follow in the footsteps of Christ day after day.

The NBS *Game*

Choose a good reputation over great riches; being held in high esteem is better than silver or gold.

— PROVERBS 22:1 NLT —

Have you ever been the victim of "friendly fire"? This happens when someone says something negative about another person behind his or her back and, then everyone believes it and spreads the story further, free of charge. How tragic that even those on the right side of the friendship and of the faith continually gossip about each other. I have noticed that there are three basic elements present in most back-stabbing stories. I refer to this as the "NBS game"; that is, "Naming, Blaming, and Shaming." Those who play this dangerous game like to give others a bad name behind their back. With their sharp tongues (against which the book of Proverbs warns us), they say things like "I wonder if so-and-so is a Christian." Then, the blame part kicks in when they accuse this person of all kinds of bad things. And then the shaming part follows. "We need to avoid contact with her. She is dangerous."

This NBS game happens without the accused knowing about it. Do you know this game? Are you aware of people who are playing it at present? Intervene immediately. Stand up for the integrity of the accused when you find yourself amongst NBS players. Exhort the guilty ones in the name of Jesus.

Fail Forwards!

If we confess our sins, He is faithful and just and will forgive us our sins and purify us from all unrighteousness.
— 1 JOHN 1:9 NIV —

The best countermeasure against sin is simply to avoid committing it! See to it that you are never in the presence of sin. Take shelter with the Lord, and you will be safe. But if you should stumble and fall, then at least do it forwards. Yes, *fail forwards*! That is, go forward and take your sins directly to the Lord. Of course God hates sin, but He nevertheless invites all wrongdoers to lay their sins at His feet immediately so that He can deal with it effectively.

Take your broken heart to the Holy Trinity without fail. He forgives and forgets. He does not keep a record of sinful deeds that have been confessed in the name of Jesus. God removes all the information from His heavenly records immediately. He wipes the slate clean of everyone who sincerely asks for His forgiveness.

If your life seems to be chaotic and out of control at present, take it to the right place at this very moment. Lay your messed-up life at His feet, receive His redemption, and begin over again with a grateful heart. Yes, renounce all sin and live in obedience to God!

Controlling Your Thoughts

Humble yourselves, therefore, under God's
mighty hand, that He may lift you up in due time.
— 1 PETER 5:6 NIV —

"Does one's brain sweat if you think hard?" someone asked the other day on Twitter. Well, to think always takes up energy. Our brains have relatively little energy available, about 40 watts' worth. That's why our mind is the original energy saver! When it can take shortcuts without thinking, it does exactly that! Your mind has many "routes," "scenarios," and "maps" stored in your subconscious about all those experiences from your past. You don't even remember these, but your mind uses exact maps to determine your behavior here and now—unless you deliberately intervene!

If we don't *continually* establish new, God-honoring thought patterns in our minds, we will be the victims of our own stereotype or even of destructive thoughts. Fortunately we are not slaves of our present thought patterns. We can and need to intervene. How? Well, by choosing to arrest those negative thoughts that rush through our heads in the name of Christ and to refocus our thoughts on Him. If not, our old thoughts will continually program us in the wrong direction. Actively arrest destructive and negative thoughts. Focus on Christ. It will set your mind free to think God-honoring thoughts.

Focusing on Christ

*Whatever is true, whatever is noble, whatever
is right, whatever is pure, whatever is lovely,
whatever is admirable—if anything is excellent
or praiseworthy—think about such things.*

— PHILIPPIANS 4:8 NIV —

Your brain is the original energy saver. It constantly uses
all those experiences, emotions, and thought patterns from
the past to dictate your behavior, emotions, and feelings
here and now. Your old thoughts can keep you captive for
the rest of your life if you don't deliberately choose daily
what and *how* you want to think every day. Therefore, Paul
tells us in Ephesians 4 not to get stuck with weak minds
that think sinful thoughts all the time. He knows all too
well that our thought patterns can degenerate into useless,
addictive routines.

In the same breath, the apostle Paul writes in 2 Corinthians 10 that we need to take our thoughts captive. Every
one of them needs to be arrested in the powerful name of
Christ. Those thoughts that fuel anger, suspicion, bitterness,
and immorality need to be unmasked time and again and
handed over to God. Such thoughts need to be identified,
unmasked, and refused free access to our minds. Otherwise
we can become prisoners of addictive thoughts and accompanying behavioral patterns. Renewed minds offer the key
to a new understanding of Christ. Let's focus our thoughts
on Christ and be free!

Accountability

"I tell you that everyone will have to give account on the day of judgment for every empty word they have spoken."

— MATTHEW 12:36 NIV —

When we think we can live all on our own for God, like a brave spiritual "Rambo," we are missing the point. In 1 Corinthians 12:13, Paul says that the one Spirit made us into one body, the living body of Christ. That is why we are now accountable to others. Subsequently, many Christians today have mentors that keep them accountable regarding how they live.

Recently, I encountered a more handy term than "accountability," namely "editability." Derived from "edit," it refers to the work of book editors. They ensure that their writers succeed. The publishers of world-renowned authors guide their authors behind the scenes and enable them to write their best sellers!

A Christian mentor is someone who guides me to enable me to reach my goal in God's kingdom. An effective mentor needs to guide me to proactively serve the Lord and other people on the road ahead. Like a great editor, they not only find my faults but guide my strengths, leading to a deeper growth. Are you allowing someone to hold you accountable today? To edit your life?

April

Editing Life

*Friends come and friends go, but a
true friend sticks by you like family.*

— PROVERBS 18:24 THE MESSAGE —

Each of us needs to be in a healthy, growth-oriented relationship with someone else who "edits" us to make the right impact for God. We aren't islands! We need each other's constant advice, shaping, intercessory prayer, exhortation, and encouragement. If you don't have someone like this in your life, it's about time! Pray that God will send the right person to assist you in your spiritual growth. Be specific: Ask the Lord to make you transparent so that the right mentor will easily find you.

By the way, how many people are you mentoring at present? In whose lives are you investing some of God's good gifts on a daily or a weekly basis? Listen, you really need to be a mentor for someone else. You need to constantly share what you've received from God. Become a "publisher" for at least one other person who is busy writing a good story to honor God with his/her life. Pray today that God will show you exactly who it is that you need to "edit" to serve God and others more effectively. As a follower of Christ, you must actively influence and encourage people around you to live godly lives.

A Safe Haven

*The heartfelt counsel of a friend is
as sweet as perfume and incense.*

— PROVERBS 27:9 NLT —

It seems to me that safe people are as scarce as safe places. Who or what is a safe person? It is someone in whose presence you can open your heart. It is someone with whom you can just be yourself without fearing that he or she will use it against you. A safe person will always protect your integrity in front of others—and always enjoys speaking to God about you.

Shedding tears is a gift from God to wash our insides clean of hurt and pain. But our tears are not safe with everyone. Some see it as a sign of weakness or an inability to stare life bravely in the eyes. How great that the Lord made some people so free that they are safe havens for those around them. With these folks you can be fragile and broken. And even sensitive. In their presence you find healing for your tired soul.

Do you know safe people? Cherish them! Thank God over and over for them. Are you someone like this? Not? Then get to know Romans 12—learn how to mourn with those who are mourning and to rejoice with those who are rejoicing. There you will also learn how to associate with the humble and to dry the tears of others.

Unique

Thank You for making me so wonderfully complex!
Your workmanship is marvelous—how well I know it.
— PSALM 139:14 NLT —

No two people on earth share the same fingerprints. But did you know that our "eye prints" are equally unique? The developer of the Iris ID, John Daugman of Cambridge University in England, has already compared the "eye prints" of thirty million people. No one of them is the same. Each of us also has twenty-three pairs of chromosomes that can combine in 8,388,608 different ways. Every one of us is unique.

However, not only our fingerprints and our eyes tell us that we are unique, valuable, and special. God confirms it over and again in the Bible. Just take Psalm 139:14, where David writes how the Lord put us together in a wonderful way. We are the climax—the magnum opus—of all God's works here on earth. Maybe that is why Vincent van Gogh once said that Christ is the greatest artist ever. However, according to Van Gogh He works with living pieces of art instead of dead statues.

Why do we talk so destructively about ourselves if we are so uniquely sewn together? Why do we so eagerly focus on our shortcomings? Notice that there's only one you in the whole universe. Let your one and only life produce continuous heavenly music for God. Make good sounds with those opportunities you have at your disposal.

Light Years

*The prayer of a righteous man
is powerful and effective.*
— JAMES 5:16 NIV —

A snippet of good news especially for you—the distance between heaven and earth is shorter than you've ever thought. On the day that the feet of Jesus touched the earth, this distance shrunk dramatically. On that day the chasm between heaven and earth was bridged forever. No longer do we have to rely on our own attempts to reach God. Such attempts will come to nothing in any case. Jesus Christ really is the only connecting road between God and us.

The best way to keep to Christ's road is through prayer. The minute you start praying, you are present in the throne room of the Almighty. By way of a simple prayer in the name of Jesus, you are transported to the presence of God in a divine instant. A prayer spans the distance between heaven and earth faster than any text message.

The speed of prayer easily beats any high-speed Internet connection. For a prayer to overtake the speed of light is plain sailing. Banish any distance between heaven and earth today in your prayers. Connect to God in the name of Christ.

The Right Name

*"My Father's will is that everyone who looks to
the Son and believes in Him shall have eternal life."*

— JOHN 6:40 NIV —

Here is a vitally important rule for you to remember until that very moment when you take the first step on the other side, the side of death. Remember it for the rest of eternity: When you stand face-to-face before God and He wants to know why you are there, you must appeal immediately to the only Savior in the entire universe.

Declare that you know the name of the One on whom you have built all your hope: Jesus Christ. He alone is your Lord! This simple confession will unlock the doors of eternity for you. Jesus will be there to welcome you to an everlasting feast!

What a privilege to know the most important Person in the universe by name. What an honor to have the most exclusive name of all on one's lips and to speak it with respect and love, giving it a place of honor in one's heart. You should never become used to this privilege. You should let the Spirit guide you to stand before our great God with a sense of wonder time after time. Respectfully give praise to His name in your every prayer.

The Right Connections

If you declare with your mouth, "Jesus is Lord,"
and believe in your heart that God raised
Him from the dead, you will be saved.

— ROMANS 10:9 NIV —

Remember that the only "legitimate" way you can have a conversation with God is by knowing a second name of equal importance: that of Jesus! No one can reach God except through Him (John 14:6; Acts 4:11-12). If the words that you speak profess the name of Jesus, and if you believe in Him with all your heart (Rom. 10:9-10), then you have the only key to unlock the door to true life forever. Only the saving grace of His name can give you this unbelievable guarantee.

The warranties that large international companies provide on their products are valid for a few years at the most, but not for ever. But Jesus guarantees His work of redemption in your life forever! Jesus has promised in black and white that everyone who submits to Him will receive everlasting life in His heavenly home (John 5-6). Not even death can bring this new life to an end. In fact, this is the start of true life! This is the first time that you are really going Home.

Today and every day, use the correct Heavenly Connection if you want to live in God's home!

God Goes about Quietly

I know the LORD is always with me.
I will not be shaken, for He is right beside me.

— PSALM 16:8 NLT —

Simply by speaking, God can quiet a violent storm in an instant! Just ask the seafarers in Psalm 107. One day they saw the calm sea around them suddenly turn into violent waves; their boat rolled to and fro uncontrollably. They realized that they were in serious trouble. There and then they started to pray. All at once, God performed a miracle. He calmed the waters; something He likes to do! God addressed the giant waves to calm down when His people started to pray.

Still today, the Lord walks quietly on stormy waters. The most powerful winds cannot blow Him off course, especially not when His children flounder helplessly in dangerous storms.

Even when the winds are at their strongest, the Lord calmly reaches out to His people. He knows when they feel trapped and helpless. He knows their feelings of fear and despair when giant waves wash over their lifeboats. When they anxiously call for help He hears every word. He will constrain the winds that blow all round them at once. In no time He will clear the dark clouds that have gathered above them. He will also do it today. All you have to do is ask!

The Shadow of His Wings

Whoever dwells in the shelter of the Most High will rest in the shadow of the Almighty.

— PSALM 91:1 NIV —

God always knows where you are. He watches your movements closely, 24/7. He can trace you in no time at all, wherever you might be wandering. Each earthly address where you spend your time is recorded in the heavenly books. You will never be able to change your address quietly without God discovering it in a divine instant. That is why He knows full well when you land in real storms. You can be sure that He will be there in the blink of an eye.

Always know that when you feel caught up among giant waves, the Lord is very close to you. You are too precious for Him to allow gales to blow you away from Him. You are one of God's very special possessions, and He will speak out to calm the storms round you. He will protect you. Ask Him to do it!

Remember to bow to Him in thankfulness afterwards. Honor Him for being with you in your dark hour of need. Worship the only Lord who can change even the most intense darkness, surrounding you with the brightest light and turning your night into day!

A New Creation

*Imitate God, therefore, in everything you do,
because you are His dear children.*

— EPHESIANS 5:1 NLT —

The name God uses to address everyone that bows before Jesus is "child." "How great is the love the Father has lavished on us, that we should be called children of God! And that is what we are!" (1 John 3:1). "He who did not spare His own Son, but gave Him up for us all—how will He not also, along with Him, graciously give us all things?" (Rom. 8:32). God calls us His children. Through the blood of His Son He has made us part of His heavenly family. Thus, God is our Father and we are the special children of His kingdom! He loves us all equally and for the same length of time: forever.

To God we aren't mere numbers in an ID document. No, God calls us His *beloved children*. We share in all the privileges that go along with this name of honor, such as a permanent place to sit at His feet as well as a brand-new life.

Wow, we should rejoice that God has chosen this incredible new name for each of us. Naturally our lives should reflect that we are part of the family of the kingdom of God; indeed, that our Father is the King of all creation.

Beyond the NOW

*God has said, "Never will I leave
you; never will I forsake you."*

— HEBREWS 13:5 NIV —

One can so easily become blind to everything but one's own circumstances. Then it's easy to fall back on that old evergreen complaint: "The Lord has forsaken me." Listen, it is definitely not true. Your own feelings and circumstances should never be the yardstick against which you measure how far (or near) God is from you. Don't think that God is far away simply because you feel that it is the case. Don't let your troubles make you believe that He has forgotten you because God will never forsake you in difficult times.

We allow our feelings to lead us by the nose far too easily. Whenever it feels as if the road to heaven is closed, we decide that God has given us up as a bad job. Yet the Bible tells us that not even dire circumstances can ever separate us from Him (Rom. 8:31-39).

God proved that we are extremely valuable when He sent His only Son to make us His permanent property. We are so important that God sent His Spirit to transform us into permanent dwellings for the Almighty.

In Step with God

*I will teach you wisdom's ways and lead you
in straight paths. When you walk, you won't be
held back; when you run, you won't stumble.*

— PROVERBS 4:11-12 NLT —

Keep pace with the rhythm of the Lord. How?

Make time for the Word (Psalm 1): Make time in your daily program to read God's Word. The Bible must be your daily guide. You must replenish yourself regularly with the right kind of good news.

Make time for prayer: To really hear God's voice, you have to switch off the noise around you: the TV, the radio, the telephone, as well as your busy schedule. You have to put aside quiet time for sitting alone at the feet of the Lord (Matt. 6:5-6). Choose a quiet garden or a room, where noise won't disturb you, and where you are also able to silence the noise within you.

Make the right kind of friends: Instead of keeping company with people who are frivolous or devoid of any hope, you should rather spend time with people who uplift you as a person. Make a point of befriending people who can teach you to walk close to the Lord. Your role models and mentors should be people who walk the Lord's road of grace every day.

In God's Hands

"I know you well and you are special to Me."

— EXODUS 33:12 THE MESSAGE —

Asaph, one of the believers in the Bible who always went against the grain, wrote in Psalm 73:13 that he had been near to losing his faith after he had seen the prosperity of wicked people compared to his own suffering. Fortunately the Lord opened his eyes to see what it was all about (v. 17). Asaph came to realize that God deals with sinners in His own way (vv. 18-20). He also learned that the Lord never forsakes His children. God is the Rock where people who are afraid can hide (v. 23). Listen to Asaph's words: "My flesh and my heart may fail, but God is the strength of my heart and my portion forever" (v. 26).

The Lord will never forsake us, not even when we are in revolt against Him. That is why Asaph confesses, "When my heart was grieved and my spirit embittered, I was senseless and ignorant; I was a brute beast before You. Yet I am always with You; You hold me by my right hand" (vv. 21-23).

Well, there you have it—the true facts! Do you believe it? Or do you listen to all the noise in your head?

The Joy of Life

*"Come to Me, all you who are weary
and burdened, and I will give you rest."*

— MATTHEW 11:28 NIV —

One of the reasons for our rushed lives could be our desire for more earthly possessions. We exhaust ourselves in order to afford a new car, house, holiday, furniture, the children's education—we worry today about the problems and expenses of tomorrow.

But listen to this: God measures out grace only "one day at a time" (Matt. 6:11). He provides in all our needs—one day at a time. But when we appoint ourselves as the architects, owners, and builders of our plans, our faith diminishes while the speed at which we live increases by the day, so much so that we begin to devise plans to get even more unnecessary food on the table.

The solution is to hand over full control of the building plans of our lives to God. He should be the only architect of our life's house. Then we will move forward in the right direction, one day at a time. We will no longer have unnecessary man-made building plans in our lives that sap our energy and swallow our faith. Peace and simplicity will become the most precious possessions we have—gifts bestowed upon us by the Lord!

Cease-Fire

*He Himself is our peace, who has made
the two groups one and has destroyed
the barrier, the dividing wall of hostility.*

— EPHESIANS 2:14 NIV —

The peace of Christ proclaims that there is no more *enmity* between heaven and earth. His death and resurrection constitute the cease-fire that connects God and us. There is no other road to God. Only Jesus brings true peace and can guarantee that it will last. The peace of Christ gives the receiver permanent access to God. If we follow Jesus' road of peace, we are assured of a place at the throne of God.

Read what Paul says in Romans 5:1-2: "Therefore, since we have been justified through faith, we have peace with God through our Lord Jesus Christ, through whom we have gained access by faith into this grace in which we now stand. And we rejoice in the hope of the glory of God."

There is no more punishment from God. Peace equals good news. This means that there is no condemnation for those who are in Christ Jesus (Rom. 8:1). The peace of Jesus brings about peace between people on earth who fight with one another.

Company

"For where two or three gather together as
My followers, I am there among them."
— MATTHEW 18:20 NLT —

God loves the wrong kind of people. He loves sinners, enemies, rebels, and good-for-nothings. For that reason He devised a master plan to free all His enemies that He loves so dearly from the death traps of sin. He needed only one Man to carry out this master plan. Not hordes of angels, super beings with laser guns, or an army with mega bombs. No, He needed only one person who didn't carry dangerous weapons or wear shiny clothes. I am talking about Jesus, of course!

One day Jesus took a decisive step that had an everlasting effect on world history. He decided to exchange His heavenly honor for a humble life here on earth. No red carpets were rolled out in His honor during His wearisome journeys on earth. Stripped of all glory, Jesus braved our dusty dirt roads to tell sinners and outcasts about the kingdom of God.

Jesus wants to be present in the company of everybody, and that includes you. Kneel before Him. Give yourself to Him unreservedly. In exchange, everlasting new life will be your gift.

Set Your Sails

*Don't you realize that your body is the temple
of the Holy Spirit, who lives in you and was given
to you by God? You do not belong to yourself.*

— 1 CORINTHIANS 6:19 NLT —

Do you want the power of the Holy Spirit to swell your life's sails? Well, be assured of the following:

Know that the Spirit lives in you (1 Cor. 3:16; 6:19): The Holy Spirit was given to the church of Christ (Rom. 8:9). He transforms you and other believers into temples of the Almighty. He changes your life into a temple of the living God.

Know that the Spirit is the Guarantee that you will reach the finish line (Eph. 1:13-14): The Spirit guarantees that a heavenly feast awaits you. He guarantees that you will reach the finish line safely because you believe in Christ. He also guarantees that He will be with you wherever you are on your journey. He will make sure that you reach the eternal home of the Lord safely.

Let the Spirit fill your life every day (Eph. 5:18): Your life should be like an empty vessel that is filled with the Spirit each day. Be the clay in His hands for Him to model. Ask Him to fill the vessel of your life to the brim with life-giving water, enough to spill over to others.

The Heavenly Gardener

"Remain in Me and I will remain in you. Those who remain in Me and I in them, will produce much fruit."

— JOHN 15:4-5 NLT —

God lets Jesus, His heavenly Gardener, till the garden of your life so that you may bear more fruit to His glory. He plants a nameplate next to your life that reads, "Under the special care of the heavenly Gardener!" Therefore, as far as He is concerned, you have to prepare for a blessed year. He is going to shape and mold you so that His Word takes deeper root in your heart. You will have new insights into the words of the Bible.

What is more, you will find it much easier to carry the burdens of others on your shoulders. In short, this time is going to be God's season of grace for you, a special year for you to grow and bear fruit!

Embrace this bonus year. Go to those places where living waters flow and living bread is handed out. Make time to go to church, to pray, and to study God's Word. Leave the rest to God! He will see to it that you bear the fruit that He requires. He will gather the crop at the appropriate time. All you have to do is be a willing tree in the hands of the heavenly Gardener.

How Far Away?

He tends His flock like a shepherd: He gathers the lambs in His arms and carries them close to His heart.

— ISAIAH 40:11 NIV —

Are you one of those who wonder how far away God is from you? Maybe you feel that today He is very, very far. Well, the Bible tells you exactly how far away He is from you at this very moment. Listen, GOD IS ONLY A PRAYER AWAY! And no farther. He really is only a call-for-help away; no farther than a single, humble prayer asking for help. He is as close to you as the time it takes you to speak one sentence in the name of His Son. Yes, God is as close to you as that.

Jesus removed the distance between God and you. Now, God is very near. You don't need binoculars or a telescope to see His goodness. And you don't have to shout at the top of your voice to get His attention. He is only one prayer away. That is all! When you address Him in the name of Christ, the last bit of distance is removed! Then you are as close to Him as a single prayer!

I repeat: When you pray in the name of Jesus, there is no distance between you and God. He is as close to you as that one prayer!

Wake Up!

"The LORD your God is with you, the Mighty Warrior who saves. He will take great delight in you; in His love He will no longer rebuke you, but will rejoice over you with singing."
— ZEPHANIAH 3:17 NIV —

Do you live in a make-believe world? If so, open your eyes! It is time for your appointment with Destiny! Leave all your unfulfilled dreams behind, because the Lord's heavenly ladder extends down into your life today. God's plan for your life will turn into reality. As you deliberately begin to live your life in His company, you'll become aware that you walk on holy ground every day. You will realize that you are in the presence of the One who holds heaven and earth in the palm of His hand. What a privilege to know that the most powerful Person in the universe accompanies you wherever you go.

Maybe you will come across a few important public figures in the course of your life, but the most important One, who is with you right now, is the living God. He is always close to you, whether you are among believers and friends, at work, or at home. Be grateful that God honors you with His personal presence! Bow down before Him. From now on invite Him every day to be the Guest of Honor in your life!

Your Life Story

Surely the LORD is in this place.
— GENESIS 28:16 NLT —

Can you recall Jacob's dream (Gen. 28:10-22)? He dreamed about a ladder and saw angels climbing up and down. All of a sudden God was there, too. He promised Jacob that He would be with him. Jacob then awoke and exclaimed in shock: "Surely the Lord is in this place, and I was not aware of it" (v. 16). What a mistake not to recognize the Lord when He is with you!

Fortunately, Jacob afterwards honored the Lord by marking the spot with a rock and naming the town Bethel, the House of God. In that way a very ordinary town suddenly became the residence of God, and Jacob, in turn, became a brand-new person!

Jacob's rock proclaimed God is here. By the way, do the stories of your life also reflect the presence of God? Is your life a holy shrine to His honor? Is your life a Bethel—a house of God? Do you realize that the Holy Spirit lives within you when you bow before Jesus? Dedicate your whole life to being the living house of God. Let your every word, every deed, and every thought shout it out—God is here! Bethel!

The Master

*"No one can serve two masters. Either you
will hate the one and love the other, or you
will be devoted to the one and despise the other.
You cannot serve both God and money."*

— MATTHEW 6:24 NIV —

Do you work yourself to the bone for a better future for yourself and your family? Then let me tell you that you are deceiving yourself, for if you are a workaholic, you have become a stranger to everyone. What is the use of working yourself to death for the future while your life, here and now, is devoid of meaning? There is no guarantee on the reverse side of a dollar bill that reads: Possession of this currency guarantees happiness. No, what one could read there instead is, "Whoever loves money never has money enough; whoever loves wealth is never satisfied with his income. This too is meaningless" (Eccles. 5:10).

There is nothing wrong with making money, but something is seriously wrong if your attitude towards money changes your role from manager to slave. The god of money does not share you with anyone. It demands your loyalty twenty-four hours a day. The result? It steals all your joy in life, your family, and your friends. Stop wearing yourself out for possessions, or you risk losing everything in the end! Bow before Christ instead. He is the Lord of mercy and can guarantee your true happiness and wealth!

On Your Doorstep

Let the morning bring me word of Your unfailing love,
for I have put my trust in You. Show me the
way I should go, for to You I entrust my life.

— PSALM 143:8 NIV —

"A man can do nothing better than to eat and drink and find satisfaction in his work. This too, I see, is from the hand of God" (Eccles. 2:24). You will find true happiness when you break bread with those who are close to you. The cup of your life will run over with joy when you spend happy times with family and friends.

The true joy of living awaits you on your doorstep each day. All you have to do is to make each time you break bread or visit with friends and family a festive occasion. Treat everyone sharing your meal as a special guest. Each one has come into your life to lighten your burdens and to ease your way.

If you are far from your loved ones today, take a lesson from the early Christians. They reserved a seat for the living Lord at their communion table. Why don't you do that? Invite the Lord to be the Guest at your table, even if you're only having a simple piece of bread. There is no doubt that He will accept your invitation to celebrate with you! He is sure to free you from your feelings of loneliness today.

Living the Plan

*"I know the plans I have for you," declares
the Lord, "plans to prosper you and not to
harm you, plans to give you hope and a future."*
— JEREMIAH 29:11 NIV —

When you bow before Jesus, every story of your life with a bad beginning and a dreary end is wiped out! Then you become part of a brand-new story, the master story of God! All of a sudden, your yesterdays, todays, and tomorrows are fresh and new, and eternal new life unfolds before your eyes. Yes, the complete story of your life is rewritten by only One Man.

Do you know that suddenly there will no longer be a single report in heaven containing damning evidence about your sins of yesterday? No mark of the hurt you caused a loved one or of any other personal tragedy in your life? Your name is entered only once in the books of heaven and that is in the Book of Life. It has been written in the blood of Christ. Believe it. See it. Experience it. Live it!

Jesus transforms sinners into new people, into children of God. He prepares a new road for everyone who holds on to Him as their Lord and Savior. May you once again behold Jesus, the One who changes the destiny of all for ever.

Your Facial Muscles

A cheerful heart brings a smile to your face.
— PROVERBS 15:13 THE MESSAGE —

I heard about a boy once who found a dried leaf in his mother's Bible and asked her: "Mom, is this the fig leaf that Adam used in the Garden when he wanted to hide his nakedness?" Cute, no? We should have more humor in our lives, don't you think? We should make more time for laughing and being jolly. Do we not serve a God of joy? In His kingdom joy wins. In His presence there is no place for sulking and wearing a long face (Rom. 14:17).

Perhaps we shouldn't take ourselves and others so seriously. Perhaps we should be more lighthearted about life—not that we should be frivolous. A believer once made the remark that "God must have a very good sense of humor since He made human beings like us!" Whenever you are about to fly off the handle, ask yourself if it is really worth getting upset about. Try laughing out loud at yourself and others—or rather with others—for a change.

God gave you many facial muscles, most of which get absolutely no exercise if you don't laugh. So, what are you waiting for?

The Voice of the Spirit

The LORD delights in every detail of their lives. Though they stumble, they will never fall, for the LORD holds them by the hand.

— PSALM 37:23–24 NLT —

God devised a wonderful plan to make sure that we never forget His name. He sent the Holy Spirit to all who follow Christ. Read Romans 8:15-16 to see how the Spirit does it: "You received the Spirit of sonship. And by Him we cry, Abba, Father. The Spirit Himself testifies with our spirit that we are God's children."

Listen carefully and you will hear the Holy Spirit in your heart calling to God lovingly and compassionately today. He is the inner voice that calls to our wonderful heavenly Father on our behalf! It is the task of the Holy Spirit to form an intimate, never-ending bond between you and God. He sees to it that you are always very close to God, even when you don't experience it!

Open your ears today and listen carefully so that you can hear His voice deep in your heart. Hear the Spirit conversing with God about you, calling out to the Father on your behalf. Allow the Spirit to give you the assurance that God is your Father, a loving Father who cares about every little detail of your life.

Source of Joy

"Are you tired? Worn out? Burned out on religion?
Come to Me. Get away with Me and you'll recover
your life. Walk with Me and work with Me—watch
how I do it. Learn the unforced rhythms of grace."

— MATTHEW 11:28–29 THE MESSAGE —

Where can you find joy? In a well-stocked checking account or an expensive holiday? A new house? A well-paid job? Yes, surely joy can be found in these things, but it is only temporary. So where can you find the kind of joy that lasts? Jesus promises to give lasting joy, and He invites us in Matthew 11 to come to Him and experience it. His yoke is easy to carry, for He took our burdens on His shoulders when He died for us on the cross.

Too often, religious people give the impression that they are shouldering the burdens of the whole world. It shouldn't be like that. That is not what religion is about. It is about joy. How can one find the joy of Jesus? Simply by accepting gratefully the joy that He provides. And by using it and putting it to work. All you have to do is to collect your portion of heavenly joy each morning. Ask the Lord each day that you may experience His peace, and your request will be granted instantly.

God's heavenly joy can never be used up—He renews it day by day!

Name, Blame, and Shame

God blesses those whose hearts are pure,
for they will see God.

— MATTHEW 5:8 NLT —

People love to "name, blame, and shame" others. They usually do it behind the backs of those they want to shame and bring into disrepute. You and I have to stop this cruel behavior. We must point out that they are transgressing the rules of Jesus in Matthew 18. There Jesus teaches that when you have something against someone else, you must always take it up personally with him or her. You do this privately, honestly, and transparently. You talk face to face, never face to back!

Before you have spoken to those who are under suspicion of wrongdoing, keep quiet. Integrity is all about the courage to look each other in the eye, never in the back! It requires face-to-face transparency. Integrity is the new game plan for all followers of Jesus, never backstabbing and shaming.

Go and learn from Jesus in Matthew 18 what the rules of the gospel are. Strictly adhere to them, otherwise your relationships will be ruined.

Doubting Thomas

"My Lord and my God!" Thomas exclaimed.
— JOHN 20:28 NLT —

Poor Thomas—do you recall the first Sunday evening after the resurrection of Jesus when He visited His disciples, when Thomas was absent? Afterwards when Thomas heard what happened, he uttered in disbelief, "Unless I see the nail marks in His hands and put my finger where the nails were, and put my hand into His side, I will not believe it" (v. 25). If you are absent when Jesus is present, you miss out on LIFE.

Fortunately Jesus specializes in giving people second chances. He cares about those who are not at peace. That is why He speaks the language of peace when they are within earshot. Eight days later, when Thomas turned up at a meeting of the disciples, Jesus arrived too. The first words that He spoke were, "Peace be with you!" (v. 26). Jesus demonstrated that the peace He offered could transform doubting Thomases in the blink of an eye when He invited Thomas to touch His wounds with his doubting fingers.

Thomas fell to the ground and called out, "My Lord and my God!" (v. 28).

Yes, skeptics gladly kneel before Christ when they experience His peace. He opens their eyes so that they recognize Him as the Lord!

Powerful Prayer

*"Ask, using My name, and you will
receive, and you will have abundant joy."*

— JOHN 16:24 NLT —

Change all your prayers into regular, sincere conversations with God. Choose a few Bible phrases to express your love for Him throughout the day, such as "Lord God, You are good" or "Praise the Lord." Continue doing this in times of crisis. Remind yourself in the words of the Bible that God will always be with you, and say it out loud to Him. "You shield me and keep me safe from harm because I walk close to You" or "The Lord is my Rock, my safe Haven."

Learn to use the Bible effectively by letting it become your guide in prayer also. Speak to God from His Word each day. Use the Psalms to help you share with God your own joy and sadness, your distress and pain. Be brief, sincere, and to the point. Say what you have to, and say amen. Make prayer the heartbeat of your whole life before God. Continue to pray for everyone that crosses your path. Pray until heaven opens up in front of you.

Remember, the most important lesson of all is to always pray in the name of Jesus Christ.

Submit to His Will

*Submit to God, and you will have
peace; then things will go well for you.*
— JOB 22:21 NLT —

Prayer cannot be separated from the rest of your life. There is no such thing as rattling off a few quick prayers to still your conscience while carrying on as you wish. In John 15:7-8 Jesus tells us that if we remain in Him, we will receive what we pray for. A life of obedience to God is the road to, and the result of, a life of obedient prayer. Obedience to God changes the way you pray. Your prayers do not revolve around your own selfish needs then. They don't sound like someone shopping for groceries—"pass this, give me that, do this, help me here." No, then your prayers shift the attention away from yourself to the glory of God and the coming of His kingdom.

Believe me, prayer is a serious matter! Prayer is to speak with the King of the universe. Prayer can be a wondrous adventure if you pray in submission to God's will. If you do, the floodgates of heaven will be open above you night and day, because God hears and answers prayers such as these.

Go on, knock on the doors of heaven in the wondrous name of Jesus and see what happens!

May

From the Beginning

If anyone is in Christ, the new creation has come:
The old has gone, the new is here!

— 2 CORINTHIANS 5:17 NIV —

The basic rule of grace in the kingdom of God is: FROM THE BEGINNING, ONCE MORE! Every day with God is like a new day. He gives us a clean slate every morning! He is not able to recall our sins of the previous day if we sincerely asked for His forgiveness.

Psalm 103:12 says, "As far as the east is from the west, so far has He removed our transgressions from us." There is no place in heaven to store away the records of all the wrong we did in the past. They were tossed in the heavenly garbage can long ago. God's fatherly heart does not think back on the sins we have confessed and for which we have asked His forgiveness in the powerful name of Jesus.

God farms with grace. Forgiveness grows profusely on His heavenly farm. He forgives and forgets. God's bonus year for forgiveness, His year of second chances, has just arrived on the world market! Christ hands out this bumper crop of grace to everyone. Go on, just ask Him, and He will erase the bad records against your name in heaven forever!

Giving Time

Make the most of every chance you get.
These are desperate times!
— EPHESIANS 5:16 THE MESSAGE —

If you are serious about your relationship with God, then give Him one of your most prized possessions today: your time! Most Christians don't think of this when they put things on the altar for the Lord. They offer their possessions, money, Sundays, and more, but not many give over their daily programs to the Lord!

To live a powerful Christian life, you have to give over your watch and your precious diary to the hands of the Lord. You have to learn to synchronize your time with the time of the Lord. If not, you will spend all of your time on the wrong things.

Day-to-day faith is about surrendering your diary to the Lord each morning for Him to overwrite your priorities in heavenly ink with His heavenly ones. Your faith is truly at work when you repeat this giving-away exercise day after day and year after year.

Ephesians 5:16 tells us that we should be "making the most of every opportunity, because the days are evil." Time is precious. Each day is there for you to walk with God, but if you let it slip through your fingers, you waste a precious opportunity.

Prime Time for God

*Because of Christ and our faith in Him,
we can now come boldly and
confidently into God's presence.*

— EPHESIANS 3:12 NLT —

Make time somewhere during the day to switch off your cell phone, close the door, be alone with God, and read His Word. The Lord's Word is not merely letters on paper. While you read the Bible, the Holy Spirit is always at work burning these letters into your heart. The heavenly seeds that He sows in your heart while you dwell in His Word will quickly take root in your mind, as well as on your hands and feet.

The blessings you reap if you are prepared to invest time to seek the face of the Lord will be beyond belief, because every time you do this you find yourself in the Holy Spirit's sphere of power and attention. Every time you do this, your life is molded to the glory of God by the most powerful person in the universe!

There are no shortcuts on the road to spiritual success; however, there are right roads! If you want to follow the main road of faith, one of the most important routes to take is that of setting aside special time for God each day. Oh yes, also dedicate the rest of the day to God as well! Do this every day.

Focus on Jesus

Therefore, since we have been justified through faith,
we have peace with God through our Lord Jesus Christ.

— ROMANS 5:1 NIV —

God loves us from head to toe, despite all our spiritual weaknesses and shortcomings. Heavenly peace reins between Him and us who believe in Jesus Christ, even though we sometimes make a mess of things. That is what the Bible tells me, and I believe it with all of my heart and soul. I believe that God calls me His child, and that He isn't on my trail to punish me.

Of course that doesn't mean that I have a license to do as I please or to sin. But I know that there is permanent redemption through Jesus. In His presence I get a second chance every day, even though it may be my thousandth or millionth second chance!

Realize that God sees all His children through the cross of Jesus. Know that the light of the cross is the light on the road of your life, and that it erases all those crooked roads from the past.

Rejoice in the grace that you receive freely. Be satisfied with what God does in your life. Allow His Spirit to root out everything that is wrong, and keep your eyes fixed on Christ.

Filling Your Mind

Blessed are those whose ways are blameless, who walk according to the law of the LORD. Blessed are those who keep His statutes and seek Him with all their heart.

— PSALM 119:1-2 NIV —

When you travel on an overcrowded train or bus, or when you are caught in a traffic jam in your car, don't just sit there staring lifelessly into thin air. Do a valuable mind exercise instead. Think about what you read in the Bible last night. Become excited once again about the latest knock-out news you discovered in the Bible, and let the expression on your face show it.

In order to remember the Word of God, you need to read it regularly, of course. Charge the spiritual batteries of your mind with heavenly power every single day. Let your thoughts revolve around the living words of the Bible in traffic jams, at work, and at home.

Take the words of Psalm 119:97 to heart: "Oh, how I love your law! I meditate on it all day long." Wait, don't merely read these words. Live them out as well! Spiritual success is guaranteed if they spill over from your head to your hands and feet.

In His Arms

He will order His angels to protect you wherever you go. They will hold you up with their hands so you won't even hurt your foot on a stone.

— PSALM 91:11-12 NLT —

The well-known religious reformer Martin Luther once wrote how his wife, Katharina, emerged from their bedroom one morning wearing funeral clothes, and to his question "Who has died?" she challenged him with her answer, "Your God." She explained that this could be the only reason for his gloom. Her words jerked Luther from his dark pit there and then.

David describes his own "dark pit experience" in Psalm 88. Listen to what he says: "I am counted among those who go down to the pit; I am like a man without strength. I am set apart with the dead, like the slain who lie in the grave, whom You remember no more, who are cut off from Your care. You have put me in the lowest pit, in the darkest depths" (vv. 4-6). Ouch! It is no fun to plod around in a dark pit.

Are you living in a dark pit at the moment? Look around you—even there God is at your side. He does not stand at the top watching you struggling to get out in your own strength. Hear the voice of the Lord right next to you in the dark. See Him switch on a bright light of hope right there where you are.

One Day at a Time

*Live happily with the woman you love through
all the meaningless days of life that God has
given you under the sun. The wife God gives
you is your reward for all your earthly toil.*

— ECCLESIASTES 9:9 NLT —

God takes note of what you do with today's borrowed time. Don't wait for other people to make your life more enjoyable. Don't think life owes you anything. If you do you are going to sulk your life away. No, be brave! Surprise everyone. Dare to call today a day of celebration. Choose the joy of sharing some bread with friends. Put aside celebration time with your children and your spouse (vv. 8:15; 9:9). Forget about an unnecessary appointment; cancel a boring meeting. Start living, because you have only today to do it. Don't waste time. Only if it is the will of God will you see the sun rise tomorrow. But that is still a day's journey away. In the meantime, live life to the full.

God gives life in twenty-four hour portions of "one day at a time." He does not guarantee the next five years of life ahead of time. No, He gives us only today's sunshine, rain, and life. At this very moment you are experiencing your own portion of abundant goodness from heaven. You are alive, right? Your heart should be full of hope and gratitude because God has given the green light for you to be alive today.

The True Facts

*"I'll be with you as you do this, day after
day after day, right up to the end of the age."*

— MATTHEW 28:20 THE MESSAGE —

"The Lord doesn't care about me anymore. Why does He let all these terrible things happen to me?" Have you ever said words like these? Or have you thought it perhaps? Of course you are not alone if you feel like this sometimes. Many people have the same thoughts.

What are the true facts? Well, let me remind you of Jesus' last words on earth a few minutes before His departure to heaven: He assured us that He would be with us until the end of time. Jesus will never, ever leave us—we are too precious to Him. He will accompany everyone who believes in Him to the end of the road.

Are you going to join all the grumblers of the world who complain, "No one's burden is as heavy as mine," or are you going to see the Lord who holds you safely in His hands today?

Sliding Backwards

*Rather, you must grow in the grace and
knowledge of our Lord and Savior Jesus Christ.
All glory to Him, both now and forever! Amen.*

— 2 PETER 3:18 NLT —

If you don't walk with Christ day after day, you fall behind. If all your time is taken up by your busy program, and you neglect God by putting aside special time for Him, don't be surprised if you are half dead spiritually. The fact is, you reap what you sow: spiritual poverty! Learn to put your time at the disposal of the Lord so that you can reap His blessing at the right time.

If you want to keep pace with the daily program of heaven, you have to make each day a special day of God. Do not put aside only Sundays for the Lord, but make each day, from Monday to Saturday, the special day of God. Every morning when you wake up, thank Him for being alive. Declare this day a day of celebration. Make an official announcement at the doors of heaven that you are going to dedicate the full twenty-four hours, yes, each of the 1,440 minutes, to the Lord.

But remember, God hears you. He will take you at your word. What He will do immediately is to overwrite all your appointments and meetings, and your social and recreation programs, with His heavenly program.

Good Deeds

*"I'm telling the solemn truth: Whenever you did one
of these things to someone overlooked or ignored,
that was Me—you did it to Me."*

— MATTHEW 25:40 THE MESSAGE —

Life goes by all too quickly. Do not let the few years you have been granted slip through your fingers. Do you really gain anything by making a lot of money but losing the very people who are close to you? Above all, what do you gain if you are so busy that you don't have any time for God and you lose Him, too? Then you have literally lost everything!

Do the right thing here and now: go back to God immediately. He will receive you with open arms if you come before Him in the name of His Son. Also, go back to your loved ones—they will receive you as their honored guest.

Do something good for someone in the name of the Lord today. Do not go to bed without having spoken a kind word to someone or having performed a loving deed for someone in need. In Matthew 10:42, Jesus gives us the assurance that God will notice it if we give a cup of cold water to the most insignificant of His followers to drink. The smallest gesture of love is recorded in the most important place in the universe.

The Robber of Faith

*"That is why I tell you not to worry about everyday
life—whether you have enough food and drink,
or enough clothes to wear. Isn't life more than
food, and your body more than clothing? Can all
your worries add a single moment to your life?"*

— MATTHEW 6:25, 27 NLT —

Do you know what one of the biggest stumbling blocks is that crosses the path of believers regularly? *Worry*! It is a robber of faith. Worry kills our trust in God. In the parable of the sower (Matt. 13) Jesus tells us that the seed of the Word falls in four places. According to Him, 25 percent reject the gospel outright. But, a full 75 percent embrace the Good News. Can you believe it? Three out of every four people are very religious initially! Unfortunately, 50 percent of all those who hurriedly bow before God throw in the towel eventually. Why? Well, there are two reasons: (a) the demands of religion, and (b) worry! Those who hurriedly say yes to God all too soon backslide into the bad habit of worrying and running after money. Tragic, but true!

You have one of two choices—either you take God at His word when He promises to take care of you, or you try to do it yourself. If you carry out your daily tasks patiently, the Lord will provide you with food at the right time. He who was there yesterday will be at His post tomorrow and the day after that.

Two Loaves of Bread

*"Therefore do not worry about tomorrow,
for tomorrow will worry about itself.
Each day has enough trouble of its own."*

— MATTHEW 6:34 NIV —

One day, someone told me that the future looked very bleak indeed. I asked, "What future are you talking about? The future a week from now or the future in a year's time or in ten years' time? Because at the moment we are right in the middle of exactly that future about which we worried so much about ten years ago!" Despite that, all of us are surviving somehow! We are living last year and last week's future, here and now! Today is yesterday's tomorrow that we worried ourselves sick about. Incredible? No, it is grace! It is all thanks to God! He is true to His Word! He has cared for us exactly as He promised!

Can you recall how you worried about your future a few years back? Well, that future has arrived. Are you without food today? No? Do you have enough warm blankets for tonight? *Yes!* Will you have enough money and supplies for the next month or so? Undoubtedly! Will you make it through the next year? Definitely! Now tell me, what are you worried about? To worry is nothing but a vote of no confidence in your heavenly Father!

Harsh Words

*Remind everyone about these things, and
command them in God's presence to stop
fighting over words. Such arguments are useless,
and they can ruin those who hear them.*

— 2 TIMOTHY 2:14 NLT —

Beware of biting words; the kind that hurt others. Ban them from your lips. Train your tongue not to return evil for evil. You don't have a free pass to be rude or to let bad language escape your lips. You don't have to be like everyone else. You are the property of the Lord. He has the exclusive rights to your life, and that goes for your tongue, too.

Keep your cool when you get involved in an argument. Yes, you may say what you need to say, but do not change into a hooligan when you disagree with others. Make your point in a controlled and sincere manner, never with boxing gloves. This does not become children of the Lord.

"And the Lord's servant must not quarrel; instead, he must be kind to everyone, able to teach, not resentful. Those who oppose him he must gently instruct, in the hope that God will grant them repentance leading them to a knowledge of the truth" (2 Tim. 2:24-25).

Good Medicine

Watch your words and hold your tongue;
you'll save yourself a lot of grief.
— PROVERBS 21:23 THE MESSAGE —

Drench your tongue with the Word of the Lord. Entrust your lips to the Holy Spirit, and your words will be edged in silver. Check your anger with gentle words. Challenge a sour face with a few friendly words. Compliment sincerely whenever necessary. Encourage others. Don't be afraid to speak your mind if others have made a mess of things, but never gossip behind someone's back. Be honest. Let your love for the Lord guide you when you reprimand wrongdoers. Sometimes you have to be strict with others as Paul instructs us when he says: "Correct, rebuke and encourage—with great patience and careful instruction. For the time will come when men will not put up with sound doctrine" (2 Tim. 4:2-3).

Of course it will take courage to swim against the tide and have God's language upon your tongue. But remember, the Rock on which you are standing is never shaken, even though you might be. Speak wisely about the Lord to others, even though you say only a few words.

Ask the Lord to load the right language onto your tongue, and leave the rest up to Him. He will turn your words into good medicine.

Don't Go AWOL

Above all else, guard your heart,
for everything you do flows from it.
— PROVERBS 4:23 NIV —

The other day someone told me about one of his colleagues who maintained that he and God had a good relationship. According to this man he liked doing sinful deeds and God liked forgiving sin. This is pure nonsense! You being a follower of Jesus Christ places you on duty for Him full-time. If you are a believer, there is no such thing as "time out" to live the way you want to. If you do wrong you are going to be "AWOL"—Absent Without Leave. If you do that, you are a lax disciple in your duties.

Do not give up territory to the enemy. Remain at your post, whether you are at work, among friends, or in church. Even if you are the only believer among thousands—be strong! If you are with your back to the wall at work—persevere! Remember, the Lord is there with you. He will never ever leave you in the lurch. Do your duty faithfully among people who do not kneel before God.

Remember, they take note of your example. Your actions speak louder than your words. Your fearlessness in being the Lord's anchor-person makes a deep impression on them, whether they say it or not.

Carrying the Flag

*Light shines on the righteous and joy on
the upright in heart. Rejoice in the LORD,
you who are righteous, and praise His holy name.*

— PSALM 97:11-12 NIV —

I once read a story about two armies who entered into battle in the American War of Independence. One of the generals, realizing that his soldiers were losing badly, ordered them all to fall back immediately. But the flag bearer, who flew the colors of the army right at the front, refused. In haste, the general asked a messenger to go and instruct the man to fall back immediately. But the flag bearer refused once again. Then he sent back the following message to the general, "No, Sir, I'm not falling back. Please instruct the soldiers to march forward to me!"

We are the flag bearers of the gospel. Often you and I find ourselves alone on hostile territory. Perhaps we all feel like falling back. Don't! Instead, call fellow believers through your actions and words to join you at the front, where you are on duty for the Lord.

Plant the flag of the gospel right at the front in His honor. Be strong for the Lord. You are never alone in any event. The One who is stronger is with you. The Lord controls every trench on the battlefield, each piece of ground where you may find yourself.

Jesus' Affliction

Let us run with perseverance, fixing our eyes on Jesus,
the pioneer and perfecter of faith.
For the joy set before Him He endured the cross.

— HEBREWS 12:2 NIV —

Jesus did not suffer on the cross to benefit Himself. Definitely not. Jesus came down from heaven for people like you and me. My only destination was death until Jesus came and changed everything. With the blood He shed for me on Calvary, He wrote the words "paid in full" over all my sins!

Jesus' way of the cross is still the only way of life. There is no other way to God. Only the road of Jesus is the right road. His cross is the only eraser of sin. When I stand before Him with a broken heart, He erases my sin in the split of a heavenly second. He erases every fingerprint I left on sin and every footprint I left behind on the detours of life. Christ gives me a brand-new identity; He makes me a new person from head to toe.

Calvary tells the story not only of the death of Jesus but also of a new life for me. It is not only about suffering but also about restoration. I took my stand at the cross of Jesus. Now I can really live for the first time! Glory to God, for the victory bells are still tolling loudly.

The Vine

"I am the vine; you are the branches. Those who remain in Me, and I in them, will produce much fruit. For apart from Me you can do nothing."

— JOHN 15:5 NLT —

The scene is Luke 13:6-9: The parable of the fig tree that did not bear fruit. The main characters: God (the Owner), Jesus (the Gardener), and me (the tree without fruit).

The solution to not bearing any fruit: A season of grace! Jesus undertakes to fill my life, inside and out, with heavenly water and fertilizer. He does not simply grant me a year's grace to see what I will do with it. That would not be true grace because it would still leave the ball in my court. Divine grace does not work that way. No, Jesus gives me a chance now! He takes sole responsibility for seeing to it that I bear fruit. Jesus puts His name in jeopardy. He takes the chance Himself.

Do I have to do anything? Yes, I only have to be in the vineyard! That is all. Christ looks after the rest. He does the watering and the fertilizing. I simply have to be there in the season of grace when He works on my life.

Where is the vineyard? The vineyard is where the Word is. The vineyard is when I pray. The vineyard is where believers get together and spread the gospel. Be there!

Omnipotence

*"And surely I am with you always,
to the very end of the age."*

— MATTHEW 28:20 NIV —

Nothing can ever separate you from God's love—not even the biggest crisis you have to face. Nothing in life is a match for the power and love of God, absolutely nothing. Paul assures us of this amazing fact in Romans 8:31-39. You are the special property of the Lord because you believe in Christ. You are so precious to Him that He carries you in the palm of His almighty hand night and day. You are never alone, not for a single moment.

Even though you may feel defenseless and weak at times, you are still a member of God's winning team. Eternity has a permanent place in your heart. You are on your way to the heavenly winner's circle. Keep on believing that. Do not allow your emotions to play games with you. The Lord is not far from you merely because you feel that way. The Word promises that God is always near.

Although you may feel that the prayers you send up get stuck at ceiling height, you must know that it is your feelings running away with you once again. God is omnipotent—He is with you. Believe it and be free!

His Yoke

*Carefully build yourselves up in this most holy
faith by praying in the Holy Spirit, staying right
at the center of God's love, keeping your arms open
and outstretched, ready for the mercy of our Master,
Jesus Christ. This is the unending life, the real life!*

— JUDE 20-21 THE MESSAGE —

Are feelings of hopelessness and worry your best friends at the moment? Well, then, you are keeping the wrong company! They are going to rob you of your happiness and of your faith. Do something about it, today. "How?" you ask? Resign from this hopeless brigade. Write a letter of resignation in which you declare that from now on you are not going to let any negative feelings or worries into your heart. If you give free entry to these feelings one more day, they are going to rob you of your faith eventually.

In the parable of the sower in Matthew 13, Jesus warns that worry is a big robber of faith. Be warned: The more you worry, the weaker your faith will be. On the other hand, the greater your faith in God, the more you trust in Him. His shoulders are broad enough to carry the cares of the whole world and to provide for everyone's needs. There is no reason why He will not carry yours. He was prepared to give up His Son to die for you, so why would He not care about every small detail of your life? Believe it.

Standing in the Wind

Pray in the Spirit at all times and on every occasion. Stay alert and be persistent in your prayers for all believers everywhere.
— EPHESIANS 6:18 NLT —

The Day of Pentecost was not windless—anything but. On that day a mighty, heavenly gale-force wind of the Spirit started blowing through our dead and dying world. When the Holy Spirit came down on that day, His wind and fire gave new life to the entire church. People who had been scared before started speaking about Christ fearlessly all of a sudden. At every turn they found their tongues had been loosened. An abundance of power was available once again—supernatural power to witness, to sing, to serve, and to make miracles happen!

The heavenly wind of the Spirit is still blowing today. His power is no less now than it was on the Day of Pentecost—only you and I restrict His power. Perhaps we no longer believe that He has remained unchanged to this day and that He will remain so forever after. Let us ask the Spirit to fill our souls once again (Eph. 5:17). Let us spread our sails to catch the wind—the right wind: the wind of heaven!

If we stand in the wind of the Spirit, we will boldly speak about our great God. Then this broken world of ours will be full of hope again: heavenly hope!

Living Temples of God

*Don't you realize that your body is the temple of
the Holy Spirit, who lives in you and was given
to you by God? You do not belong to yourself.*

— 1 CORINTHIANS 6:19 NLT —

Paul tells an unbelievable story in 1 Corinthians 6:19-20.
He writes that we were bought by Jesus when we were still
enslaved by sin and death. He came searching for us on
the market square of sins. On that day His blood was the
method of payment by which He made us His property.
Isn't it unbelievable that Jesus has such abundant love for
the wrong people—for sinners such as you and me? Well,
that is precisely what Christ is like. That is why He buys
sinners, even today. His specialty is saving the broken and
the dead.

There is another important thing that Jesus did when
He bought us. According to 1 Corinthians 6:19, He gave us
over to the lifelong care of the Holy Spirit. There and then
the Holy Spirit transformed us into temples of the living
God. Now we are His final earthly home before the Second
Coming. The Spirit builds living temples in honor of our
Father. He transforms us into living dwellings in which God
can live and work.

We have been set apart permanently to reflect God's
greatness. Therefore, we have to live up to, speak up to, and
do up to His great name! Let's do it!

When Bad Things Happen

God is faithful; He will not let you be tempted
beyond what you can bear. But when you are tempted,
He will also provide a way out so that you can endure it.

— 1 CORINTHIANS 10:13 NIV —

"This isn't fair. I have been serving the Lord for years, but now everything in my life is going wrong. Why does God allow this? Why doesn't He help me?" Have you heard these types of remarks? Well, many feel this way. They think God is failing them. Is this true? No, of course not. God doesn't take off as soon as His children have tough hills to climb.

However, God's presence does not mean that you will experience prosperity, happiness, and wealth always. He does not guarantee that you will never be faced with dangerous situations. God's Word promises that He will always be near, even when you are in need. Call on Him. He will help you but in His own way.

Even though you may feel like you are being led like a lamb to the slaughter and that life is knocking you down, know that you are never alone. The hands of God your Father enfold you. You are safe in His arms, even though you may be bleeding. He will dress your wounds with His Spirit and fill your life with hope and strength. He renews His true care of you every day. The sun of His righteousness will shine on you each day.

Too Little Too Late?

We fix our eyes not on what is seen,
but on what is unseen, since what is seen is
temporary, but what is unseen is eternal.
— 2 CORINTHIANS 4:18 NIV —

That terrible feeling of "too little too late" often clings to you when you leave the church building after a service. Suddenly you feel as though you are the Lord's naughtiest child who can do absolutely nothing right. Well, here is some good news: Christ starts over every day with each and every one who feels that way, including you! He promises this in this verse.

Jesus is not really as disappointed in you as others would have you believe. He is continually busy transforming you and His other children into the image of God. It happens without you even seeing it. In the same way you cannot see a tree grow, you cannot see yourself growing spiritually. But do not despair. Put yourself in the hands of the Lord, and leave your spiritual growth in His care. He will let it happen. Stop focusing on all your mistakes. Place them at the feet of Christ and leave them be.

Stop thinking that you are constantly doing too little too late. To do this is to lodge a vote of no confidence in the work of the Lord. And that is not at all true.

Eyes Like Elisha

*The LORD will be at your side and will
keep your foot from being snared.*
— PROVERBS 3:26 NIV —

Elisha had very good eyes. He was able to see the invisible realm of God. Do you recall that night he was besieged by enemy soldiers (2 Kings 6)? His servant was petrified when he saw they were surrounded. Elisha, however, told him that their own numbers surpassed the numbers of the opposition by far. This did not make sense to his servant. His arithmetic told him that one plus one made two, and he and Elisha made only two, and they were badly outnumbered by the opposition. Then Elisha prayed to God to open the servant's eyes. All of a sudden he saw a mighty heavenly army surrounding them.

Do you have eyes like Elisha, too? Do you see God by faith, or are the problems around you the only things you see? The Almighty stays near His earthly property at all times. The superior heavenly force is on the believer's side.

However, that does not imply that we will never go through difficult times or that we will never be hurt. What it does mean is that nothing will ever be able to wrest our fate from the hands of God. We are the precious possessions of the Lord. Therefore, He is with us always.

Today

The Lord has done it this very day;
let us rejoice today and be glad.

— PSALM 118:24 NIV —

You must make some vitally important choices again today. What are they? You must choose where to leave your fingerprints and footprints. Will your fingerprints be displayed on the same old sins and all your bad habits of yesterday again today? What about your footprints? Will they perhaps be left on the road of life where the lonely, the helpless, and the hurting find themselves? Or maybe not?

It is your choice whether to touch the lives of others with the love of God or whether to ignore them. Fortunately, you know which choices you need to make. As a follower of Jesus, the Spirit of God will speak to your heart to make the right choices today. So, what are you waiting for?

Serve the Lord today by making a deliberate choice to take someone else's burdens on your shoulders. Serve God by walking with someone for two miles instead of the one mile they've asked for. Serve Him by deciding to defend someone's integrity when others talk behind his or her back. Serve God by deciding to entrust your life to Him anew right after you have read these words.

More Than a Spectator

*Live a life filled with love, following the example
of Christ. He loved us and offered Himself as
a sacrifice for us, a pleasing aroma to God.*

— EPHESIANS 5:2 NLT —

You should do something special with the portion of life God has lent you today. Remember that you receive life only one day at a time. You don't know if you will still be here tomorrow. You are fortunate to have received today as a gift from heaven. Do something special with it. Live and use each and every second of these twenty-four hours to the glory of God.

Do not let worries or problems spoil your day. Erase each concern from your mind with a prayer right away. Do not allow the wrong people to pull you down into their sinful way of life. Speak only words of encouragement when others around you make nasty remarks. Share a friendly word with a colleague at work who has become a victim of grumpiness. Send an encouraging text message to a friend whom you haven't seen in a long time. Pray for someone who the Lord has placed in your thoughts.

Do not be a passive spectator of life. Play only on the playing field of the Lord today. Live with hope. Realize once more that you are the Lord's prized possession. Jesus Christ bought you with His precious blood.

It Works!

*The earnest prayer of a righteous
person has great power.*
— JAMES 5:16 NLT —

Prayer works. The other day I heard about a poor community in an African township that set up prayer tents. Suddenly the rate of crime in their area decreased dramatically. The chief of police asked the organizer of the prayer movement to put up more tents in areas with a high crime rate because it had such a real effect on the well-being of that community. Isn't it wonderful to hear stories like this?

Praying is speaking with God Himself. It is a personal appointment in the heavenly throne room with the King of the universe. Prayer is about being in the presence of the Father by the Holy Spirit through faith in Christ. That is why offering a prayer to the Father in the name of Jesus is so powerful. God is the Hearer of these prayers. He opens the heavenly gates to everyone who seeks His countenance in humility and faith.

James 4 says that we do not receive because we do not pray, and when we do pray our prayers are self-centered. These are the two big hindrances in the path of answer to prayer: not enough prayer and self-centered prayer. See to it that these hindrances are removed from your heart when you approach God.

The Speed of Prayer

"God, have mercy on me, a sinner."
— LUKE 18:13 NIV —

Two of the shortest prayers in the New Testament are to be found in the Gospel of Luke. The one is in Luke 18:9-14 where the tax collector prays, "God, have mercy on me, a sinner." There and then, in a moment of heavenly grace, his prayer is answered. Jesus says that this man went home a changed person—someone whose relationship with God had been set right.

The speed of grace is always eons faster than the speed of light. It strikes you every time when you stand naked and bankrupt before God with nothing else to offer Him than your sins and broken life. There is no speed limit to God's grace. He is always at His best when we are at our worst.

The second short prayer is in Luke 23:42 when the man on the cross next to Jesus asks, "Jesus, remember me when you come into Your kingdom." Jesus answers him, "I tell you the truth, today you will be with Me in paradise." There is no time to lose when people beg for mercy. God answers without fail and always at the speed of grace.

In Step with God

He is your example,
and you must follow in His steps.

— 1 PETER 2:21 NLT —

The right question is not "What is God's will for my life?" but "What is God's will, and how do I obey it?" Did you notice the shift in emphasis? God's will is not about me. No, it is about God, twenty-four hours a day, seven days a week, 365 days a year. It's about His honor, His plans, His dreams, and His will!

The only way my plans can synchronize with those of God is when I walk in step with Him. When my diary is replaced by the diary of the living God, and my watch is traded in for a heavenly hourglass, the right things start happening in my life. That is when God's will is done.

How does this happen on ground level in my life? Well, it all starts with prayer. Jesus taught us to pray, "Let Thy will be done!" God's will in your life is not done automatically, but you can miss out on it by being disobedient. The way to get back on track is by praying in faith, praying those getting-in-step-with-God prayers! Your life should be like clay in the hands of God every day: good quality clay that is soft and malleable.

True Life Is Really Free

Because of His great love for us, God,
who is rich in mercy, made us alive with Christ.

— EPHESIANS 2:4–5 NIV —

It is not thanks to you that you are a Christian today. You were stone dead and covered in sin when God bestowed mercy on you the first time. Christ gave His life for you when you were still a sinner (Rom. 5:8). Even then He loved you. Why? Well, because God is love. He has a wealth of kindness (v. 4) and is a full-time grace farmer.

God loves the wrong people—sinners! He constantly tracks His enemies in order that He can save them. That is why He took you back as His child when you were farthest away from Him. God saved you when you did not want to be saved. He was the One who softened your hard-heartedness. He was the One who delivered you unto life once again.

On top of that, Christ removed your heart of stone and replaced it with a heart that loves Him. You have received the greatest heavenly gift ever: a new life, compliments of the living God. All of that just because you bow before Jesus as your Lord. Believe this good news wholeheartedly every day and live abundantly!

June

First Aid

*He has removed our sins as far
from us as the east is from the west.*
— PSALM 103:12 NLT —

When sin makes you stumble, do not give up and lie down in the mess. That is exactly where the enemy wants you: wounded and without hope! No, if you have stumbled, do the following:

Confess your sin: Remember the words of 1 John 1:8-2:2 that tell us that if we confess our sins, God is faithful and just and will forgive us. His Son, Jesus Christ, is our only Advocate and Intercessor at times like these.

Accept the redemption of God: When you commit sin you must immediately confess it before God in Christ. At the same time, you must know that Jesus will expiate your sins. In turn, God is a righteous Judge; He will redeem you because the sacrifice of His Son is sufficient for you and all others who approach Him with their failures and sins.

Report for duty immediately: If you place your sin in all sincerity at the feet of God, you can and must know He will grant you His divine grace for the sake of Christ. Accept His special redemption and report for duty back at the front line again.

Forgive and Forget

So what do we do? Keep on sinning so God
can keep on forgiving? I should hope not!
— ROMANS 6:1 THE MESSAGE —

In Matthew 18 Jesus teaches us that God does not work according to a quota system for forgiveness, like Peter thought. Initially, this disciple of Jesus thought that forgiveness granted seven times was more than enough. In those days the Jews believed that three times was sufficient, so Peter thought seven times was very generous. But then Jesus surprised His disciple with the heavenly formula— 70 times seven. *Ad infinitum.* Endlessly. Constantly! God does not add up the times He has granted forgiveness. He does not keep record of the number of times you have asked His forgiveness. On the other hand, you don't have license to commit sin. Paul addresses this matter very clearly in this verse.

Grace does not give you a free pass to commit sin; on the contrary. But if you commit sin, remember that you can be redeemed by God through Christ. Therefore, do not give up or allow yourself to be trapped in the mess you are in. At the same time, after you receive the phenomenal forgiveness of God, you should lavishly share it with others. Do not keep record of the times they have wronged you. Forgive and forget. Be finished with bitterness and resentment.

Never Too Late

The Lord will vindicate me; Your love, Lord, endures forever—do not abandon the works of Your hands.

— PSALM 138:8 NIV —

The other day an elderly lady told me she had been converted only recently and that it was too late for her to do anything meaningful for the Lord. True? No, not at all! It is never too late. Ask Moses. He was a full eighty years old when the Lord decided he was ready to fulfill his life's calling to lead Israel out of Egypt.

Your every word, every action, and every prayer in the service of the Lord has eternal value. Even when you give someone a cup of water to drink in the name of the Lord, it does not go unremarked in heaven (Matt. 10). When you give your last penny for the Lord, like the poor widow in Luke 21, instead of spending it on yourself, note is taken of it in the highest council chamber of the universe.

There is no age limit to being serviceable for the Lord. You don't have to be learned, great, wealthy, or whatever either. All you have to do is to use every opportunity that comes your way through God. Transform ordinary situations into heavenly occasions to reflect the love of Christ.

Being Yourself

"Before I formed you in the womb I knew
you, before you were born I set you apart."
— JEREMIAH 1:5 NIV —

An international author recently said that when he asks people who they would like to be, 90 percent say they would like to be somebody else. Why are people dissatisfied with themselves? Maybe we have become victims of an artificial world where only appearance, status, and money count. Your appearance, where you stay, what you do, and what you drive determine how successful you are. Everything revolves around living up to this man-made picture of happiness and prosperity.

God does not want you to become an arrogant person who is always concerned with appearance and possessions. Even less does He want you to be somebody else. Until the day that you die, you will only be you! Make peace with this fact. God thought it good to create you with your unique appearance, personality, and body type. If He wanted you to be somebody else, you would have been that person, right? Long before your birth, He planned you in detail. You are the end product of an important planning session by God.

Thank Him for the fact that you are you! In this week, in a unique way, live according to your God-given purpose.

Never Asleep

"Watch and pray so that you will not fall into temptation.
The spirit is willing, but the flesh is weak."

— MATTHEW 26:41 NIV —

How quickly our strength wanes. Illness, worries, and heavy schedules all too easily steal our life's fuel supply. Far too often we are tired, burnt out, and overworked. By the middle of the week, with the weekend hardly over, our flame begins to burn low again. The good news is that God never becomes tired or sleepy. Psalm 121 tells us this good news. Age and illness have no effect on Him. He is never beset by boredom. Unlike us, who often doze off, God is always wide awake. When our knees buckle and our strength diminishes, God still remains strong.

More good news from Isaiah 44 is that not only is God strong when we are weak, but He renews the strength of His tired servants. He replenishes the strength of each and every one who perseveres in waiting for the Lord! That is His promise to you too! Therefore, if you feel you are at the end of your tether, you need much more than vitamins or a weekend getaway—you need new strength that only God can provide. Knock on His heavenly door. Your portion of heavenly strength is right there waiting. Claim it in the name of Christ.

Small and LARGE

Commit everything you do to the Lord.
Trust Him, and He will help you.
— PSALM 37:5 NLT —

At times I am very aware of my weaknesses. When I trip over a stone on the road of life, I realize that I am fragile. Yes, when all is said and done, I am no more than dust and wind. Even so, this fragile old clay pot contains a precious treasure. Truly, I am never alone. The Lord is with me because Jesus is the Lord of my life. God is my constant and only wealth, my gold, my silver, my life.

Even when I am small, God is great. When I am weak, God is infinitely strong. Every time I falter, God is my rock. When I fall, God remains the strong One. What a miracle: small and large together forever—the weak me and Almighty God! What an act of grace to have been made a child of our heavenly Father by Christ. He is the one who catches me every time I fall. I know that God never leaves me on my own. He bends down to pick me up, exactly as Psalm 37 promises.

Therefore, I can walk straight ahead until the end because I am accompanied by the strongest one in the universe: Almighty God!

The Great Search

*Because You are my helper, I sing
for joy in the shadow of Your wings.*
— PSALM 63:7 NLT —

Do you sometimes long for someone so badly that it feels as if you have chest pains? Do you know that deep yearning? If you do, you will have compassion with the writer of Psalm 63 who calls out to God. He longs and thirsts for God like someone in the desert who needs water urgently. Do you know this intense thirst for God? Do you start off every morning in the desert searching for living water? And at night, when you lie in bed, do you long for God's strong hand on your shoulder (v. 7)? Does your inner being constantly shout for God? Then be assured that God can be found by every sincere seeker. He will quench your thirst. He will satisfy your longing. He will meet you where you are.

No one who sincerely calls for God does so in vain. No one who seeks His company walks away empty-handed. God lets Himself be found. He does not hide. He is not busy with other more important matters when you call on Him today. Seek and you will find! That is what the Man of Nazareth said. He knows the heart of His Father best of all.

The Hairs on Your Head

"He pays even greater attention to you, down to the last detail—even numbering the hairs on your head!"

— MATTHEW 10:30 THE MESSAGE —

Having read Matthew 10:30, which says that God even counts every hair on our heads, I told my bald-headed friend that he was really making the Lord's task easy. There is nothing left to count on his head!

God is so near, so intensely involved with us, that He makes time to get to know the details of our lives. So much so that He is up to date with "unimportant" details, such as when we lose a hair. Even if you are privileged enough to have a good head of hair, how many did you lose during the night? God knows. His care is so sincere that He knows even that! How about that for attention to detail? How about that for intense awareness and priority treatment!

God takes special care of His prized earthly possessions. We, who have been bought through the blood of His Son, are His family, His handiwork, and His property. That is why He nurtures and looks after us. That is why He carries and protects us. So, touch your hair or bald head and know that God is near. Then bow before Him in deep reverence.

A Safe Refuge

The LORD is good, a refuge in times of
trouble. He cares for those who trust in Him.

— NAHUM 1:7 NIV —

Trouble! We know all about it. We experience it in our lives. Quite often it is our best friend for too long. Well, don't take it any longer. At the least, don't be victims of trouble. Do not slide into a "pity me, please" attitude. Take care that you never sing that age-old theme song: "Nobody knows the trouble I've seen."

Choose to effectively and correctly handle your troubles. Discuss them with God regularly. Pray! Seek His countenance until He opens up heaven above you. Do not let go of His hand when you are walking in darkness. Persevere to the end. A green pasture awaits you at the end of each troublesome event. That is what Psalm 23 promises. In effect, trouble is the shortcut on the right way to where you are heading.

Fortunately, the Shepherd of your life is accompanying you and seeing you through all your troubles while you search for better pastures. From now on, give your troubles a hard time when they want to rob you of your happiness. See to it that you and the Good Shepherd, Jesus Christ, walk side-by-side always. Note how His footprints cover all your problems.

The Little that You Have

Here is a boy with five small barley loaves and two small fish, but how far will they go among so many?
— JOHN 6:9 NIV —

Of what significance can I be to God? I am too weak to really make a difference. Is that what you think sometimes? Well, that is very far from the truth. The Lord does not require you to be strong before you can start working for Him, neither does He expect you to have all the best possible equipment at your disposal. Anything but. Simply use that which you have already. Put that which you have at hand at the disposal of the Lord and watch what happens!

In John 6, we read about a young boy who had five loaves of bread and two fishes. He was only a small speck among a crowd of people of more than five thousand who were listening to Jesus. When Jesus decided to feed every-one, that small amount of food in His hands was more than enough for a heavenly feast. Jesus multiplied the boy's meal and it became enough to feed all the people.

Learn from him to give the Lord the little money, spiritual talent, and commitment that you have. Then trust Him to multiply them to bring forth a rich harvest. He will!

More Than Enough

Let us not become weary in doing good, for at the
proper time we will reap a harvest if we do not give up.
— GALATIANS 6:9 NIV —

Our basic needs are to have food and shelter every day. Our foremost need is to have our dreams come true.

Well, the Bible tells me that Christ has come to fulfill our basic needs. John 6 says Jesus is the bread of life. He takes away our hunger forever. Christ also fulfills our foremost needs. John 7 says that rivers of living water flow from us when we believe in Him. He lets us experience abundance every day. We who believe are blessed with armfuls of heavenly life—the kind that never comes to an end. Christ showers us with so many blessings each day that they overflow from our hands, feet, and lips to others.

Christ is our everything! We lack for nothing. When life is dark, He is our Light. When we are surrounded by pain and disappointment, He is our Helper. When we feel we cannot or do not want to carry on, He is our heavenly source of strength. When we are abandoned by everybody, He stays near. When storms rage around us, He walks on the water beside us. Truly, we have more than we need, now and for always.

The Good Old Days

Don't long for "the good old days." This is not wise.
— ECCLESIASTES 7:10 NLT —

How many of us long for the good old days? For some reason or other they always seem to be better than today. Or are they? Well, I can assure you that if we could go back to those times that we idolize as the best days ever, we would find fault after a short while and start longing for better days.

Perhaps that is why Ecclesiastes 7:10 cautions us not to think that the past is better than the present—because it is not wise to do so. If we did we would not live wisely and be fully aware of every moment we receive gracefully from God's hand.

We have only today to live life fully for the Lord and others. Yesterday is water under the bridge, and we can't be sure that we will see the light of tomorrow. But today is within our reach. Let us turn it into a festive day for the Lord.

Let us hand out cups of cool water to those who are going through difficult times. Let us be good to one another. Let us gladden the heart of the Lord today.

Precious Treasure

*"Wherever your treasure is,
there the desires of your heart will also be."*
— MATTHEW 6:21 NLT —

Everything that glitters is not gold. Sometimes the most precious treasures are not buried deep under the ground but can be found near the surface instead. Look around— your companion, your parents, and your children are the Lord's special gifts to you. They are your most precious earthly possessions. The Lord does not want you to struggle through life alone. That is why He gave you your loved ones. They are your helpers, your towers of strength, your biggest supporters, and your gold. They are the ones who constantly pray, stand by you, and carry you.

What are you doing for your loved ones? Do you pray for them regularly? Do you set an example for them in your commitment to the Lord? Do you set aside enough time for them? Or are you always tired when you have time to devote to them? Do you constantly have the excuse that you have more work to finish or two more telephone calls to make? If so, you have not really discovered God's special treasures. You are looking for gold in all the wrong places.

Look at your loved ones once more. Thank God for them and live close to them.

Run Like the Blazes

Run from all these evil things. Pursue righteousness and a godly life, along with faith, love, perseverance, and gentleness.

— 1 TIMOTHY 6:11 NLT —

Can you recall the film *Forrest Gump*? He ran for all he was worth right across the USA. He told himself over and over again to just "Run, Forrest, run!" And that is exactly what he did. This is what Paul tells Timothy and all other believers to do in 1 Timothy 6:11. We all have to run. What for? No, the question should rather be from whom or from what. And the answer is from *sin* of course! We should take care to not be in the same place at the same time as sin. If we are, we will get into trouble because sin is not something to play with.

However, to try and run away from sin is not enough. We have to run *to* someone, to Jesus Christ. Only then will we be safe because it is only when we run to Jesus that sin will not be able to catch up with us and temptation will lose the race.

Which wrong things in life always get you down? Does this happen because you have not decided to run away from them? If so, today is the day to take to your feet, but do so in the right direction. Run to the Lord. He is your safe haven.

An Actor or the Real McCoy?

*"When you give to the needy, do not let your left hand
know what your right hand is doing. Then your Father,
who sees what is done in secret, will reward you."*

— MATTHEW 6:3-4 NIV —

Acting is the biggest industry in the world. The stars of
Hollywood are the superheroes of today. They have mastered
the art of pretending. The sad thing is that pretending does
not only happen on film sets and in theaters but also in real
life. Some people pretend to be holier than a saint. The good
things they say when they move in religious circles are all
an act. We call it hypocrisy. It is a role you play on Sundays,
but when you are on your own, where no one else can see
you, you show your real colors. That is when you go off the
track completely.

What about you? Are you pretending to be a believer
when it suits you or are you the real McCoy? The proof of
true faith is whether you serve the Lord when no one is
watching. Do you do good things quietly without expecting
any recognition? Jesus says in Matthew 6 that when your
left hand does not know what your right hand is doing,
that is the end of role-playing. When you serve God and
worship Him when no one is near, that is the real thing.

Turning Words into Weapons

*[Believers] must not slander anyone and
must avoid quarreling. Instead, they should
be gentle and show true humility to everyone.*

— TITUS 3:2 NLT —

My tongue is not mine to do with as I please. That is what the Bible says. I should not use words randomly. Words are weapons of mass destruction or protective medicine. Depending on the mouth in which words are formed, they can be good or bad. When spoken by a fool, words are killer missiles that break and hurt others. When spoken by the wise, words are like good ointment and medicine that heals. This is what the book of Proverbs says repeatedly.

Paul says in Titus 3 that we as believers should not speak slanderous words about anyone. We should always be soft-spoken and kind. Our words may never be dangerous. They must not inflame the severely infectious situation that vile language causes in society. They must not aggravate the grave sickness that sin has brought into our world. There are enough nasty and destructive words circulating the world right now.

Let's break this evil spell by constantly speaking God-honoring language. Remind yourself to speak differently about people and to people. Speak wisely, calmly, and gently. Do not say and do things that will hurt others.

Are You a Worrywart?

Satisfy us in the morning with Your unfailing love,
that we may sing for joy and be glad all our days.

— PSALM 90:14 NIV —

Simplicity is one of the joys of life. It's true, isn't it? There is joy in the simple act of breaking bread with a good friend or family member. Simple joy is playing ball with your children or spending time with your family. And what a joy it is to thank the Lord for the blessing of each new day. Simplicity is being satisfied. It is saying the words of Psalm 23: "The Lord is my Shepherd; I shall not want."

What are you short on? Money? A better car? Different job conditions? Well, if you worry about things you lack, you will probably always be dissatisfied with what you have. Even a new car will not be enough. You will be satisfied only when you have one with a sunroof and leather seats. Or when your new training bike looks like your neighbor's.

If you worry about things you don't have, you will always want more or something different. You will always be short of something. But if you know the Lord as your Shepherd, you will truly lack nothing. You will have as much as you need.

Destined for Good Things

*We are God's masterpiece. He has created
us anew in Christ Jesus, so we can do the
good things He planned for us long ago.*

— EPHESIANS 2:10 NLT —

God has created us to devote our lives to doing good.
That is what Paul writes in Ephesians 2:10. Did you hear?
We are destined for good things and not to build castles
and monuments to glorify our own names. We have been
created to glorify our heavenly Father in the short time we
have on earth. Therefore, we must make a difference!

We do not have to change the world. We only have to
carry out the few assignments that God has in mind for us.
We only have to take part in the relationships that God has
planned for us and make a difference.

Well, have you discovered your call in life? Do you know
what the purpose of your life is? No? Then it is high time
that you start doing the right things. It is time to become
part of God's plan to repair the broken world bit by bit.
There are sure to be broken people around you who need a
piece of bread: living bread and ordinary bread! Start there.
Who knows? They have probably been destined by God to
cross your path and be part of your destiny.

Counting Your Blessings

Be gentle with one another, sensitive.
Forgive one another as quickly and
thoroughly as God in Christ forgave you.
— EPHESIANS 4:32 THE MESSAGE —

What does your balance sheet for this year look like so far? Did you use all the chances you were given? Were you more softhearted—someone who cared more about others? Did you show more compassion; a hand more open to those in need? Was your tongue coated in silver more often than it was full of venom? Were you more faithful in prayer? Perhaps you got to know God's Word a little better? Were the lives of others enriched by your friendship? Were you a neighbor to someone whose life hit hard times? Were you the one who made a positive, heavenly difference in the lives of others?

Have you enjoyed this year so far, despite the hardship around you? Have you really noticed the sunrise and felt the wind and rain through your hair? Have you listened to the voices of children playing happily? Did you feel your minister's sermon on a Sunday morning was meant for you in particular? Did you leave church with a smile on your face because you realized God truly loves you? Well, if these moments of happiness on your balance sheet top the heartache, then it has been a good year so far.

Keeping Score

*Make allowance for each other's faults, and
forgive anyone who offends you. Remember,
the Lord forgave you, so you must forgive others.*

— COLOSSIANS 3:13 NLT —

Can you recall the question Peter put to Jesus in Matthew 18:21? "Lord, how many times shall I forgive my brother when he sins against me? Up to seven times?" Actually, Peter's offer was quite generous because the Jews thought forgiving someone three times was more than enough. That closed the books of forgiveness, and feelings of hate could multiply afterwards.

Jesus' reply was that seven times was not sufficient; 70 times seven would be in order. In other words, do not count the times you forgive your fellow man, for there is no end to forgiveness. Forgiveness does not work like sums of addition. The followers of Jesus do not keep record of others' mistakes or of the times they have forgiven. They never think back on the transgressions of their friends, colleagues, and family. Christians have a short-term memory when it comes to how others mess up. On the other hand, they are not blind to their own and others' flaws. However, they talk things over without being nasty about it. They never spread ugly rumors about others behind their backs. And they do not speak maliciously towards others.

The Object of His Affection

To Him who loves us and has freed us from our sins by His blood, to Him be glory and power for ever and ever!
— REVELATION 1:5–6 NIV —

Usually we don't like people who tread on our toes, but we like those who behave the way we want them to. Fortunately, God is not like us. He likes all of us who bow before Christ, regardless of what we do or fail to do.

We are His special possessions, His favorites, always (Rom. 8:31-39). No, God does not give us a license to do wrong or to wallow in sin, but His love for us does not depend on what we do. He loves us in any case. His love does not seesaw—liking us today and disliking us tomorrow. No matter how deep we fall, God seeks us out every time. It is His choice. It is His divine nature.

God's love is not reactive. He does not first look at how we live and then decide whether He still likes us or not. No, God decided at the outset that those who believe in Jesus Christ are the apple of His eye. He likes us best of all His creatures. This is affirmed by the manger and the cross. God is love, and we are the objects of His affection.

Laugh!

A cheerful heart is good medicine.
— PROVERBS 17:22 NIV —

Recently, a church elder told me he had heard an old man next to him start to snore during my sermon. When he nudged him in the side, the drowsy man had mumbled, "Sorry, dear, I'll turn over immediately." I don't know whether the elder was just making a joke, and I didn't want to ask him, but it made me realize that my sermons might be like sleeping pills to more people in the church than I would care to know.

I realized that we should not take ourselves so seriously. Perhaps we should take life more lightly (not be flippant, of course!). The facial muscles of too many church people turn to stone when they enter the church. No wonder, as many churches still have a sign out front warning: "SILENCE CHURCH." I agree that the church is about God but that does not mean that there is no place for humor in our religious lives.

Perhaps we should look again at the many times Jesus enjoyed the company of people and celebrated with them joyously. Let us imitate Him in that!

One by One

Never tire of doing what is good.
— 2 THESSALONIANS 3:13 NIV —

The right kind of impact in the world occurs at the rate of one person, one word, and one action at a time. Real change is not necessarily brought about by great actions and programs. When the life of one person is filled with hope because of her or his contact with me, another brand-new row of bricks is laid on the road to heaven. The territory taken up by despair, death, and hopelessness decreases by one person.

When my words and deeds bring hope to the broken and when my simple actions of compassion help heal their wounds, the world suddenly becomes more bearable, humane, and safe! The sunbeams of the gospel warm our world anew.

While our world is becoming colder and more impersonal, I must be the living difference for the Lord. Everyone who comes into contact with me should have my fingerprint of compassion on their lives to show for it. Others should feel and hear the clear echo of heavenly grace in my life. One by one they should move closer to hear more about God because my life is such a powerful reflection of His love (Matt. 5).

Success

*You can make many plans, but
the Lord's purpose will prevail.*
— PROVERBS 19:21 NLT —

Success does not depend on the two horrible "M-things": money and material possessions. It is not about what you drive, where you live, or what you own. What is more, success does not revolve around our favorite word: "mine, mine, mine." People who are truly successful are people with integrity (Rom. 12). These are men and women who touch the lives of others and are a blessing to them. They make a difference to the way others live.

Won't you please become a new trademark for excellence? Let your love for God, your warmth, and your caring be an inspiration to others! Start working on a spiritual heritage, one through which you leave your footprints in heavenly rock and not in sand. Do not walk over people. No, walk with them and encourage them. Do not walk proudly in front of other people. Walk behind them and help them when they get lost. Do not tower above others; be a servant who looks after them well. Let the love of the Lord spill over to them by speaking gentle words and doing kind deeds. Make a living difference in the lives of others. If you do, you are successful in the right way in the eyes of the right person: Christ.

Why So Safe?

*"Walk with Me and work with Me—watch
how I do it. Learn the unforced rhythms of grace."*

— MATTHEW 11:29 THE MESSAGE —

Orderly, structured, controlled—do these words describe your lifestyle? Do you live within a safe, highly structured routine where everyone and everything is in its right place? Now, there is nothing wrong with a well-ordered life as such. But the question is: what do you do if an unexpected crisis descends upon you? Does the unexpected take you by complete surprise? Or is this an opportunity for growth?

Do you have the guts to see today as a clean, new page? Are you open and receptive to life's many surprises? Or is everything in your life so structured that you can even arrange your own "surprise party"? Do you still have the ability to see God's hand in a small act of kindness? Or in an unexpected smile? Or a quick conversation?

Can you surprise yourself by changing your strict daily routine to visit somebody who is lonely or to buy flowers for a loved one? Will you dare tell a colleague or a friend how God answered one of your prayers? Do you have the guts? Or do experiences like that disturb your set routines too much? Why so safe?

Use It or Lose It

*Faith is confidence in what we hope for
and assurance about what we do not see.*

— HEBREWS 11:1 NIV —

What were your resolutions for this year? Have you kept them after nearly six months have come and gone? It is quite possible that you haven't because most people who make New Year's resolutions have forgotten them by the third week of January. However, it is not too late to begin over again. How about a new resolution to persevere on the road of God each day for the rest of the year? Remember, faith operates like the "use it, or lose it" rule. You cannot cling to last year's faith—consider it used up. Faith is about keeping at it each day. Your faith must have an impact on your life here and now, otherwise it is archive material. If it does not have a daily impact, you belong in a museum for people of obsolete faith!

Faith is entrusting Christ with your most precious possession—your life. Live your life each day in the knowledge that your faith is as alive as your most recent steps on God's road.

You must choose anew each day to follow the Lord with all of your heart. You need to decide daily to be obedient to Him in all things.

Storage Space

Love does not demand its own way. It is not irritable,
and it keeps no record of being wronged.

— 1 CORINTHIANS 13:5 NLT —

Supermarkets normally require a vast amount of storage space for their stock. Perhaps you, too, require a lot of storage space in your house or apartment for food, clothes, furniture, TVs, and books. Our mind is also full of stored information. If you are a Christian, then you definitely do not have storage space in your mind for bad thoughts about other people!

True faith is forgetful. It has the effect of never holding things against people. Time after time, in your head, you have to close the little black book which records other people's misdeeds. At the end of every day we must "delete" the negative information and transfer it to the garbage can for useless information.

In 1 Corinthians 13:5 Paul reminds us that God's people never keep a record of wrongs. Neither should you. You are a new person. "Remember to forget and forget to remember" when it comes to bad things. God has renewed your thoughts, which in any event do not have enough memory or bandwidth to store resentment or wrongs.

Your Greatest Critic

The LORD has done it this very day;
let us rejoice today and be glad.

— PSALM 118:24 NIV —

We can be all too critical of ourselves. Far too often we only focus on our faults and failures. Yesterday's errors remove all the joy from today's sunshine. Are you perhaps too hard on yourself? Do you find it difficult to forgive? In that case, adopt Lamentations 3:22-23 as your new daily creed. These are life-changing words born out of the dark period directly after the Babylonian exile, when the Israelites returned to a devastated Jerusalem. Listen: The Lord's kindness never fails! If He had not been merciful, we would have been destroyed. The Lord can always be trusted to show mercy each morning.

Forget about yesterday's mistakes. Know that God's love is new every day. Today He truly makes a fresh start with you and everybody else. Today is a new day in God's kingdom. The failures of yesterday and the day before are erased by the cross of Jesus Christ.

Notice today's new gift of heavenly mercy on your doorstep. See God's footprints which obliterate your own. Today's path is so much more accessible. You can make a success of every new day!

Gear Up for God

The LORD will vindicate me;
Your love, LORD, endures forever.
— PSALM 138:8 NIV —

Your car doesn't move when it is in neutral. Neither does your faith. You have been re-created by God to do good things for Him in the ordinary moments of your life! You can't go to heaven if you remain stationary. In fact, Paul tells us in Ephesians 2:10 that God created you to devote your life to do those good deeds for which He prepared you. Are you turning this Scripture into truth?

Every moment of your life is precious. The next hour might just be a God-given opportunity in your life to do something profound in His name. During the mundane moments of your life, God sends opportunities your way.

However, no celestial warning lights are flashed. There aren't always angels who appear and shout, "Prepare yourself, God is going to start using you within 10 seconds." Instead, at the traffic light, at your desk or workplace, next to the sports field, or in class, these special moments arise out of the blue. In those moments, you dare not act like an observer or a coward. No, you must get into *sixth* gear for God.

Sing!

*At about midnight Paul and Silas
were praying and singing hymns to God,
and the other prisoners were listening to them.*

— ACTS 16:25 NIV —

The scenario: Paul and his assistant, Silas, have just been beaten to a pulp in the city of Philippi for believing in Christ (Acts 16). Half conscious, they are thrown into the maximum security jail in Philippi.

The response: Paul and Silas start singing at midnight. They sing songs of praise—not those generic favorites you and I would sing, like "I am done for," but the purest songs of praise. Despite their broken bodies and without musical accompaniment, they sing, although hoarsely, the most beautiful songs of worship ever heard.

God's response: He quiets the heavens so as to hear the pure sounds. Then He stretches out His hand to touch His broken servants in Philippi. At that moment the earth shakes and the doors of the jail swing open.

Paul reports for duty again: Although the jail's doors were open, Paul did not escape. Instead, he told the warden about being saved.

The lesson: Sing! Sing songs of praise in honor of the Lord, even though it is pitch-dark around you. Even though all your prospects seem bleak—sing! Praise God, even though there may be nothing in your life to sing about.

July

Choose Joy

*Whatever you do or say, do it as a representative of the
Lord Jesus, giving thanks through Him to God the Father.*

— COLOSSIANS 3:17 NLT —

Maybe the problem with our plans and visions is that we
set challenges that are too difficult for ourselves. We want
to achieve the impossible. But then our spirit is broken
before we have even started. Maybe we should set smaller,
more realistic goals for ourselves. And the goals should also
be enjoyable! This month choose to do something with your
life that will make your life and the lives of those around
you happier. Choose goals which reflect God's greatness
through the ordinary things you do every day (Col. 3:17).

What about the simple decision to laugh out loud at least
once a day during the month of July? Or to drink coffee
with someone once a week? Is it too much to ask to pray for
another person every day? Or to phone someone who is suffering once a week to say that you are thinking of them? Or
to secretly give extra money to somebody in need? Scatter
joy everywhere you go—God's type of joy.

You can't change the whole world and you don't have to.
But you can make your own piece of the world a happier
place. The choice is yours.

Fireproof

*If you confess with your mouth that Jesus
is Lord and believe in your heart that God
raised Him from the dead, you will be saved.*

— ROMANS 10:9 NLT —

Financial advisers regularly caution people to make the correct financial investments to ensure a safe future. Peace of mind about tomorrow ensures a better life today. Well, if you are prepared to rely on the advice of financial advisers, what about the advice of a spiritual giant like the apostle Paul? Would you rate his advice more highly than the advice of the competent people around you? Paul was privileged because he had access to the treasure house of God in heaven through prayer. And, furthermore, Paul was instructed to share God's secrets with us, free of charge!

The greatest secret which has now been revealed is that God designed an enduring insurance product which is death proof. This product was personally designed by Jesus Christ when He died on the cross for you. His instructions are simple: Confess with your mouth and believe with your heart that He is the one and only God (Acts 16; Phil. 2; Rom. 10). Then your future will be fireproof. It will also be death proof. Nothing and nobody can wrench you out of the hand of God. Therefore, you may truly live today, with great peace of mind.

Regret

*When you ask, you don't get it because
your motives are all wrong—you
want only what will give you pleasure.*

— JAMES 4:3 NLT —

A few times I have stood at a death bed. No dying person has ever said to me that they regret not having worked harder or not having made more money during their life here on earth. No, instead all would have liked to have spent more time with God and with their loved ones. A friend once was on a flight when two of the engines failed. He told me that the captain instructed the passengers at one stage to use their mobile phones and call their loved ones. No, not their bank manager or their financial advisor. When a person's life hangs by a thread, their heart yearns for their loved ones. Then they pray. And love wins!

Let's get our priorities right while we have the time to do so. Let's walk with God. Let's join the faithful in Revelation 14:1-5 who follow Jesus everywhere He goes. Then we will walk as winners on our way to the finish line. Jesus walks on the road of life. When we follow Him we won't have any regrets when our last day on earth arrives. Tomorrow's regret begins in today's choices, so choose anew to follow Christ now!

Start with Today

"Give us today our daily bread."

— MATTHEW 6:11 NIV —

Many people live in the future already. But they show up here in the present every day. In fact, they merely regard today as a fleeting moment on the road to tomorrow. Here and now is not really important. For them the meaning of life lies in tomorrow. That is a big mistake. Jesus taught us to live today, to live from here towards the future, not the other way around. In the Lord's Prayer we are taught to pray, "Give us today our daily bread," not tomorrow's bread.

In Matthew 6 we are taught not to worry today about tomorrow's problems. Life happens today. God's grace is here today. His care, love, and support as well. Tomorrow is at least a day away. A lot of water has to run into the ocean before today becomes tomorrow. What a waste of time it is if today we don't fully live to the glory of God.

What a waste to think that we are only going to get around to living to His glory tomorrow or next week. No, today is the day. Go, and receive your portion of grace from God. Give your life to Him today. Then you will be living correctly!

A Divine Opportunity

*"I now know beyond a shadow of a
doubt that there is no God anywhere
on earth other than the God of Israel."*

— 2 KINGS 5:15 THE MESSAGE —

When God called on a young Israeli slave in Naaman's household to serve Him in a foreign country, she reported for duty right there on the spot. The greatest moment in her life arrived soon afterwards when Naaman contracted leprosy. Two sentences, at exactly the right time, ensured that she become immortalized in the Bible. Her words "If only my master would see the prophet who is in Samaria! He would cure him of his leprosy" ensured that general Naaman's life would be changed permanently.

After Naaman was cured of his leprosy, he openly acknowledged that the God of Israel was the only God. He and his attendants had seen God's amazing power in action. Maybe the young Israelite did not know the incredible effect of her words. That does not really matter. The fruit of our work for God is not meant to be observed by us. As long as we seize every divine moment that God brings across our path, we are on track. On the day of Christ, He will show us whether we have utilized every divine moment or let it slip through our fingers! The choice is ours.

From the Inside Out

People judge by outward appearance,
but the LORD looks at the heart.

— 1 SAMUEL 16:7 NLT —

We spend most of our time getting our lives sorted out externally. Consider our domestic routines: our clothes are neatly packed in drawers, food is stored in pantries, and our cars are parked in garages. The greatest part of our time, money, and energy is taken up with tangible things like clothes, cars, houses, the acquisition of possessions, and our appearance.

Paul writes in 1 Corinthians 3:16 that we who believe in Christ are a temple of the Holy Spirit. We are God's new home here on earth. God does not reside in church buildings. We are His house, His spiritual temple. And yet many of our spiritual houses are derelict, because we spend too much time on our external dwellings. We believe the lie that life actually happens externally.

God teaches us that we do in fact operate differently. There is only one way to live our lives from the inside out: we must give the Holy Spirit free access to our lives, from the inside out. We must be soft clay in the sculptor's hands so that He can decorate us with His love and mercy. Then we will live the way God wants us to.

God Knows You

*You hem me in behind and before,
and You lay Your hand upon me.*
— PSALM 139:5 NIV —

You are not a biological coincidence. Psalm 139:13-14 exclaims, "For you created my inmost being; you knit me together in my mother's womb. I praise You because I am fearfully and wonderfully made; Your works are wonderful, I know that full well." God knows you inside out, from the moment you began. He knows more about you than you could ever know about yourself. Before your birth God already knew the path that your life would follow. "You know me inside and out, You know every bone in my body; You know exactly how I was made, bit by bit, how I was sculpted from nothing into something. Like an open book, You watched me grow from conception to birth; all the stages of my life were spread out before you, the days of my life all prepared before I'd even lived one day" (vv. 15-16).

God knows every thought that crosses your mind. He sees your whole existence in a flash, in all its dimensions. There is no part of your life that you can hide from Him. All your decisions, dreams, fears, and joys—literally every millimeter of your life—are known to God. He looks right through you. Don't try to understand how it works, because it isn't possible.

Passion

*"I will give you a new heart and put a new
spirit in you; I will remove from you your
heart of stone and give you a heart of flesh."*

— EZEKIEL 36:26 NIV —

Recently I heard two people discuss a church elder, one of them remarking that the elder had too little passion for the work of the Lord. This comment really got me thinking. A church leader without passion and Christians without hearts—how is this possible? I don't know, but it is really sad, to say the least. Too many Christians understand the Bible intellectually, but they have not told their hearts about it. They have the correct answers to all kinds of difficult questions, but their faces are not radiant when they talk about God and His affairs. How sad.

The gospel requires the attention of your heart. Yes, your head as well but particularly your heart. If you can't testify, as Paul did in Philippians 1:21, "For to me, living means living for Christ, and dying is even better," then you have completely missed the pulsating heartbeat of faith. If you are not excited with childlike wonder about God and His affairs, then you lack spiritual passion. If this is the case, you should sit in God's presence until you experience His glory. You should leave everything and wait upon Him until He reveals His heart to you again.

A Strong Fragrance

*Thanks be to God, who always leads us in triumphal
procession in Christ and through us spreads
everywhere the fragrance of the knowledge of Him.*

— 2 CORINTHIANS 2:14 NIV —

Faith smells. And it is a strong smell. In *The Message* Paul writes, "Everywhere we go, people breathe in the exquisite fragrance. Because of Christ, we give off a sweet scent rising to God, which is recognized by those on the path of salvation—an aroma redolent with life. But those on the way to destruction treat us more like the stench from a rotting corpse." We as Christians are Christ's aroma on earth. Some people think we smell bad. Others think that we have the scent of life. What a contrast—life and death, salvation and destruction. All of this we exude if we live close to Jesus.

It is astounding that we are God's fragrance on earth. It is so sad that some people confuse the smell we have with that of death. They can't stand us because they are enemies of the cross of Christ. Nevertheless, even though some people think we smell, it is our obligation to be Christ's aroma. We must distribute true life through our actions. How? Well, by living Christ's victory. But we must stay close to Him all the time. That is the secret. Then Christ's rejuvenating power flows through us to those who need it most today.

He Holds Me

In the same way, the Spirit helps us in our weakness.
We do not know what we ought to pray for, but the Spirit
Himself intercedes for us through wordless groans.

— ROMANS 8:26 NIV —

When Christ returned to heaven, He did not leave us to our own devices. He gave us the Holy Spirit in His place, as Helper, Counselor, Spiritual Assistant, Advocate, Savior, Intercessor, and Builder of Temples. We are no longer alone, even if no one else is present. The Holy Spirit is our permanent companion. He is with us all the time. He raises us up when we are really down and out. He intercedes for us with the Father when we do not know how or what to pray. He keeps us on the right spiritual path to the Father's heart.

When we start losing direction, the Holy Spirit immediately comes looking for us. When we try to hide from God in the darkness of our own faults and misdemeanors, He switches on a bright, spiritual light in our lives. We cannot run, we cannot hide—neither from ourselves nor from Him. The Spirit's task is to one day deliver us, safe and sound, to God the Father in His eternal heavenly dwelling (Eph. 1:13-14). This is why He consistently ensures that we stay on track. He keeps us en route to God.

Living Art

*Let us then approach God's throne of grace
with confidence, so that we may receive mercy
and find grace to help us in our time of need.*

— HEBREWS 4:16 NIV —

David states in Psalm 139 that you are a unique creation of God. The Almighty God decided that you would specifically live in these times. God sketched your life on His easel. He planned you and called you into being. And then you were born. No, you are not a coincidence. God observes your life with great interest, every day. He notes everything that you do. He hears all your words. He reads all your thoughts.

God's expectation is that you will change in order to reflect His heavenly kindness, more and more. His desire is that you will let His light shine brightly in this dark world of ours. Not only did God form you with great care and endless love when He created you from scratch, He remodeled you into a new person. God interceded in your life through Christ, because He does not want you, one of His special works of art, to go to ruin.

Give thanks to God for having created you on His easel and for re-creating you. Start achieving your unique spiritual potential.

Jesus Is the Answer

*"I am the Alpha and the Omega, the First
and the Last, the Beginning and the End."*

— REVELATION 22:13 NIV —

"Jesus is the answer!" somebody once wrote on a wall.
Someone else wrote below it: "What is the question?"
Maybe that is not such a stupid comment. Maybe we should
ask the question differently. "For whom is Jesus the right
answer?" Well, He is not the answer for religious people,
but He is the answer for sinners! Jesus gives brand-new life
to sinners who pitch up, bent and broken. He changes them
at the speed of heavenly mercy into new persons. But for
"religious" folk who think that their lives are good enough,
Jesus has nothing to offer.

So, is Jesus the answer? It depends on who you ask.
It depends on how great your need is. Are you desperate
to sort out your affairs with God? If you are desperate to
repair your relationship with God, then Jesus *is* the answer!
If you have taken your sins to Him, then you will definitely
know what I am talking about. But if you have not done it,
then it is high time you pay Jesus a visit. He has reserved a
special place for you at His feet. He will answer your most
pressing questions. Just go and ask!

Setting the Pace

Let us run with endurance the race God has set before us. We do this by keeping our eyes on Jesus, the champion who initiates and perfects our faith.

— HEBREWS 12:1-2 NLT —

In long distance races there are often "pacesetters." Pacesetters are athletes who run in the front of the pack for one or two laps to inspire the champions to achieve better times. Normally, pacesetters stop running before the end of the race. They get out of the way of the winners who break records and receive all the glory. Pacesetters are actually the unseen heroes on whose shoulders the champions stand. Maybe it is my and your calling to be spiritual pacesetters in God's world. We should deliberately create opportunities for co-believers to run past us and beat us. We should proactively invest in the lives of others so that they can grow past us spiritually.

When other Christians excel spiritually, we win. When we support co-believers to do things in a better way than ourselves, for God's glory, to worship better, to testify more powerfully, to teach or preach more dynamically, or to be better at prayer, then Christ's message wins. In these circumstances, we contribute in a modest way to set the pace for God's athletes. The emphasis then falls in the right place—on God and on others, not on ourselves.

Not Ashamed

*"If anyone is in Christ, the new creation
has come: The old has gone, the new is here!"*

— 2 CORINTHIANS 5:17 NIV —

I could hear the excitement in my daughter's voice when she told me that she had tickets to watch her favorite Christian band. The tickets for the show had been selling like hot cakes. My daughter just had to be there. Their music plays an important role in her spiritual formation and in her daily life. Therefore, she told everybody about it.

Her excitement made me wonder if my heart beats for Christ in the same manner as her heart beat faster when she had the opportunity of seeing her favorite Christian band performing live?

After thinking about this, the words of Paul in Romans 1:16 obtained a fresh, new meaning for me. "I am not ashamed of the gospel, because it is the power of God that brings salvation to everyone who believes: first to the Jew, then to the Gentile."

How can I remain silent about the best news of the day and about the headlines for the year? How can I remain silent when Christ is the only power in this powerless world? How can I stop rejoicing when He still changes lives?

Taste!

*Taste and see that the L*ORD *is good.*
— PSALM 34:8 NIV —

"You do not want to leave too, do you?" Jesus asked the disciples after many had turned away (John 6). They had just heard that they should follow Jesus radically, but they weren't prepared to do so. They weren't prepared to eat His flesh and drink His blood, as He explained to them. The demands of discipleship were too high, and the cross they had to bear was much too heavy. Peter's answer was equally direct and straightforward: "Lord, to whom shall we go? You have the words of eternal life!" (John 6:68).

If you "taste" Jesus' words, your hunger will disappear. It is like eating eternal food. You can never go away from Him once you have swallowed His living words. It gives eternal energy forever! But you first have to eat His words to really understand what Peter meant. How do you do that? Well, just ask Jesus to pronounce living words over you. He will do it immediately! Then you will ingest bread which will satisfy your spiritual hunger forever. You will never want to leave Jesus, because then you will die of spiritual hunger.

Before You Speak

Set a guard over my mouth, Lord;
keep watch over the door of my lips.

— PSALM 141:3 NIV —

A person thinks six times faster than he talks. Academics calculate that the typical person talks at approximately one-hundred words per minute, but that they think at 600 words per minute—with visuals and all! Well, if that is true, then it means that I have to be more cautious with my words—because they don't just happen automatically.

Too many dangerous words swirl around in my head before they leave my lips. For this reason I should pray Psalm 141:3 as if my life depends on it. I must beg God to place a guard in front of my mouth and allow Him to keep watch permanently over the door of my lips. Where my thoughts start, I must only allow those that are good and pure. If I don't, I will think foolish thoughts. Even worse, I may speak negative words in the company of other people.

In that event, my words will become weapons of destruction and not a soothing balm or good medicine. I must place my thoughts and my words, like clay, in God's hands today. Then other people will experience healing in the presence of my words.

Get Out of the Boat

Jesus immediately said to them:
"Take courage! It is I. Don't be afraid."

— MATTHEW 14:27 NIV —

To walk on water is not normal. Ask Peter! You have to climb out of your boat before you can walk on water with Jesus. And that requires a fixed stare in His direction and a secure grasp of His hand. But is walking on water really as difficult as some people think? Yes and no! Yes, walking on water is difficult for those unused to doing so!

For those who never risk talking about their faith proactively or who never stay obedient to God through thick and thin, life's storms can be devastating. But for those who time and time again risk following Jesus even in the midst of a storm and who are not embarrassed to be carriers of the cross, sometimes they walk on water. It does not scare them. It is also not impossible.

Jesus lifts us above every storm—provided that we place our hand in His! Don't let life's storms cause you to let go of His hand. Look past your crises—look towards Him, who is greater! Walk towards Him. That is the secret.

Not for Sale

*Truly my soul finds rest in God; my salvation comes
from Him. Truly He is my rock and my salvation.*

— PSALM 62:1-2 NIV —

Two Simons in the town of Samaria (Acts 8): Simon the
sorcerer and Simon Peter. Simon the sorcerer was known
as "The Mighty." The other Simon was known as Peter,
the Rock, the one upon whose testimony Christ built His
church (Matt. 16). Simon the Powerhouse versus Simon the
Rock: worldly sorcery compared to heavenly power. No
contest! Simon the sorcerer was immediately stumped when
he saw how Peter communicated the gospel to people in
Samaria. The power of the Spirit that worked through Peter
changed their lives from the inside out. Then the sorcerer
tried to purchase this supernatural power.

What a mistake to think that God can be purchased
with money! The Spirit works in His own way. He is never
for sale. His power cannot be copied. Thank God, He works
charitably and completely free in the lives of those whom
He changes into temples of the Almighty. The Spirit changes
ordinary people into rocks who can bravely testify about
Jesus, not into sorcerers who try to impress with tricks.

Let Him use you as one of His rocks so that people
around you may change in the right way, too.

Our Awesome God

*"My Father, who has given them to Me, is greater than all;
no one can snatch them out of My Father's hand."*

— JOHN 10:29 NIV —

A few years ago my wife and I traveled through Turkey with a wonderful group of people, and one afternoon we experienced a solar eclipse. For a few minutes the moon moved across the sun, and the world around us was pitch dark. Everybody who experienced it was overwhelmed, as was I. Once again I realized just how big and mighty God is. I was in awe over His power. He has the power to push the moon quietly across the path of the sun. He can extinguish the sun when it suits Him. But the tenderness with which He guards His creation so that the planets remain in orbit day after day is too much for me to understand.

Psalm 8 cries out, "What is man that You are mindful of him?" In the greater scheme of things, we are a handful of nothings—little bits of dust in life's massive machine. Yet God concerns Himself with tiny human beings like us. He creates us out of dust, and He lets us live in front of Him, daily. He even loves us. God holds us, Christ's sheep, lovingly in His hands (vv. 28-30). Praise His name!

Little People

*"Whoever welcomes one such
child in my name welcomes Me."*

— MATTHEW 18:5 NIV —

Jesus compared His followers to little ones (Matt. 18). No, not strong ones or important ones. Not supermen with X-ray eyes that fly around from one spiritual heroic deed to the next. Not powerful lions or giant elephants. No, little ones! Leaders and followers in Jesus' group are vulnerable! Power is not their strong point, but faith is! Status and fame does not mean anything to them, but respect does! They care for each other. They constantly pray for each other, support each other, and cry and laugh together. They do life together in the presence of their Father in heaven.

Jesus' little ones do not have a high opinion of themselves. They have no reason to because they know that everything that they have is through grace. They never try to push to the front of life's queues, because it is not about them. It is only about God and His gigantic love for a world that is in the ICU. Therefore they worship Jesus day and night. They talk about Him and to Him. They sing about Him. And they gladly serve the ones that He sends across their path daily.

Awe

Put yourself aside, and help others get ahead.
Don't be obsessed with getting your own advantage.
Forget yourselves long enough to lend a helping hand.
— PHILIPPIANS 2:3–4 THE MESSAGE —

The world is becoming cynical. Nobody believes anything good about anybody else anymore. When somebody is successful, she or he is maligned. When somebody wins, others "steal" his or her medal by making sarcastic comments behind his or her back. Nobody is safe from the cynical comments of other people. Should we not trade in our cynical hearts for hearts full of wonder? How? Well, start by doing what Paul recommends in Philippians 2. Start by treating others as more important than you. Notice that God gives His grace in large quantities to the people at work and in the church. Remember, you are not the only person whose prayers are heard. See the beauty in friends and family despite the scars that life has inflicted on them. For a change, look past their faults; look until you see how God also blesses them with His grace.

Awe makes you smaller and others bigger. As you become smaller before God, your cynical nature disappears. The more Christ's heartbeat echoes within you, the more you discover the beauty in others. And then you become the restorer of God's creation and not the inflictor of scars.

Against the Stream

*Imitate God, therefore, in everything you do,
because you are His dear children.*

— EPHESIANS 5:1 NLT —

"It won't work." "Don't even try." How many times have you heard statements like these when you have a dream? Don't listen to such comments. If Moses listened to all the prophets of doom on the way to the Promised Land, Israel would have collapsed into the desert sands of Egypt. If Elisha started trembling when the enemy armies surrounded the town of Dothan (2 Kings 6), like his slave did, he would have disappeared from all memory. If Paul listened to Luke and his co-workers who tried to prevent him from returning to Jerusalem (Acts 21), a large part of the Roman Empire would not have heard the good news of Christ.

If Martin Luther listened to the advice of his peers, he would never have stood up against the church of his day and, in so doing, would have never launched the Reformation. If Mother Teresa had relied on human support and finances, she would never have gone to Calcutta and changed the plight of the poor and sick.

And you? Do you constantly lend your ears to a stream of pessimists, or do you listen to the calling of the Spirit within your heart?

In His Service

> *"Whoever wants to become great among you must be your servant, and whoever wants to be first must be slave of all."*

— MARK 10:43–44 NIV —

You can place your napkin in one of two places: on your lap when you eat or over your arm when you serve others. By the way, Jesus' favorite followers are not those being served at the table but those serving: those who are the waiters, the slaves, and the servants. That is what He says in Luke 17. His followers who make a real difference stand in the back of the line. For Jesus, first is always last, and last is always first. For Him, the back is in front, and the front is at the back. This sounds upside down, and it is. Being a Christian is topsy-turvy. Jesus really turned our world upside down!

Jesus does not call His "upside down" followers lions. Instead, He calls them sheep. Not elephants, but lambs. Jesus came to earth wearing modest clothes, and He spent most of His time among the "wrong" crowd of sinners: weaklings, strangers, sick people, people who had been shunned, the lonely, homeless, and despised. In the same way, He expects us to follow in His footsteps. Therefore, Jesus' modern heroes are those who live back to front and upside down by becoming servants to the forgotten.

God Likes Me

"We believe that we are all saved the same way,
by the undeserved grace of the Lord Jesus."

— ACTS 15:11 NLT —

God does not owe us anything. He is not in our service. What can we do for Him so that He owes us anything in return? In Romans 11, Paul says that God does not like us as a result of who we are. No, He loves us *despite* of who we are.

This is called grace—the type Paul refers to in Romans 5: "At just the right time, when we were still powerless, Christ died for the ungodly" (v. 6).

"God demonstrates His own love for us in this: While we were still sinners, Christ died for us" (v. 8).

"If, when we were God's enemies, we were reconciled to Him through the death of His Son, how much more, having been reconciled, shall we be saved through His life!" (v. 10).

Powerless, sinners, enemies—that is who we were when God encountered us; we were by no means strong, victorious, or nice! He loved us when we were knee deep in muck. Despite ourselves—that is how God likes us most! His love says so much more about Him than about us. That is what He is like. He does not owe us anything, and yet He dispenses grace to us every day.

All You Need

"My grace is enough; it's all you need."
— 2 CORINTHIANS 12:9 THE MESSAGE —

"It's mine!" Those are the words of a two-year-old if you dare take his toy. And if you don't return it promptly, there is war, because it's "mine!" Some adults also live in this manner. Everything in the shops, every new product, has their name on it. "Mine" is what they say to themselves when they see a new car, CD, clothes, furniture, video camera, laptop, or cell phone. There is no rest for their soul until that item has also become theirs. As soon as the item has been purchased, they want something else.

We live in a world which continuously creates one desire after the other. We never have enough things that can be regarded as "mine." If we don't guard against it, we can become prisoners of our desires. That is why John warns against a continuous desire for things that have to be exhibited on the "must-have" shelf (1 John).

As a believer, I often say that the Lord is my Shepherd. Well, then, I should have such a deep desire for His love and mercy that I make His love "mine" with everything that I have in me. Only then will I really have enough.

Math

If God is for us, who can be against us?
— ROMANS 8:31 NIV —

Are you afraid of the dark? Does that small portion of life that is yours to live every day get you down? Well, then you have to do the right thing: Pray! Ask God to open your eyes wide for a change. Start doing heavenly math. That will make you realize that one plus one is a winning equation when it's God plus you!

Take Elisha when he was surrounded by the Arameans (2 Kings 6). That morning his servant got up and feared for their lives. Elisha asked God to open his servant's eyes but still he could see nothing else than the Arameans on all sides. He was paralyzed with fear.

Elisha's words, "Those who are with us are more than those who are with them," did not help. According to the servant's arithmetic, one plus one made two, and that was far less than the army that surrounded them—until God opened his eyes. Only then did the servant understand heavenly mathematics. He discovered that one plus one is always the majority when that one is God. With God on your side, you are a winner. With Him on your side, you will always be the majority.

Waiting for Instructions

"Be still, and know that I am God."

— PSALM 46:10 NIV —

Do you often feel like changing everything and everybody around you? Are you always on some or other mission? Why? Is this really God's plan for your life—to change others so that they can be better people? Do you really know what He wants you to do, or do you just decide by yourself?

If you want to be Atlas, carrying the world's misery and problems on your shoulders, I have bad news for you: You can't be everything to everybody. In the long run, you will be nothing to nobody! You do not have to change the whole world. You are not the savior of the church or the only answer to all of mankind's problems.

Instead, you are only one person. But wait, at least you are *you*; you are one person with the spiritual potential to be yourself every day. Stop trying to be everything to the rest of the world. You might miss out on the real "you" that God created you to be. Be still in His presence until you hear where He wants you to be and what He wants you to do. And then, show up where He wants you and wait on further spiritual instructions!

Opposites

> *Since we live by the Spirit,*
> *let us keep in step with the Spirit.*
> — GALATIANS 5:25 NIV —

What is the opposite of rushed? Or hasty? It's not peaceful, slow, or unhurried. Certainly not if you are walking along God's route. The opposite of all these words is: "Keeping pace with God!"

Do you live in the fast lane? If yes, you should get with it and get into the same rhythm as God. See what His speed and rhythm is and adjust your own accordingly.

God's speed is not always the same. Sometimes you will experience a season of grace. When this happens, God wants to spoil you with His blessings. At such times peacefulness is a pre-requisite—neutral or first gear, as it were. At other times He might send you all over the place on urgent missions. This is a season of activeness and being busy. Third, fourth, or fifth gear is then required.

To live in pace with God removes all frenetic urgency, irrespective of whether you sit, stand, or run with Him. If you live close to God, according to Isaiah, even if others tire, you will fly on the wings of an eagle (Isa. 40:31).

Fast Enough for God

*So I never lose sight of Your love, but keep
in step with You, never missing a beat.*
— PSALM 26:3 THE MESSAGE —

Do you sometimes feel like pushing the cars in front of you out of the way, because you are in such a hurry? Do you always try to finish the sentences of others, because you don't have time for small talk? Does somebody who unexpectedly visits you at home disturb your routine? How impatient are you?

There is nothing wrong with being efficient and fast. Just don't be too fast for God. That's all. Remember that He created the world one day at a time. He reduced His speed from celestial speed to walking pace. Genesis 3 tells us that God actually strolled with the people that He created. Talk about a reduction in speed! The eternal God adjusted to a one-day-at-a-time speed. Why can you not achieve that, too?

Get in pace with God, one day at a time. This is the speed of God's creation, which is also His relaxation speed. At the end of the day He sat back and enjoyed His creation. Adjust to that speed. Then you are living fast enough! You will always be on time and in time for the most important things!

Carpe Diem

Satisfy us in the morning with Your unfailing love,
that we may sing for joy and be glad all our days.
— PSALM 90:14 NIV —

God likes today so much that He made it. He made it especially for us to fully enjoy! He planned it, and it arrived just in time! It's only a result of His grace that today has been added to the world's calendar. God wants us to experience today in all its splendor and beauty. We should not save our energy for tomorrow. Tomorrow is still far away. Do not do what Shirley Valentine did when she said, "I got lost in unused time!" It is terrible to get lost in that way. Too many people are lost in time. They keep waiting for better days instead of creating something today, in God's name!

For a change, be excited about the most important day in your life—today! Today has the right spiritual DNA, because it was uniquely created by God. And He gave it to the occupants of this world, including you. Don't pack today away in the storage cupboard of so many other wasted, unlived days. Your daily portion of heavenly bliss awaits. Consume it and live today!

Radical

Trust in the Lord and do good.
— PSALM 37:3 NLT —

Sometimes spiritual opportunities arrive only once. Perhaps this is why the friends of the disabled man in Matthew 9 did something really radical. They decided to break down the roof of Peter's house to lower their disabled friend down to Jesus. Talk about extreme—tearing down a roof to get a sick friend to Jesus. Remarkable! The next day Jesus could possibly be gone and then the chance of a lifetime to bring their sick friend to Him would have disappeared.

Jesus couldn't ignore their pluck. All of a sudden they were in Jesus' personal space, in His face. That is radical faith. That is what happens when people only have one chance to change the world and to help others. Roofs have to be broken down. Appearance and etiquette are much less important than rejuvenating lives through Christ.

You have been nominated as an impact player in God's kingdom to make a difference today. Let your light shine. Leave your stamp on for all twenty-four hours that you have. Ensure that people who spend time with you in this time take note that you are a representative of Christ. Let your presence count!

August

God's Way

The Lord directs the steps of the godly.
He delights in every detail of their lives.
— PSALM 37:23 NLT —

Frank Sinatra sang, "I did it my way." One day I would like to sing, "I did it God's way." In fact, I want to sing it tonight before I go to bed. I do not want to postpone my walk with God one more day. Days come and go! Opportunities abound, but sometimes days to walk with God only arrive once. There are more than enough wasted, unused days in my life. I want to stop wasting time in such a senseless way.

As Paul said in the letter to the Ephesians, I want to redeem my time. I will start by living and experiencing today, which I have received by the grace of God, in the right way. I can't afford to waste today. I want to welcome Jesus into my life today, as a special honored guest. Then I will use my time effectively.

I know that Jesus never waits until tomorrow or the next day to help. He sets His watch to the needs of broken people. His diary is overflowing with appointments with people who have sinned. That is where I want to be, with those people: the hurting, the broken, and the lost.

The Right Thing

*"If anyone, then, knows the good they ought
to do and doesn't do it, it is sin for them."*

— JAMES 4:17 NIV —

Confucius once said, "To know what is right and not to do it, is the greatest deed of cowardice." James took it one step further by saying that he who knows how to do good and does not do it, sins—a contravention of God's will. James regards a life that is lived expressively as the best evidence of faith in God. Faith cannot be merely expressed by a few confessions in church or in discussions between people about what is right and wrong. Faith must become daily experiences. Faith in God must be spoken, done, seen, heard, and felt. Otherwise faith is just words in the wind, cowardice, or even worse: sin! Did you hear that?

How much of what you know is demonstrated every day in your life? Perhaps I should not ask you this question, but rather your colleagues, family, friends, a shop assistant who helped you, or the guy at the grocery store. What will they say after having been in your company? Do they experience the love of God in your life? Well, why don't you ask them?

The Price Tag

Jesus said, "I am the Road, also the Truth, also the Life. No one gets to the Father apart from Me."

— JOHN 14:6 THE MESSAGE —

The road to heaven has been irreparably damaged. Sin is the cause. None of us can get back to heaven on our own. Not even the nicest things that we do are sufficient or enough to create a new stairway to heaven. Every ladder that we erect is based on precarious foundations!

We need somebody to bridge this divide between God and us. If somebody does not build a path from heaven back to earth, we would be in a quandary. Somebody who is very powerful, big, strong, and merciful has to help us. Fortunately there is such a person—Jesus! He has already bridged the divide. Where no road existed before, He has built a road with His own life. His journey to us was the most expensive road in the universe. It opened a new road to God, a road with protection against sin and death.

If you are worried about the travel costs, Jesus has already purchased and paid for the ticket for your journey. Believe in Him as God over your life and just stay on His track daily.

The Power of His Name

Never stop praying.
— 1 THESSALONIANS 5:17 NLT —

Prayer should be a daily way of life for us all. Prayer is our regular, from-the-heart communication with the one and only living God. That is why Paul wrote, "Never stop praying." But remember to shoulder other people's problems when you stand in the presence of God. Place the names of the people around you before Him. You can even pray for those whom you do not know. Carry their needs to our Father in heaven; intercede for those who are suffering.

Instead of staring into space when you have stopped at an intersection, pray a sentence for the person in the vehicle next to yours. Or pray for the people sitting next to you on the bus. Maybe you are the only person who will ever pray for them. Who knows? Your one-sentence prayer could just be the missing link to open doors, in heaven or on earth, for them. Pray regularly until the heavens open for the persons for whom you are praying. Most importantly, always remember the words of John 16:24 to pray in the name of Jesus Christ. Then mercy rains down!

Out of Control

"You will call on Me and come and pray to Me,
and I will listen to you. You will seek Me and
find Me when you seek Me with all your heart."
— JEREMIAH 29:12-13 NIV —

Sometimes my prayers are nothing more than pious presentations to God of my own plans. Actually, they are disguised (or undisguised) instructions, including all the necessary requests about precisely how and when it should happen. In fact, I am often so busy communicating my own needs to God that I forget to seek His presence unconditionally. I try, way too often, to stay in control of things, specifically through my prayers. That's a mistake! The essence of true prayer is being out of control. It means trusting God with everything. It means confessing that everything that I am and everything that I have comes from Him.

God, and God alone, is in charge of my life. True prayer means becoming devoid of myself. My prayers should never be disguised attempts to regulate God's calendar and activities or to fill up His day with my selfish trivialities. For this reason, I submit myself in childlike belief and trust to the will of God. For this reason, I kneel without any conditions before God, dependent and full of wonder. From now on, that is how I will live—dependent on my Father's grace! I will pray to honor Him. That's all that matters.

Faith Is...

*Faith is being sure of what we hope
for and certain of what we do not see.*
— HEBREWS 11:1 NIV —

Faith is:

- The certainty that Christ did everything that I could not do myself, on my behalf, to make things right between me and God.
- To expect everything from God. Faith is not something that I have in me. *My* faith is never the issue, as if it is measurable. Faith just means that I place all my trust in Christ. He makes a new life possible!
- Not a manner of changing life into a safe or predictable environment. Faith does not isolate me from surprises, shocks, disappointments, unexpected happiness, or uncertainty. Ask Paul, who writes in 2 Corinthians 4 that he is also perplexed sometimes.
- A lifelong adventure. Faith asks the gut to follow Jesus in a courageous way, even if you do not know where the path is taking you because you lifted His cross onto your shoulders.

Faith is the certainty of Christ and His gift of salvation, even if you are not sure of what the next twenty-four hours holds in store. It is the courage to trust Him today with your life and your eternal future.

Creating Opportunities

*Let us not become weary in doing good, for at the
proper time we will reap a harvest if we do not give up.*

— GALATIANS 6:9 NIV —

Many people caution you to wait for the right moment.
However, the problem is that many people wait for the right
opportunities until the day they die. They spend their lives
waiting in vain. For them, life is like a traffic light that never
changes to green. I think it works the other way around,
actually. God's way is always a green traffic light. You learn
what His will is while you are on the move.

Of course there is space for standing still in our spiritual lives. But faith is not one long sequence of silent, passive moments in a celestial reception. Instead, it is about the
right activities. Faith happens. And it happens in real life. It
means seizing every spiritual opportunity, like David who
accepted Goliath's challenge to Israel, as a wonderful opportunity to praise God. While the Israeli soldiers wondered
how they could annihilate such a giant, David in turn wondered how he could miss such an enormous target with his
five missiles! Do the same. Create opportunities to praise
God every day! Live abundantly in praise of Him! Just do it!

Internal Radar

Set your sights on the realities of heaven, where Christ sits in the place of honor at God's right hand. Think about the things of heaven, not the things of earth.

— COLOSSIANS 3:1-2 NLT —

Did you know that in your brainstem there are a group of cells that are known as the "Reticular Activating System" (RAS)? The function of these cells is to determine which stimuli should get priority. Test yourself—let's say that you intend to buy a new car. Before long you will notice the kind of car you would like to buy is everywhere.

In normal language we can say that these RAS cells in our brains function as a radar system. What has this got to do with faith? Everything! If our relationship with Jesus is really the dominant priority in our lives, then our RAS system will be focused on seeing and creating opportunities to praise Him. Too many Christians' radar systems are focused on other things—money, possessions, work. God is not really the first priority on their radar screen, and they just use pious religious language on Sundays. How do you rectify this? Deliberately place Christ first in your thoughts. Read Romans 12:1-2 and Colossians 3:1-2 and focus your thoughts on God's will. Then your internal radar system will change rapidly. And when that happens, your life comes into sync with your new priorities.

Foolishness

*Everything that we have—right thinking and right
living, a clean slate and a fresh start—comes from God
by way of Jesus Christ. That's why we have the saying,
"If you're going to blow a horn, blow a trumpet for God."*

— 1 CORINTHIANS 1:30–31 THE MESSAGE —

Paul writes that the cross is foolishness to many. Have you ever considered the meaning of this Scripture? Or the meaning of his challenging words in 2 Corinthians 13? That Jesus was crucified in weakness? Foolishness and weakness—these are the words that describe the greatest and most profound act of rescue in the history of the universe. In human terms a king does not hang on a cross. And yet Jesus specifically chose this humiliating route—a choice that seems foolish to the world. In this strange way, God's power is demonstrated. When Jesus hung on the cross powerless, an earth-shattering spiritual rescue operation took place.

Foolishness is a characteristic of the gospel. What does it tell us? At least that we should rid ourselves of our preconceived ideas about the gospel being a human success story and a magnificent display of power. It also requires us to walk the humble route with Jesus. This will not lead to our winning all the popularity contests, but it will place us on the only course with an "eternal" destination—a route following the Shepherd.

Action

> *Don't just listen to God's Word. You must do what it says. Otherwise, you are only fooling yourselves.*
> — JAMES 1:22-23 NLT —

Most New Year resolutions do not last long. Why? Well, scientists say that if good intentions are not converted from theory to practice within seventy-two hours, then they are merely a waste of time. We could just as well not have made the decision.

Therefore, the motto is ACTION! This sounds like a spiritual message too. In James 1, he says that good decisions without actions are empty. One could just as well look into a mirror and immediately forget how they look when you walk away. And this seems to be a common problem, considering how many mirrors there are in our houses and stores!

Faith in Christ that is not converted into action is a dead faith. Let us decide here, on August 10, to do the following:

- Let us commit the rest of this year to electing at least one lesson out of each sermon we hear and to implement it within twenty-four hours.
- Let us pray every day for at least one other person by name.
- Let us carry at least one other person's burdens every week.

A Prayer Away

"And when you pray, do not keep on babbling like pagans, for they think they will be heard because of their many words. Do not be like them, for your Father knows what you need before you ask Him."

— MATTHEW 6:7-8 NIV —

In his remarkable book, *Practicing the Presence of God*, written in the 17th century, Brother Lawrence says that in the course of the day you should pray several short, effective prayers rather than one long, lifeless prayer aimed at merely easing your conscience. Jesus taught us in Matthew that God is not impressed by a shower of words. He is not interested in long prayers. That's not the point. Prayer is never an arm-wrestling session with God. In any event, we do not have anything with which to impress Him. God really needs nothing from us.

Prayer always requires faith, obedience, and humility. It always asks that we submit our will to His Word. Do you also want to pray effectively? Then change your prayers into honest, open discussions with God. Also, learn to use the Bible effectively as your most important prayer guide. Talk for shorter periods, but more often, and with God, using the prayer guide: the Word.

Use the Psalms to assist you in communicating your joy and sadness, your needs and pain, in your own words to God.

In His Hands

*"So don't worry about tomorrow,
for tomorrow will bring its own worries.
Today's trouble is enough for today."*

— MATTHEW 6:34 NLT —

I don't know what the future holds, but I do know who holds it! Do you believe that? If you do, you should live differently today. Why? Because tomorrow's uncertainties cannot and will not happen without God's knowledge. When tomorrow arrives, He will be there. He will report for duty, just like every other day. God will definitely be on time for tomorrow. Even if unexpected problems arise, if bad things like illness or crime come knocking at your door, God will not be absent. He will not be too busy with other urgent matters.

Your life does not escape God's attention for a single moment. Did you hear: Your life will not escape His attention ever! He didn't forget about you yesterday, it will not happen today, and He will not forget about you in the future. God holds you—your times, seasons, and years. Believe this, and live with a light heart.

Live joyously in God's abundant love.

God's World View

*So from now on we regard no one from a worldly point
of view.... Therefore, if anyone is in Christ, the new
creation has come: The old has gone, the new is here!*

— 2 CORINTHIANS 5:16-17 NIV —

Martin Luther said a Christian is, in the same breath, both
righteous and a sinner. In ordinary language, Luther meant
that you can view your faith from two vantage points—
either from your own perspective or from God's. When you
look at your side of the matter, you notice all your mistakes.
When you view the matter from God's perspective, you
notice that He performed spiritual surgery on you some
time ago to make you new and acceptable in His eyes. Read
the verse again.

Before we were saved, we were sinners in God's eyes,
but that era is fortunately behind us (Rom. 5:6-8). God has
accepted us as His children. Jesus is our God, before whom
we now kneel. And God is very happy with us. Even better,
He really likes us! We are members of His new family! Royal
blood courses through our veins. Believe the best news
that you will hear this week, namely that Jesus' death on
the cross fundamentally, dramatically, and comprehen-
sively changed the perspective from which God views all
His children.

A Light Ahead

Since we have been made right in God's sight by faith, we have peace with God because of what Jesus Christ our Lord has done for us.

— ROMANS 5:1 NLT —

God loves us from head to toe, even though we have many spiritual faults. There is peace between Him and us, even if we sometimes take the wrong path. The Bible says so, and I believe it with my whole heart. I believe that God calls me His child and that He is not continually trying to catch me sinning in order to punish me. Of course I do not have a license to remain in sin. Never. But I do know that Jesus always dispenses grace. From His spiritual home, a second chance is offered every day; even if it's my thousandth second chance!

Recognize the fact that the light of the cross shines over your life, twenty-four hours a day, and that it erases all the kinks in the road. Look away from yourself. Look properly; look at God. Recognize His spiritual kindness and live! Believe in what the Bible says, "This righteousness from God comes through faith in Jesus Christ to all who believe" (Rom. 3:22). Celebrate with the Word, "Therefore, there is now no condemnation for those who are in Christ Jesus" (Rom. 8:1).

Detours

*So, if you think you are standing
firm, be careful that you don't fall!*
— 1 CORINTHIANS 10:12 NIV —

"I know all the detours." "I often get distracted." Do you also say these words? Do you know from experience about straying from God's path of truth and righteousness? Are you familiar with the self-incrimination when realizing that the same old sin has you faltering again? Are you acquainted with the hurt and shame which takes hold of you when you think about how much you have stumbled around in the dark? If you are, then you know about falling down.

It is strange how things can derail people. As soon as you think you are on track, some terrible thing derails you. It is no wonder that Paul warned the Corinthians that they must not assume that their faith is so strong that they will never do wrong (v. 12). Sin takes hold of you at the most unexpected moments.

What can you do about this? Make mistakes in a forward-falling manner! In other words, take your sins directly to God. Of course God hates sin. It is against His will. It offends Him. And yet He invites sinners to lay their sins down in front of Him, in Jesus' name. Do it now!

Dangerous Prayer

"Very truly I tell you, my Father will give
you whatever you ask in my name."

— JOHN 16:23 NIV —

Remember, every prayer that is sent to heaven in the name of Jesus Christ is a direct link with God. Never go alone to heaven's door. Rather knock in the name of Christ. This is what Jesus teaches us in John 16. If you rely on your own resources, you will be too weak to stand before God. When you stand before God holding the hand of Jesus Christ, He invites you in, time and time again.

Prayer is never removed from life as it happens. Put differently, we cannot whisper a quick prayer and then proceed to live as we wish. Jesus says in John 15:7-8 that we should stay attached to Him, just like the branches of a vine are attached to the stem, and then we will receive what we are praying for.

A life of obedience to God is a requirement for powerful prayer. It ensures that our prayers do not merely dwell on our own needs. Then our prayers do not sound like shopping lists that instruct God all the time with "do this; do that; help here; give there." No, instead, the extension of His kingdom in the lives of others should be the most important matter on our prayer agenda.

Pay it Forward

*"I have been a constant example of how you
can help those in need by working hard.
You should remember the words of the Lord Jesus:
'it is more blessed to give than to receive'"*

— ACTS 20:35 NLT —

Give away something of yourself: a precious few seconds, a few cents, a gift, a set of clothes, a visit to someone who is lonely, a prayer, a gentle hand on someone's shoulder, or a listening ear. Paul tells us that Jesus said it makes us happier to give than to receive. Believe it; do it! One of the pillars of the gospel is to give. Jesus is the perfect example of this. He gave everything. His own life was His gift to all of us.

Giving brings your life in sync with the gospel. Then you live according to the basic tenets of God's kingdom. In this world everybody wants to receive as much as possible. In God's world, His people give a part of themselves. The more they give without expecting to receive something in return, the more heavenly joy streams into their world. And their gloom becomes brighter.

Eventually they are only as dark as a morning dawn, and on a good day the darkness disappears completely! To give genuinely is to have something of God's character. It results in experiencing abundance with God.

Overflowing

You, however, are not in the realm of the flesh but are in the realm of the Spirit, if indeed the Spirit of God lives in you. And if anyone does not have the Spirit of Christ, they do not belong to Christ.

— ROMANS 8:9 NIV —

Do you lack spiritual power? Do you long for the experience of God's presence in your life? Then listen to what Jesus says in Luke 11:13 (THE MESSAGE): "If your little boy asks for a serving of fish, do you scare him with a live snake on his plate? If your little girl asks for an egg, do you trick her with a spider? As bad as you are, you wouldn't think of such a thing—you're at least decent to your own children. And don't you think the Father who conceived you in love will give the Holy Spirit when you ask Him?"

Our heavenly Father offers the special power and guidance of the Spirit to everybody who asks for it! What are you waiting for? Pray and receive! Open your life today to the Spirit for a brand-new experience. He is our heavenly Father's gift to every believer. He will guide you along the correct path and on no other path! He will show you where you fit within the framework of God's plans. Place yourself in His hands, like an empty vessel, and trust Him to fill you with living water. Then you will bubble over with the right kind of power and love!

By Your Side

*"No one can snatch them away from Me, for My Father
has given them to Me, and He is more powerful than anyone
else. No one can snatch them from the Father's hand."*

— JOHN 10:28-30 NLT —

Nothing shall separate you from the love of Christ if you
know Jesus as the Lord and sole Ruler of your life. This
truth is shared by Paul in such a compelling manner in
Romans 8:31-39. You are God's precious property because
Christ wrote your name in the Book of Life. Every day you,
together with all of God's children, fit neatly into the palm
of His hand. You are God's sole property, bought and sealed
by His Spirit.

Even when you are weak, you are still God's property.
You are somebody with eternity in your heart. You are en
route to the finish line. Believe it. Don't ever allow your
emotions to play games with you. You are not far away
from God merely because it sometimes feels that way. The
Gospels state that God is always near.

If you think that your prayers do not rise above the roof
of your home, it is merely your emotions fooling you. God
is everywhere—all around you. Stop trying to find God in
the distance. He is close by. Believe it and be free!

A Mere Observer

*Share each other's burdens, and in
this way obey the law of Christ.*

— GALATIANS 6:2 NLT —

Are you suffering under the yoke of life's innumerous heavy burdens? Are despair and fear your closest companions? If so, you should really do something about it. "What?" you ask. Well, resign from and banish those negative emotions. Do it right away! Don't allow fear or despair to reside illegally in your heart. Also, refuse to allow a difficult work environment, loneliness, or poverty to steal your freedom in Christ. Refuse to let illness and other calamities steer you off God's course.

You must do something special with this part of life that has been "lent" to you. Remember that you only have one life. Use it with wisdom! Live every aspect of it exclusively for God. Use kind words which express God's mercy to give hope to the people around you. Talk in uplifting terms when your colleagues use trite, negative, or depressing language. Share a friendly smile with somebody at work, or send a supportive text message to a friend. Don't be a passive observer of life. Play on God's playing fields with love and service. Make a real difference. God's sunbeams will suddenly shine again.

The Connecting Line

To the only God our Savior be glory, majesty,
power and authority, through Jesus Christ our Lord,
before all ages, now and forevermore! Amen.

— JUDE 25 NIV —

On most gravestones there are two dates—a date of birth and a date of death. They are connected by a short line. That short line is known as life! What happens between your date of birth and date of death is actually what your life is all about. You don't have any control over those two dates in your life, but you do have control over your life in between them. You control where it leads—to God's city or to the city of death! Most people will not remember the dates on which your life started and ended, but they will remember the life you lived in between.

So, what are you doing with your life? Are you living a life that is worthy of imitation? Are you creating happy memories in the hearts of others? Are you leaving footprints that others can follow which will lead them to God? Do your fingerprints bring hope and joy to people's lives? People will not just remember you with compassion, God will also know you well. And even better, your real life will start on the other side of the second date on the gravestone!

Out of Control

Sensible people control their temper;
they earn respect by overlooking wrongs.
— PROVERBS 19:11 NLT —

I once read about a British pastor in his early twenties who had a congregation of more than a thousand people in London about 200 years ago. He worked himself to death to keep them happy. At the age of twenty-nine, he had a fatal heart attack. On his deathbed this talented young man said that God had given him a Bible and a horse. Now that he had worked his horse to death, what did it achieve? God needs healthy people, not people who work their horses to death and then have little energy left for His service because their health has failed.

If your life is in chaos, it is not caused by your boss, activities, schedule, diary, or your studies. You are the cause. Don't point fingers elsewhere. You make that fatal decision every day to work yourself to the bone. You are not a victim or a passive observer of your busy life. You alone choose to follow that path! Nobody else forces you to damage your body.

Slow down. Realize that God is the God of your life. He will provide your needs.

Don't Be an Addict

*Anyone who competes as an athlete does not receive the
victor's crown except by competing according to the rules.*
— 2 TIMOTHY 2:5 NIV —

There is a difference between a few busy seasons in your
life, which happen to all of us, and a schedule that is permanently filled to capacity. In everybody's life there are
busy periods, but if it happens every day, then something
is wrong!

Workaholism has become a socially acceptable illness—
everybody does it. When do you have this terrible disease?
Well, when it robs you of precious time that you should
have spent with God. Or when it alienates you from your
loved ones.

When you have no time left for God, for others, for
yourself, or just for doing nothing, then you are addicted
to your work. When you collapse dead tired into bed every
evening just to wake up tired the next morning and begin
rushing again, then you are held captive by your work.

Listen up: it is not just a bad habit to be hurried all the
time, it is a sin. You are living outside God's will because
you are living outside the speed limits that He determined
for your body. Trust God to give you what you need daily
(Matt. 6:25-34). Show that you believe it by living at a
slower pace!

Taking Responsibility

Jesus declared, "I am the bread of life.
Whoever comes to Me will never go hungry,
and whoever believes in Me will never be thirsty."

— JOHN 6:35 NIV —

The other day somebody told me that he has no other choice than to work sixteen hours a day. Says who? He does! Who knows, maybe you think you don't have any other choice than to live as rushed as you currently do. There has to be food on the table and the house has to be paid for—not to mention school fees, the car, retirement. In this process of running around at the speed of light, you don't see God's plan for your life any longer, because you don't set aside prime time for Him.

You have changed into a full-time workaholic. You have forgotten one of the basic lessons of being a Christian, namely to ask God humbly for your daily bread (Matt. 6:9-13). You are denying your faith through the way you live your life. With weak excuses you flog yourself toward the hospital and the grave.

Have you forgotten that your heavenly Father wants to take care of you and that He *will* take care of you? He knows precisely what you need (Matt. 6:25-33). Trust Him for a change.

Don't Get Stuck

The world is unprincipled. It's dog-eat-dog out there!
The world doesn't fight fair. But we don't live or
fight our battles that way—never have and never will.

— 2 CORINTHIANS 10:3-4 THE MESSAGE —

If you are held hostage by negative thoughts, do what Paul recommends in 2 Corinthians. Take every negative thought captive that threatens to invade your thinking. Do it in the name of Christ immediately. Deliver that thought to Him, and let Him deal with it. Give all other destructive thoughts to God as soon as you realize they are gathering in your heart. Be on the lookout for unwelcome thoughts that get caught up in hate, bitterness, lust, hopelessness, and other destructive things. Notice them in advance and stop them in the name of Christ.

Remember that no temptation that is too strong for you will ever come across your path (1 Cor. 10:14). God never allows you to have tempting thoughts that you cannot say no to. Know that every temptation that comes across your path has been assessed in heaven before it reaches you. Therefore you can say no. You can resist every temptation in the name of Christ. Neither you nor any child of God has any excuse to succumb to temptation.

Celebration

"Be happy about it! Be very glad!
For a great reward awaits you in heaven."
— MATTHEW 5:12 NLT —

It seems that you can't make it through the year without hearing a few complaints about the commercialization of Sundays and other religious festivals. As far back as I can remember, religious fanatics have complained about this. Does complaining help reduce the misuse of festive days? I doubt it. Will the exploitation of Christmas, for example, suddenly stop because some churchgoers are opposing it? Probably not! Maybe another solution? What about a more personal one? Meaning, you and I who honor Christ as our Lord should wear the generosity of the holiday spirit year round.

Our yearlong festivities should tell of the Child in the manger who brought a new kind of peace among us. Our words, but especially our deeds of compassion towards others, should always tell of our Lord's heavenly generosity.

Then life in our area will look different 365 days a year. We decorate that little piece of world inside which we live, work, and play with the right kind of joy every single day. We don't have to sing with the choir of faultfinders, criticizers, and protesters.

A Carefree Life

Always be full of joy in the Lord.
I say it again—rejoice!
— PHILIPPIANS 4:4 NLT —

Learn from a few important lessons from Jesus' favorite people. I refer to children, of course. Learn how to play and relax. Learn not to take yourself too seriously. Think of yourself as a child in a grown-up's body. Make time to laugh and play every day, to be careless, fun-loving, and expressive. Share humorous stories. Laugh. It will add many joyful years to your life as well as life to your years.

Wouldn't it be a wonderful thing if joy, playfulness, rest, and relaxation were a constant part of your life for the rest of the year? Your quality of life will change dramatically when you deliberately choose to celebrate life in the presence of our good Lord. Your relationship with Christ and others will look quite different if each of these relationships is surrounded by joy and happiness. You will discover the Lord in surprising new ways when you begin to trust Him with everything in a childlike fashion.

When you get into the rhythm of choosing day after day to live a carefree life, divine joy will be something you experience every day.

Tapping the Drum

This will be a sign to you: You will find a baby
wrapped in cloths and lying in a manger.

— LUKE 2:12 NIV —

Do you know the "pa rum pump pum pum" refrain from
The Little Drummer Boy? This song tells the story of a boy
who wants to play the drums with all his might for the
child in the manger.

The arrival of Jesus calls for festivity. That's what the
three wise men realized when they saw His star. Their gold,
incense, and myrrh herald of the arrival of the Child of
Peace here on earth.

But the coming of Jesus is about so much more than just
presents. It's about us becoming living presents to others.
Just as Jesus came to give Himself away without any pre-
conditions, He turns us into gifts to those around us.

But there's more about the coming of Jesus that we need
to know. If we only stand in awe at His manger, we haven't
yet walked far enough. We also need to bow down at the
cross of our Messiah. The manger calls for the cross. The
gifts of the wise men call for the gift of Jesus to us all. His
own life is the real gift. His precious life is God's ultimate
gift to the whole world.

Jesus is new life for us all. That's why we celebrate His
coming the whole year round.

Bearing the Cross

"Whoever wants to be my disciple must deny
themselves and take up their cross and follow me."

— MATTHEW 16:24 NIV —

Gordon Wakefield writes that there can never be a hint of true Christianity without a cross—the cross of Christ that we bear, and each of us bearing our own cross. From the manger to the cross, from Bethlehem to Calvary, and from there all the way to my own life—that's the nutshell story of faith. From the cross of Jesus to the cross that I have to carry on His behalf—that's the new route that I follow.

When I become part of Jesus' story, it turns me into someone who is crucified and cross-bearing in the same instant. The story of Jesus says loud and clear that my life started over from square one.

At the manger, the cross, and the empty grave I find my new identity. From there I also find the daily direction for my life. Jesus is my only compass. His arrival, His death, and His resurrection are the reasons for my existence. That's why I can tap my own little drum for Him today, even while there's a heavy cross resting on my narrow shoulders. That's why I can follow Him all the way, because He sacrificed all for me as well.

"Where No Man Has Gone Before"

This is My command—be strong and courageous!
Do not be afraid or discouraged. For the LORD
your God is with you wherever you go.

— JOSHUA 1:9 NLT —

The Star Trek generation knows about "boldly going where no man has ever gone before." This is perhaps the cliché of all clichés. People just love this slogan. But few practice it. Few ever wander out into unchartered territory.

People love to play it safe—safe places, safe neighbors, safe jobs, safe friends, safe circumstances—that's all part and parcel of the safe package called "the good life." No wonder there are so many safe Christians and safe churches around. What a safe, boring, and snoring bunch "churchianity" has turned into!

Let's boldly go places for Jesus. Follow Jesus on His terms! Follow Him into the gutters, streets, inner cities. Live for an audience of One, even if you have to do it alone!

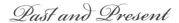

Past and Present

*Create in me a pure heart, O God,
and renew a steadfast spirit within me.*

— PSALM 51:10 NIV —

Once, I thought I had to impress other people. No longer. As a follower of Jesus, I don't want to impress; I only want to share impressive God-stories.

Once, I thought I had all the answers. No longer. As a follower of Jesus, I trust God with the unknowns in my life.

Once, I had everything under control, or thought I did. No longer. As a follower of Jesus, I surrender all control to God who is in charge of everything.

Once, I enjoyed receiving more than giving. No longer. Now, as a follower of Jesus, I experience the joy of giving and sharing with people around me.

Once, nothing impressed me much. No longer. Now as a follower of Christ, I see beauty everywhere.

Once, I talked mostly about God. No longer. As a follower of Jesus, I talk more to God.

Once, I was only excited about complex theological ideas. No longer. As a follower of Jesus, I am just as excited about interacting with people who follow in His footsteps.

Once, people had to listen to me most of the time. No longer. As a follower of Jesus, I take more time to listen to others.

September

Wait a Minute

*Their responsibility is to equip God's people to do
His work and build up the church, the body of Christ.*

— EPHESIANS 4:12 NLT —

"Religion is just a money-making scheme." How many times have you heard expressions such as this? However, nobody complains when big businesses make excessive profits or pay their directors preposterous bonuses. I'm not trying to justify the fact that some churches or ministries have excessive funds. But to automatically think there is a problem when some churches show a healthy monthly income, while turning a blind eye to businesses who keep on feeding the monsters of capitalism and consumerism, is not the answer either.

To blindly criticize the church for not getting it right, while more than 80 percent of all new businesses fail within their first year of existence, is surely not the way to go. Yes, some local churches make a mess of their calling. They are stone cold. But to generalize is dangerous. Why are we so critical of ourselves in church, but we forget to use the same yardstick when we look at other institutions in society? More often than not, I am shocked to see the poor state of leadership in many businesses—their lack of vision, team building, trust, and conflict-handling skills. Many churches get it right. They follow in the footsteps of Christ. Praise God for them!

Dare

*Do everything readily and cheerfully—no bickering,
no second-guessing allowed! Go out into the world
uncorrupted, a breath of fresh air. Provide people
with a glimpse of good living and of the living God.*

— PHILIPPIANS 2:14-15 THE MESSAGE —

It is rather foolish to expect different results while you keep doing the same thing. Maybe you know these words. But do you believe them? Or are you a sheep? Repetition brings familiarity, and familiarity creates a feeling of security. Therefore, some people stay caught up in unhealthy situations for years. The fear of the unknown is a much greater threat to them than the fear of existing bad circumstances. It overrides the courage to explore new territory.

You will have to make a few very courageous choices if you don't want to remain a lifelong prisoner of yourself and your circumstances. You have to move forward in the name of the Lord if you want to discover new horizons. If you remain where you are now, you will never grow even one inch further in the right direction. Listen again: If you remain where you are now, you will never grow in the right direction. The Lord created you to be a lifelong explorer. There are thousands of treasures hidden in His Word and in His world for you to discover. Consider new things. Dare to make new choices. Go and live this challenge!

Deeper into the Storm

When Jesus woke up, He rebuked the wind and the raging waves. Suddenly the storm stopped and all was calm.

— LUKE 8:24 NLT —

Paul didn't just talk about what he wanted to do for Jesus one day. He knew daydreams wouldn't achieve anything. He had to rock the boat. No, he had to get out of the boat to walk the on water with Jesus. The only safe place was to wander deeper into the storm with Christ. Risk-taking was the new name of the game. That's why Paul refused to be a conformist. He became ignorant to the concept of "caution." It was banned from his vocabulary forever.

No longer did Paul play according to the rules of the religious game; he made new ones. He created an entirely new playing field. In Philippians 1:21 Paul expresses his new life purpose in a nutshell: "Alive I'm Christ's messenger; dead I'm his bounty" (THE MESSAGE) or, "For to me, to live is Christ and to die is gain" (NIV). It is straight-forward, simple! No strings attached. To live is to be in community with Christ. It is to constantly share in His grace and wholeness. Jesus is the reason why Paul got up every morning; why he sang praises in prison after being beaten; and why he endured hardships, rejection, disappointment, and suffering without giving in. Join him.

No Professionals

*You are the ones chosen by God, chosen for the high
calling of priestly work, chosen to be a holy people, God's
instruments to do His work and speak out for Him, to tell
others of the night-and-day difference He made for you.*

— 1 PETER 2:9–10 THE MESSAGE —

Following Christ is not intended for professionals, but
rather amateurs. If you were to research the etymology of
the word "amateur," you would realize that it is originally
associated with words like "lover" and "suitor." Therefore
only amateurs should report for duty to God. Amateurs
understand that their service to the Lord is not something
that happens part-time or after hours. Neither are they
volunteers. No, they follow Christ full-time, constantly,
over and over again, and every single day.

Amateurs serve God full-time because they are simply
overwhelmed by His kindness. They are jubilant because,
despite who and what they are, God accepts them unconditionally. No wonder that, contrary to accepted behavior,
they will choose to follow God. They help, pray, serve, seek,
support, reach out, and encourage. They give themselves
whole-heartedly in service to the Lord and His work. Their
hearts beat passionately. Their emotions are on a high—the
real *agape*-driven type! Their servitude flows from their
hearts through their hands, feet, and lips.

God's Hope

*Let us hold unswervingly to the hope we
profess, for He who promised is faithful.*

— HEBREWS 10:23 NIV —

Many of us read leadership books by internationally known business gurus, or attend their seminars, as if their best-sellers automatically turn them into the ideal role models to follow. Do we really think that they, or the big companies of this world, get it right all the time? Don't get me wrong, I don't have a problem with listening to leadership specialists or reading their books as such, but to think they have all the answers, while we in church still don't get it, is a huge mistake.

Perhaps the biggest mistake is to still use these dated categories; those "we-they," or "church-business" categorizations. Secondly, many local churches are not doing too badly. Christ is faithful. After 2,000 years He still looks after His interests here on earth, including all local churches who follow the Jesus way. No, Jesus did not give up on His people.

Through the work of the Spirit, He is in our midst. He cares for us. He listens to our prayers. He helps us out in our hour of need. He works through us in so many beautiful ways. That's why the church offers real hope to the world.

Small Is the New Big

"Whoever wants to become great among you must be your servant, and whoever wants to be first must be slave of all."

— MARK 10:43-44 NIV —

"Small is the new big." Small is important. It's so important that it overtook big recently! When small is present in church, relationships are more personal. Small is also closer. Small is more effective. Small is face to face. Small is not as expensive. Small is faster. That's why small is the new big thing in relationships. Success and big, large, and extra-large were too close for too long. Success was correlated with large numbers, huge crowds, abundant resources, and colossal incomes, but those days are gone. They should never have existed in church in the first place. It's now the turn of small.

Small churches, small Bible studies, small gatherings, small services, small outreaches, small discussions, small prayers, small forms of assistance—that's what really changes the world. Just read the Gospels again. Jesus was in-to small. Huge crowds, big tithes, impressive religious struc-tures—all of that left Him cold. Jesus loved individuals. That's why He spent so much time with His group of twelve disciples or with outcasts such as Zacchaeus, the Samaritan woman, the Syro-Phoenician woman, and Cleopas. Jesus was big on small. He had all the time in the world to care for individuals. He did relationships at the speed of one person at a time.

Ordinary People

With minds that are alert and fully sober,
set your hope on the grace to be brought to you
when Jesus Christ is revealed at His coming.

— 1 PETER 1:13 NIV —

Fame is no longer the sole territory of big companies, large corporations, or Hollywood stars. If you don't believe me, ask Funtwo, who played his guitar from his Korean bedroom to the tune of more than seventy million viewers. We live in a new world. It's out of control, fast, and furious. Today's heroes are ordinary people. You don't need a special costume with an "S" on your chest to make an impact.

Ordinary people change the world today. Now it's about mustard seeds, not spiritual giants and mighty believers. That's why we must take a closer look at Jesus. The real Jesus who got lost behind 2,000 years of Christian art, religious ceremonies, cathedrals, and religious professionals didn't wear special costumes or fly around in space crafts. Jesus came as Himself, dressed in the clothes of slaves and outcasts. Jesus' favorite people were the lost, the downtrodden, the poor, and the lonely. His "weapons" were words of grace and His healing presence. The Jesus that we need to look out for today is He who turned heaven and earth upside down by becoming a servant of all. Let's find Him. Let's follow Him.

First Line of Contact

*Never be lazy, but work hard and
serve the Lord enthusiastically.*

— ROMANS 12:11 NLT —

Recently an acquaintance of mine stopped at an accident that had just occurred and assisted a person who was seriously injured. Suddenly the man grabbed his hand and whispered, "Pray for me. I'm dying. I don't know God." My acquaintance answered, "I know a pastor who lives close by. I'll get him to pray for you." The man told the medical assistants to take care of the injured person and sped off to fetch the pastor. But he wasn't at home. He rushed back to the scene, only to hear that that the person in the accident passed away shortly after he left.

"What happened to this guy's soul?" he asked me. But his next question bowled me over. "Why aren't pastors at home when we need them?"

"Why didn't you just pray for the man?" I asked. "Me?" he asked with a shocked expression. "I'm not trained for that." "We just have to do what we have to do when the Lord calls us!" I replied. "We are heaven's first line of contact. We are on duty at all times. We don't have to know how to pray, help, or care. We just have to report for duty and leave the rest in the Lord's hands."

Rinsed Clean

By a single offering he has perfected for
all time those who are being sanctified.

— HEBREWS 10:14 ESV —

Growing up, my mother was always very confident in the principle of "rinsing it off." If anything made contact with the floor, it was never so dirty that a little rinsing at the sink couldn't solve. A dropped hotdog? A fumbled slice of cheese? An especially elusive grape? Anything was made fresh under tap water. But I knew that water was never enough. Those foods were dirty.

Your sin has stained you. It is tempting to think sin is not that big of a deal because it doesn't seem to have immediate consequences in your life, but it has left its mark. And no amount of good deeds are strong enough to wash away what has been done.

At the cross, Jesus did the impossible for those who trust in Him: He made the stained sinner clean. Every one of your sins was counted onto Jesus at the cross. Do you know how many sins that leaves on you? None. In God's eyes, through faith in Christ, you are the purest thing on earth, as if you'd never sinned to begin with. Jesus' washing was not a half measure, like a dropped apple under tap water; there is no stain of sin on you Jesus has not rinsed away.

Gucci to Share?

In everything set them an example by doing what is good. In your teaching show integrity, seriousness and soundness of speech that cannot be condemned.

— TITUS 2:7–8 NIV —

James Twitchell wrote a book in which he talks about the never-ending love affair that the world has with luxuries and that owning luxury items apparently brings beauty to our lives. Furthermore, it binds people from different social groupings together, according to him. Isn't it a pity that people need to justify their insatiable hunger for material possessions in such tragic ways? And yet Twitchell writes one thing that really shook me: "If Americans can't share God, why not Gucci?" Can you believe it?

What a tragedy that in Twitchell's opinion luxury can be regarded as more unifying than religion. This should not be true. We as believers should be a far better advertisement for God's love. We should be magnets drawing people closer to Him. As followers of Jesus we should live as servants to do all we can for others. But it is not too late to demonstrate true beauty; the kind of beauty that has lasting value. You can try to make a noticeable difference today! Be the one who shares God's love so profusely that it actually leaves people speechless. Then they don't have to be victims of earthly possessions or a never-ending culture of consumerism.

Treasures in Heaven

*"Whoever becomes simple and elemental again,
like this child, will rank high in God's kingdom."*

— MATTHEW 18:4 THE MESSAGE —

A few years ago Arnold Schwarzenegger, the famous Hollywood star and governor of California, said something more amazing than some of the "famous" expressions he is known for, like "I'll be back," or "Hasta la vista, baby!"

He was trying to convince people that more money would not make them happier, saying, "I now have $50 million, but I am just as happy as when I had $48 million." Absurd! But in an equally absurd world, where spending money on luxury items is becoming increasingly common, such statements should not surprise us.

How do we find that dividing line between "enough is enough" and "more" when we are only thinking in monetary terms? When will we learn from the book of Ecclesiastes that those who regard money as everything will never have enough?

When will we start trusting in God as our heavenly Father who promises to give us everything that we need daily? Or are these nothing more than pious words from my perspective?

The Active Word

*"It is the same with my word. I send it out,
and it always produces fruit. It will accomplish
all I want it to, and it will prosper everywhere I send it."*

— ISAIAH 55:11 NLT —

"Actions speak louder than words." Many quotes like this downplay the importance of words, especially compared to actions. The truth of this quote is that words can be hypocritical. But speech is an action, and an action that can reach further than any hand can go. An encouraging word is an act that can uplift a friend's heart. A heartfelt letter can move someone to tears. A statement of warning can save someone's life. Words can affect the world in ways deeds can't.

God has acted mightily in your life by sending you His Word. Knowing that you would someday have His Bible, God acted by speaking the words of Scripture so that they would reach you and impact your life. Every time you read God's Word, God is speaking to you, an act that can reach further than any human hand can go. How amazing! Have you submitted to God's work in your life today by reading His Word?

A Walking Miracle

"The very hairs on your head are all numbered."

— LUKE 12:7 NLT —

In his book *The Arithmetic of Life and Death,* George Shaffner views life from a mathematical perspective. He calculates that the mathematical possibility of inheriting twenty-three chromosomes from your mother is one in a million. The same applies to the twenty-three chromosomes you received from your father. If you multiply these two, you will come to the conclusion that the chance of you being you is one in one-hundred trillion. Mind boggling! On top of that, if you remember that the same is true of your parents, as well as their parents, then even mathematics is silenced. All you can do is bow down in adoration before our great Creator God! He really cares about the detail of our lives.

As human beings we are the remarkable workmanship of God's detailed creative power. How can people so easily point fingers at Him, accusing Him of lovelessness? Shouldn't we be the accused? What will be left of us if God starts interrogating us and putting the facts on the table from His side? Let us rather humble ourselves in worship and adoration before Him.

Real Power

When I am weak, then I am strong.
— 2 CORINTHIANS 12:10 NLT —

I never associated God's power with weakness until I had to translate 2 Corinthians into a modern-day version of the Bible a few years ago. When I read that when Christ hung on the cross in weakness, the biggest power in the universe was actually at work (chapter 13), I was blown away.

God's power in its purest form is always revealed in human weakness. This doesn't make sense to people who associate power with massive attendances and miracles. Well, it even took Paul a few prayers to come to grips with God's definition of power. Up until that point he was highly successful. But then Paul had a quarrel with a church leader in Corinth. He left the city humiliated (chapters 2 and 7). To add insult to injury, flamboyant preachers came to Corinth who were real show stoppers (chapters 10-13). Paul approached God three times in prayer to remove these afflictions.

Eventually God showed Paul that it's not about power but about grace and weakness! This simple message changed the course of Paul's entire ministry and his style of leadership forever. Hereafter, his letters are much more gentle. Learn from Paul. Learn to become weak in God's service.

Valuable Lessons

*"In repentance and rest is your salvation,
in quietness and trust is your strength."*

— ISAIAH 30:15 NIV —

Paul discovered that God's true power is revealed in human weakness. In this paradox, the true character of God is revealed. When we are weak, His glory is revealed. In order for this to happen we need to learn the following three lessons about weakness in God's presence:

Lesson one: *It is never about us!* God is always the only power supply in the church.

Lesson two: *We don't have to experience divine power before God gets to work*. He works in spite of what we see, feel, or experience. We should never trust our feelings when it comes to God's presence.

Lesson three: *We'll always experience a lack of spiritual power*. There is not a single text in the Bible about people asking God to cut down on the supply of power in their lives. The constant complaint of insufficient power in the church is not necessarily a sign of small faith as people tend to think. Perhaps it serves as part of God's strategy to lead us to total dependence upon Him. The apostle Paul learned this lesson the hard way. Please learn it the easy way today.

I'm Shot

The LORD your God is gracious and merciful.
— 2 CHRONICLES 30:9 NLT —

In the film *Black Hawk Down,* an officer looks at a vehicle filled with wounded soldiers. Then he spots a private named Othic and orders him to drive. Othic responds, "But, I'm shot, Colonel!" Then the colonel reacts with an amazing truth: *"Everybody's shot! Drive!"* What a metaphor for our own lives.

We all get wounded sometimes. Everybody's shot, actually! But we can still drive, because *God is gracious and forgiving.* He's not like us. When He forgives us, we stay forgiven. God doesn't have the time or the energy to keep on reminding us of the wrongs of yesterday or the day before. No, He already pushed them out of the way because Jesus keeps on clearing our records.

The really great news is that God doesn't have a notorious little black book tucked away somewhere in heaven to remind Him of the nasty stuff we all did somewhere in our distant, or not too distant, past. That black book was torn up ages ago when Jesus pleaded our case before Him successfully! In spite of our sins, wrongdoings, etc, God takes us in His service day after day. He loves us in spite of everything we do.

Living Icons

*God created human beings in His own
image. In the image of God He created
them; male and female He created them.*

— GENESIS 1:27 NLT —

God created us in His image. The Greek word *eikon* that
the New Testament uses for the term "image" is familiar
to some of us. The word "icon" stems from it. At least we
know about icons on our computer screens and icons in
those impressive Orthodox churches. Icons are images. In
our case, human beings are living images of God. We are
visible reflections and representatives of the living God.
This is the breaking news right at the start of the Bible in
Genesis 1. This amazing text tells us that we share in God's
divine likeness. Not even sin destroyed all of this.

We share in God's DNA, His character, and His heart.
We humans have a common heritage as a species—we are
made in the image of God! Our abilities to learn endlessly,
to feel deeply, to live in harmony with others, to have
compassion, to love, think, rethink, and to innovate is part
and parcel of the heart of our all-loving Father. Great news,
or what! That's why Dennis Anderson said, "You cannot
see faith, but you can see the footprints of the faithful. We
must leave behind 'faithful footprints' for others to follow."

Blame Shifting

*"I tell you that everyone will have to give account on the
day of judgment for every empty word they have spoken."*
— MATTHEW 12:36 NIV —

After hearing the same old line for the umpteenth time
that people are tired, overworked, and fed up, I catch
myself actually believing some of them. Apparently, these
excuses give people a valid excuse to be rude, ill-mannered,
aggressive, and insensitive. To be honest, I'm not Mr Love-
able myself. I'm probably just as unfriendly as many others
around me. I wish I could conveniently shift the blame
somewhere else. But it won't solve anything. Really, it won't!

Blame shifting doesn't work, at least not since the beginning of time. If you don't believe me, just ask Eve and
Adam. They were the first pros who started this destructive
game. Fortunately, God didn't buy into it. God has the full
picture. He knows that our lives will have a radically different outcome when we exercise ourselves in the spiritual
discipline of accepting responsibility for our emotions,
words, and deeds. Blame shifting seems like an easy way
out. It's easier to blame the past, the present, the economy,
the government, or the church than to get involved. In the
end we pay a high price. We slowly but surely disconnect
from God and our true self. What a terrible price to pay.

Who Am I?

We are God's handiwork, created in Christ Jesus.
— EPHESIANS 2:10 NIV —

"Who am I?" Do you ever ask yourself this question? Well, to be honest, I don't do it all that often since I made peace with the person whose body I occupy! I don't believe in introspection all that much. Years of stringent soul-searching routines, which formed part of my spiritual growth exercises, really didn't help me grow in the right direction. In the end it actually left me with more guilty feelings than ever before. It made me toxic, not healthier. It filled me with feelings of failure and doubt.

Fortunately, over the past few years, I realized that I don't need to beat myself up over every negative emotion, thought, or intention tucked away in the dark corners of my soul. I really found my purpose in life, namely to love Christ and serve others who cross my path. I know that I have to keep my focus on Jesus and forget about the rest.

My identity is not determined by other people's perceptions or views. I don't need to please people all the time. I only play for an audience of One. What about you? Have you sorted out your purpose in life?

Reflecting His Love

*Imitate God, therefore, in everything you do,
because you are His dear children. Live a life
filled with love, following the example of Christ.*

— EPHESIANS 5:1-2 NLT —

Do you remember the earliest term that some people used to refer to the first Christians? If you say "believers," you are not quite right. They were called "People of the Way" (Acts 9:2). The first believers were not known for what they knew but for the way in which their lives were a testimony of their faith in Jesus. They did not have a confession of faith but lived a life that confessed their faith. In all the right ways, their lives spoke louder than their words.

The testimony of the first Christians was a daily testimony. Others saw how they loved the Lord and one another and how they supported people in need. Their testimony was founded in a magnetic lifestyle of prayer, compassion, and simplicity. That is why they were known as people of the Way—the Way of Jesus. Their faith was clearly visible in their new relationships. What a pity that today we are known more for confessions of faith on paper than for our lives filled with love for God and others. How sad that the main conversations of churches often revolve around "purity of doctrine" without conversations about "purity of life." Are we missing something or Someone?

Forget Un-Faith!

Believe in the Lord Jesus, and you will be saved.
— ACTS 16:31 NIV —

"I don't believe in God." "God doesn't exist." How often do we hear remarks such as these! It has become fashionable for people to confess their un-faith. Hollywood actors do it; sport stars do it; business people do it, even preachers do it. Un-faith is the in thing! People believe in un-faith to set them free from faith, or something like that. So, does this rise of un-faith mean that God is dethroned? A better question would be, "Was Christianity ever meant to be encapsulated in static institutions with strange rituals and professional clerics?" Is this "official" face of Christianity the correct one? I don't think so.

The church is made up of people all across the globe who passionately follow Jesus. They frequently meet in church buildings, houses, and offices, and they are the church because they love Jesus as Lord. They are magnetic because they care for each another and for outsiders. Their love for Christ is translated into new deeds of kindness towards friends, strangers, outcasts, sinners, and foreigners. They thrive amongst unbelievers. Confessions of un-faith don't startle them. They know what they know. They believe what they believe, in spite of the efforts of evangelists of un-faith who feverishly want to convert others to their faithless views.

Time Addiction

*Teach us to number our days,
that we may gain a heart of wisdom.*
— PSALM 90:12 NIV —

Time is money. There is no time for sitting around and doing nothing. That is what many people believe. No wonder we are stuck with words in our vocabulary like "waste of time," "time management," and "effective time utilization." We are told that we should save time by living more effectively.

There you have it; we are time addicts! We frequently find ourselves breaking the speed limit to each new destination in the hope of saving two or three minutes somewhere along the way, and we forget about that "saved time" when we reach our destination. No, we never really save time. We only drive up our heart rates and increase our stress levels. Did you know, the Lord never created us to live like that? It is not at all part of His divine plan that you and I should break the sound barrier every day. Or is it perhaps the time barrier?

We are built for relationships. For that we need resting time and visiting time. We also need quiet time and prayer time. Not to mention times of meditation before God. Do you ever have time for this?

Reality from God's Perspective

"I have told you these things, so that in Me you may
have peace. In this world you will have trouble.
But take heart! I have overcome the world."

— JOHN 16:33 NIV —

Here is an interesting question—how did the apostle Paul understand reality? Let's explore this question over the next few days by focusing on 2 Corinthians. Here we learn that God is in total control over the heavenly realm and the earthly sphere. The suffering of the righteous at the hands of the wicked, including Paul's own tribulations (2 Cor. 1), does not in any way diminish God's absolute control over reality. To the contrary, His divine power is actually revealed in the weakness of Jesus on the cross (John 13:4) and in the ministry of His apostle (John 12:1-10). Therefore, suffering serves a divine purpose.

In an ironic way, hardships, such as those Paul endured, point to the presence of God's power. On the last day when God will visibly triumph over all powers of evil and when His universal rule will be finally established, all the pieces of this divine plan will fall into place. God will bring a final end to the suffering of the faithful. All of this is the result of the death and resurrection of Christ. Praise His name!

A New World

*Anyone who belongs to Christ has become a new
person. The old life is gone; a new life has begun!*
— 2 CORINTHIANS 5:17 NLT —

In our discussion that started yesterday on Paul's perspectives on reality (2 Cor.), a second point becomes clear:

The final stage of history has already dawned on earth. The "Messianic era" commenced when Christ brought salvation to His people, hence, Paul's statement in 2 Corinthians 5:17 that the old *aeon* or era has passed away, the new has come! Paul was in the privileged position to decipher history. He had an "insider's insight" into the great cosmic drama that was played out on the stage of history and in the midst of the believers' lives in Corinth!

Thirdly, Paul knew that the present world would rapidly pass away—soon to be replaced by a new cosmic order (2 Cor. 4:16-5:10). History is swiftly moving towards that fateful day when evil will finally be destroyed and the righteous vindicated. This will happen on the Day of the Lord when all people will appear before the judgment seat of Christ (2 Cor. 5:10). The world as people know it will be transcended. From this triumphant perspective on the Second Coming, Paul knew that the present with all its problems and crises would work for the future glory of the Lord (2 Cor. 6:1-13).

God's Reality

No, despite all these things, overwhelming
victory is ours through Christ, who loved us.
— ROMANS 8:37 NLT —

Let's continue our question from the previous two days—how did the apostle Paul understand reality in 2 Corinthians? He knew that Israel's history served as the prefiguration of the new time of the Spirit and Christ (Rom. 3:1-18). However, the time of Christ, which inaugurated God's new time of salvation, also overlaps with the works of the Evil One.

However, the god of this world, who has blinded the minds of unbelievers (Rom. 4:4), and those evil powers that masquerade as God's angels (Rom. 11:14) are no real threat to His power. The works of the enemy in the spiritual realm will not derail the inauguration of God's ultimate era of salvation. History has continued to run its predetermined course, in spite of various forms of evil and catastrophe, and will continue to do so until the final return of Christ.

Lastly, the present is the convergence point of God's intervention through Christ. New life is already here, but it is not yet fully revealed. Salvation is a present reality, yet all must still appear before the tribunal of Christ. But the scales have been decisively turned. The weight is now on the side of God's eternal glory!

"I Ain't Afraid of No Ghost"

The Spirit God gave us does not make us timid,
but gives us power, love and self-discipline.

— 2 TIMOTHY 1:7 NIV —

You may know the song from the *Ghostbusters* movies—"I ain't afraid of no ghost." Well, we bump into ghosts all the time. We are constantly haunted by our own fears. A shocking piece of research states that the older we grow, the more our brains form synaptic links that are related to fear. Why? Is it because life is so dangerous or because people are so toxic?

Perhaps we continue to live on the fringes of our own lives—those fringes where fear reigns unchallenged. Freedom begins when I encounter my inner fears. How? There's no quick answer. But one way is to listen to my inner self-talk. An awareness of my inner discussions will bring me into contact with my fears. Then I'll begin to see them for what they really are—pale ghosts!

God's freedom is always an inner freedom. The freedom that the Spirit brings moves me away from the fringes of my life to my inner self. His freedom lets me discover the true me. Only then will I grasp His freedom that sets people free. That's when I sing, "I ain't afraid of no ghost."

Imperfect Leaders

Work hard and become a leader.
— PROVERBS 12:24 NLT —

Do you remember all those well-known leadership mantras of yesteryear, the "leadership is everything" type? Or that well-known one, "Everything rises and falls with leadership"? Perhaps leadership is somewhat overrated. Perhaps this interest in leadership is merely a baby-boomer generation thing! Or perhaps the problem lies elsewhere. Perhaps the problem is our fascination with leaders, especially in church.

Good leaders, the godly sort, always make bad idols. It's as simple as that. True leaders don't like the spotlight. They don't crave attention. Yes, they have a teachable point of view, but they never mistake this fact for good leadership skills. Christ-like leaders know how to make tough calls, which often makes them unpopular with the masses. They know how to take risks which make hero worshippers very uncomfortable at times.

That's why leaders who follow in the footsteps of Jesus don't like any excessive interest in themselves or in their work for the Lord. Their one and only dream is to serve Christ and His people. True leaders are His lifelong servants.

Lukewarm

"So, because you are lukewarm—neither hot nor cold—
I am about to spit you out of My mouth."

— REVELATION 3:16 NIV —

Since the time of the early church, we have been stuck with human thermostats in churches all around the globe. These individuals want a safe, convenient Jesus. Therefore, they regulate the temperature of Jesus' story to make Him predictable. In this process they've "domesticated" the real Jesus and His life-changing teaching about the kingdom of God. The result: we are left with a gentle Jesus, a tame Jesus, a suburban Jesus, a weird freedom-fighter Jesus, a pious Jesus, you name it.

People naturally want a safe Jesus. A Jesus who's values perfectly line up with their own. What is so enticing about a Jesus who is a mirror image of ourselves? We get to keep everything we hold dear: the beliefs, lifestyle, and feelings we enjoy. A controlled Jesus will never ask anything hard from us or ask us to give up anything we really want.

How sad that we had to turn down the temperature of the gospel to make it more comfortable for ourselves. Let's stop this nonsense. Let's follow Jesus all the way to the cross and with His cross on our shoulders!

Dignity

*"Since you are precious and honored in my sight,
and because I love you, I will give people in
exchange for you, nations in exchange for your life."*

— ISAIAH 43:4 NIV —

The famous American interviewer and TV personality Larry King once said that the words that made the biggest impression on him ever were those of church leader Martin Luther King Jr. when he was refused admission to a hotel based on his skin color. He stood quietly in front of the hotel door, and when the hotel owner asked him what he wanted, Martin Luther King Jr. replied in one short sentence, "My dignity!" That was all.

Dignity is what most people today are still asking for—the poor child in school who is overlooked by everyone; the shop attendant and the security guard who silently go about their work; the elderly person in the retirement home. And you and me as well. We all want a bit of dignity and decent treatment from other people. And that is how it should be because the Lord created all of us in His image.

Therefore, each one of us has value to Him. We carry eternity within us. If God values us so much, then we should also treat one another with the necessary respect. We should be aware of one another's dignity and respect and help defend that dignity.

The Strength to Listen

My dear brothers and sisters, take note of this:
Everyone should be quick to listen,
slow to speak and slow to become angry.

— JAMES 1:19 NIV —

Have you ever felt like someone was hearing you but not listening? You might even feel confident that they could repeat what you had just said, but they still don't seem to be truly paying attention. We may assume that listening is a passive activity, as you are the one receiving information while the other person speaks. But true listening takes work; it is an activity that requires strength of will, patience, and wisdom.

Listening requires willpower to break focus with any and every distraction to give your full attention to the speaker. It requires patience, kindly waiting as the speaker shares. And it requires wisdom to assess what is being said with generosity and insight. Listening is not an activity for the lazy, hurried, or foolish. Will you discipline yourself to listen well today? The next time someone is talking to you, grow in character by listening attentively and well!

October

No Sympathy

But thanks be to God! He gives us the victory through our Lord Jesus Christ.

— 1 CORINTHIANS 15:57 NIV —

Many moons ago the Rolling Stones had a hit song with *Sympathy for the Devil*. Some radio stations banned the song, while many preachers warned people not to listen to it. Yes, the devil is always big news. People love to sing about him, talk about him, and make jokes about him. In spite of all of this, few take him seriously.

No wonder C. S. Lewis in *The Screwtape Letters* once wrote these famous words: "There are two equal and opposite errors into which our race can fall about devils. One is to disbelieve in their existence. The other is to believe, and to feel an excessive and unhealthy interest in them. They themselves are equally pleased with both errors."

An unhealthy interest in the devil can lead to an obsession with the occult. On the other hand, to ignore the presence of Satan leads to arrogance and a destructive belief in the power of the self. Evil is a reality and can be found in destructive structures, selfish lusts, and Satan's spirits. A battle is still raging for the hearts, souls, and minds of people. There is a war going on! The outcome of this battle is not a secret. Jesus is the victor. He has overcome evil!

The Winning Team

With God we will gain the victory,
and He will trample down our enemies.
— PSALM 108:13 NIV —

To follow Jesus is to be on the winning side of the battle. It is to be in the presence of the One who hands out abundant life here, now, and forever. However, to be a disciple of Jesus is definitely not a walk in the park. It's no easy route.

To be a disciple of the Messiah is to live against the grain. It is to live dangerously in the storms. It is to be a living example of God's brand-new day in the kingdom. It is to know that His *shalom* is a present reality in Jesus. Actually, this is the battle cry and victory song of His followers!

Jesus is the only one strong enough to fight Satan. He already conquered the forces of darkness at Calvary. Jesus rose from the dead. He sits at the right hand of God. He has all power in heaven and on earth. Through faith in Him the Evil One is cast out! To live for God is to fight the battle the right way.

To live victoriously and beautifully for Jesus is to show no sympathy for the devil.

Carbon Footprint

In Him all things were created.
— COLOSSIANS 1:16 NIV —

Did you know that each time you switch on a light in your house, light a fire, or drive your vehicle, you're affecting the environment? Did you know that the way you think about the world's natural resources (water, coal, oil, fresh air, soil) is part and parcel of your faith in God? Religion is not just about God and you in isolation from the rest of His creation. God is the Creator of the entire universe, and His creation is in ruins.

Fresh water, coal, and other natural resources will most definitely run out soon if we continue to use them at a rate faster than they can replenish themselves. Researchers tell us that this is already happening all around the globe.

Each person on earth has a carbon footprint. We produce carbon emissions directly or indirectly, which have a combined negative short- and long-term effect on our environment. But the good news is that we have the capacity to make a difference. Did you know that every kilowatt hour (kWh) of electricity we choose to avoid saves over a kilogram of carbon dioxide being released into the earth's atmosphere?

Stopping the Rampage

He causes us to remember His wonderful works.
How gracious and merciful is our LORD!

— PSALM 111:4 NLT —

According to some scientists, carbon dioxide (CO_2) is the major contributor to global warming. It has led to a rise in the earth's average temperatures by nearly 33.8 °F over the past thirty years. Shocking, or what! Global warming could still raise our average temperatures by between 34.5 and 41 °F by the end of this century. Let's do something about it. Let's use less electricity. Let's use energy-saving devices and ensure the survival of God's beautiful earth for the next generation. How? Well, by becoming green and environmentally friendly.

Did you know that by installing an 11-watt compact fluorescent light in place of a normal 60-watt light, you will save 570 kWh over the lifespan of the fluorescent? This will save at least 570 kg of CO_2. God's creation is in trouble. Rivers are polluted. Clouds of smoke fill the skies. Natural forests are being destroyed.

Let's protest in the name of God. Let's stop the destruction. Let's take up our responsibility as caretakers of God's beautiful earth. Let's get it out of the intensive care unit through our prayers and our involvement in projects to protect the environment. Let's just do it!

Eternal Fellowship

*We proclaim to you what we have seen and heard,
so that you also may have fellowship with us. And our
fellowship is with the Father and with his Son, Jesus Christ.*

— 1 JOHN 1:3 NIV —

In the Bible, God divulged a secret about Himself to us that we would never know otherwise: He is one God in three persons, The Father, Son, and Spirit. This is who God is in His being—a perfect relationship of love and union. Being made in the image of God, you and I are designed after God to be in relationship with others.

Loneliness is a hunger that gnaws at our core because it taps into one of the base qualities that makes us human—to be in relationship with others.

But God has done something beyond imagination for those who trust in Jesus: He has shared His relationship with you. The Father has adopted you and invites you to call Him "Father," the same name Jesus has called Him since before time began. The Father has invited you to love and trust His beloved Son, with whom He is well-pleased. And both the Father and Jesus share the very Holy Spirit with your heart. You are never alone. God has swept you up into the relationship He has had for all time!

Holiness

*Joyful are people of integrity, who follow
the instructions of the Lord. Joyful are those
who…search for Him with all their hearts.*
— PSALM 119:1-2 NLT —

You can't cheat your way to holiness. Recently, I attended a conference in St Antonio, Texas where the theme was "The Jesus Way." One evening I listened to one of my spiritual heroes, Eugene Peterson. In his presentation he stressed that there are no spiritual steroids for holiness. You have to live a holy life, one day at a time.

The Jesus way is not complicated. You just stay the course, day after day. You walk the walk and talk the talk every single day. There are no shortcuts, quick fixes, or spiritual escape routes. To follow Jesus is a daily commitment. You must walk in the same direction, week in and week out.

Follow the Lord, in spite of all evidence pointing in the other direction. Walk behind Jesus and remain right there, even when all logic tells you to overtake Him or to do it your own way. Never take shortcuts. You can attend all the worship experiences in the world and listen to the best sermons ever preached, but you cannot cheat your way to holiness. Follow Jesus all the way, or get left behind. Repeat this rhythm day after day. This is the holiness route. It is the simple route—the route to life.

Expect the Best

*"In everything, do to others what
you would have them do to you."*

— MATTHEW 7:12 NIV —

We are programmed to expect the worst from others. And to hold it against them for as long as possible. When we hear a negative story about somebody, we instantly believe it until proven wrong by the facts. And then some people still say stuff like, "Yes, but..." When we read an unsubstantiated gossip story about someone in a newspaper, we spread it further without thinking. When we receive a harmful text message that puts a church or one of its leaders in a bad light, we forward it to our circle of friends or tweet about it. Is this right? Heavens, no! We are called to expect the best from others at all times. And to treat them that way.

How different the texture of our lives would be if we treated others with dignity. What beautiful lives we'll lead when we start caring for others as Christ cares for them. Then we'll protect people's integrity by not believing gossip about them. Then we'll stop participating in the spread of negative stories and no longer keep unhealthy perceptions alive.

Then we won't allow people to talk badly about others in our presence. We'll stop the virus by becoming the antiseptic!

Commitment

*A man will leave his father and mother and be united
to his wife, and the two will become one flesh.*

— EPHESIANS 5:31 NIV —

Far too many movies have the same recurring theme: A
meets B. They fall in love—well, sort of. But then, at the
wedding ceremony, A decides not to go through with the
marriage. Feelings of guilt, uncertainty, remorse, and a
truckload of other emotions cause A to abandon B in the
presence of all the wedding guests. *Runaway Bride*, *Mama
Mia*, *The Proposal*, you name it; they all have different takes
on this theme. Are we afraid of commitment? Is marriage a
fetish of some sort?

And then there's the ever-present public audience in
these marriage-mania movies. They are always there to
applaud the hero who gets the girl in the end. Funny how
the kiss and make up scene must always takes place in front
of a huge audience who must give their blessing to the final
choice.

Angst about commitment is rife. But why is commitment
so difficult? It shouldn't be. When A and B spend time in
each other's presence and get to know each other well, they
will know long before any public ceremonies whether they
are meant for each other. Not so? And if they seek the face
of God above all, they will have the answer.

Your Soul Mate

Marriage should be honored by all,
and the marriage bed kept pure.

— HEBREWS 13:4 NIV —

Too many relationships between men and women are purely physical. They never get to know each other's hearts. After the initial flares of passion, the partners discover that much more is needed to keep the relationship going. The physical stuff cannot keep a relationship strong. It works the other way round, actually—but within the beautiful space of marriage! The secret to happiness for any relationship is to first seek your soul mate. This is a matter of prayer also. Let me rephrase: Begin your search for a soul mate by seeking the face of God long before you enter into any relationship. Never seek His face afterwards. It's always God first, all other relationships second.

Ask God to show you the right person to spend the rest of your life with. If you are married already, ask Him to open your eyes to discover the true inner beauty of your partner. Fall in love with him or her all over again. Otherwise you'll be a runaway bride or groom forever and never be content. Your marriage is God's special gift to you to fill your life with true happiness.

Just Say So!

Do not let any unwholesome talk come out of your mouths, but only what is helpful for building others up according to their needs, that it may benefit those who listen.
— EPHESIANS 4:29 NIV —

We are all builders. Some of us build thick walls of seclusion and bitterness around ourselves. Others build bridges. Wall builders isolate themselves from life. They lock bitterness and hatred in their hearts that grow ever colder and harder. They mutate into disillusioned, difficult people. What is really sad is that people like this still hang around in churches. Not even their faith changes their cynical disposition.

Bridge builders are open and approachable. They love to live for God and other people. One of the most important bridges you can ever build includes one small word. I am referring to the word "sorry"! This is a magic word. It is like heavenly glue that the Lord gives you to fix broken, earthly relationships. It breaks down walls between people in the twinkling of an eye and transforms walls into bridges. Hardened hearts are softened when a sincere apology is heard. Unfortunately, I sometimes hurt other people. But if I learn to say that I am sorry, then I'm building in a worthy manner.

Trade in Your Troubles

*Then Jesus said, "Come to Me, all of you who are weary
and carry heavy burdens, and I will give you rest."*

— MATTHEW 11:28 NLT —

Some people are so pessimistic that they start with the
obituaries when they pick up a newspaper. What a tragic
way of life to always notice the bad things first. Listen, there
is a better way! Turn over your problems to Jesus. Stop
trying to carry your burdens on your own. Your shoulders
are not broad enough. You are going to stumble and fall.

According to Matthew 11, Jesus offers you the exchange
of a lifetime. He asks you to exchange your worries and
burdens for His heavenly peace. Did you hear that? You
can leave your problems with Christ in exchange for His
heavenly kindness. His shoulders are strong enough for
your distress and that of the rest of the world. What are you
still waiting for? Grab the opportunity of a lifetime to give
the right kind of peace permanent residence in your life.

Then all the pessimism and misery that threatens to
overwhelm you will disappear like mist before the morning
sun.

The Heartbeat of Life

*A nap here, a nap there, a day off here, a day
off there, sit back, take it easy—do you know what
comes next? Just this: You can look forward to a
dirt-poor life, poverty your permanent houseguest!*

— PROVERBS 6:10–11 THE MESSAGE —

Do you sleep through your own dreams every night, or do you experience them wide-eyed during the day? Do your dreams ever come true? Do you already live a small part of those plans God sowed in your heart as recently as yesterday? Or are you still stuck amongst the hopeless, waiting for better days to descend upon you from out of the blue? Are you actively present in every moment of your life, or are you still planning how you are going to engage in real life? Well, then you are missing the true adventure.

Life happens one day at a time. God delivered it early this morning with heavenly compliments right to your doorstep. All you need to do is fill the day with all the right ingredients. Nobody else can do it on your behalf. You must choose to love the Lord and to have an open heart and a merciful hand for others. You have to decide to live the right kind of life proactively.

Dare to do this! If you put this choice off until tomorrow, you are once again twenty-four hours too late.

Mistakes

*Praise the LORD, my soul, and forget not all His benefits—
who forgives all your sins and heals all your diseases.*

— PSALM 103:2–3 NIV —

I am ashamed to admit that God sometimes uses my mistakes for the good rather than my so-called obedience. It happened again just the other day. I lost my temper after receiving poor service in a shop. When I walked out of there, I felt bad about my sharp words to the shop assistant. I turned back submissively to apologize. The assistant immediately asked me why I had apologized. I shame-facedly mumbled that I was a Christian and that I had violated my life principles by speaking before considering my words. And all of a sudden this person wanted to know more about Christianity!

It is good to know that God not only works when I think He is working. It is just as nice knowing that the Lord does not really need me. It is through grace alone that He uses me with all my defects. Realizing that God loves me in spite of myself—well, that is earth-shattering good news!

Knowing that my sins and weaknesses never restrict His grace is also very liberating. But I should not be content with Him using my mistakes alone, lest I become a very poor witness and a bad testimony for our wonderful Lord.

A Hungry World

Be an example to all believers in what you say, in the way you live, in your love, your faith, and your purity.
— 1 TIMOTHY 4:12 NLT —

"If you are not a good example, at least be a horrible warning!" Nowadays there are various adaptations of these words, "Don't do as I do, do as I say!" Ouch! How can I dare expect something from somebody else when I am not prepared to do it myself? That would not be right, because it would mean that I am deceitful, a warning of how others should *not* live.

If I am a follower of Jesus, He calls me every day to live and practice His kind of life filled with love and servitude. I need to model it in all I say and do. I never have the luxury of doing as I please or hiding behind my flaws and weaknesses.

No, I answer to a Lord whose burden is light. And to a Lord who isn't always ready and waiting to judge me.

True Joy

The joy of the LORD is your strength!
— NEHEMIAH 8:10 NLT —

Where do you find true and life-changing joy? Can you find it in a checkbook that has room for a whole lot of zeros? Can you find it in a brand-new house? Or maybe in that dream holiday? How about a great new job opportunity? Yes, you will surely find some joy in all these things. Such things can also be blessings directly from our heavenly Father. On the other hand, all holidays come to an end, and a house ages with time.

Where do you encounter joy that is like a constant river that provides water throughout the year; the kind of joy that is not dependent on favorable external circumstances alone? Well, Jesus offers that kind of joy. He invites us to come to Him and get it for ourselves. Joy is the gift Jesus gives to His people. Go and claim your portion today. Don't hastily put it away in one of the drawers of life. Use your heavenly joy.

You can receive it every day! Every morning an updated portion of heavenly joy awaits you with your name and address on it.

Ever-Present

God is our refuge and strength,
an ever-present help in trouble.

— PSALM 46:1 NIV —

Sometimes we are in the presence of VIPs without even realizing it. Think of Jacob. Do you remember when he was fleeing from Esau, and he spent one night sleeping with his head against a rock? The Lord unexpectedly appeared to Him in a dream. Afterwards, rather shocked, Jacob confessed, "The Lord is in this place, and I didn't even realize it."

The biggest mistake you could ever make is not recognizing the Lord when He is with you. That would be allowing the opportunity of a lifetime to slip through your fingers! And who knows, maybe you are going to cross paths with a few famous people this year. But the most important person of all is God Himself. You will see His heavenly fingerprints in many places around you.

Don't ignore the Lord. Don't wait until He awakens you from your dreams before you realize that He is present! Make God the Guest of Honor in your life every single day.

A High Price

*"If you try to hang on to your life,
you will lose it.
But if you give up your life for My sake,
you will save it."*

— MATTHEW 16:25 NLT —

You've heard of Maximilian Kolbe, the Franciscan priest who was incarcerated in Auschwitz during the Second World War. After an inmate escaped, as was the rule, 10 prisoners were chosen to die in his place. One of them had a wife and children, and Kolbe volunteered to take the man's place and face a torturous death. He died after two weeks of torture when he was given a lethal injection of acid.

Kolbe's actions remind me of the words of Jesus that there is no greater love than when someone is prepared to lay down his life for his friends!

What do we ever sacrifice for one another? Whose lives have been enriched by us? Who knows, maybe our faith is far too safe and boring!

Giving Life to Language

*Now He uses us to spread the knowledge of
Christ everywhere, like a sweet perfume.*

— 2 CORINTHIANS 2:14 NLT —

Language is alive. Note how powerful ordinary little words like "thank you" are. Or a short sentence like "I love you!" At the same time, sharp words can cause tremendous hurt. Harsh, unkind words are like gunshots. They wound people. That is why the Bible says we should count our words before they leave our mouths.

By the way, this is not merely good advice. God made us to be able to form opinions. Our emotions are our first opinion-shapers. Some researchers believe that our emotions function up to a million times faster than our minds. If we literally take the time to count to three, our minds have the chance to catch up and control our emotions when they want to fire away with hasty words.

We should carefully mull over our words before they leave our lips. Once uttered, words have a life of their own. The damage they cause cannot easily be undone. Ask the Lord to review your words before they escape your mouth. Ask Him to transform them into medicine that cures. Utter words that give life and see what happens!

Getting by

*"Your Father knows what
you need before you ask Him."*
— MATTHEW 6:8 NIV —

One of the greatest sources of stress to ordinary salaried people is whether their hard-earned money is going to last until the end of the month. Is this your worst headache, too? Perhaps you are feeling like the person who told me the other day, "I wish I could afford living the way I do." To millions, life is a struggle for survival. Well, I have some "irrelevant" news for you: Christ says in Matthew 6 that God provides everything His children need in life. He knows our basic needs, but more than that, He knows what we need and when we need it.

God is always on time. Why would some believers find this news irrelevant? Because they do not really believe it. They work their fingers to the bone, thinking that their survival rests with them alone. They worry, as if Jesus did not intend God's promise to apply in the third millennium. They build their own futures as if God knows nothing of tomorrow.

What about you? Is this news irrelevant to you, or do you believe it? Well, if you do, be a bit more carefree about life than you were yesterday and the day before.

The Prophet Said

The Lord always keeps His promises.
— PSALM 145:13 NLT —

Recently a businessman came to see me. He was upset. "God failed me," he told me. "I lost millions of dollars in a transaction after a Christian prophet told me to go ahead with this deal." "Why are you angry at God?" I asked. "Did you do proper research beforehand?" "Well, I did, but then a friend at our church advised me to go to a Christian prophet to make sure I was on the right track," he answered. "This prophet told me God showed her that I would succeed."

"You went to a religious fortune teller, not to a prophet," I replied. The businessman objected angrily, "But prophets know about God's future plans." "Perhaps you should have read Deuteronomy 18 and other Bible texts about the functions of true biblical prophecy before you put your faith in today's self-appointed prophets. Prophecy is definitely not about solving personal matters or revealing future knowledge about our business deals, but about the revelation of God's plans for His people and His world," I told him.

Prophecy never sidesteps our personal responsibility. How sad that many believers refuse to accept responsibility for their personal choices. No wonder they blame their failures on someone else or on God.

Eternal Children

Think about things that are
excellent and worthy of praise.
— PHILIPPIANS 4:8 NLT —

The young physicist at the Polutechnikum in Zurich should have been devastated when his dissertation was turned down. Most students give up when their professors decide their research is not good enough. But this man refused to do so. His name? Albert Einstein. Failure was not an option for him. "Long live insolence!" he cried.

Hereafter, in the Swiss city of Bern, the 26-year-old Einstein spent many hours writing three important papers that caused the biggest shifts in modern science. The reason for Einstein's success? He didn't have a big ego that craved recognition from his peers. Harvard professor Howard Gardner later said that Einstein became one of the greatest scientists of our age because of his openness, honesty, and naïveté. He remained an "eternal child."

We urgently need spiritual Einsteins who refuse to go with the religious flow. Far too many believers live mediocre lives. There are a great number of spiritual leaders occupying comfortable positions in highly predictable church environments. Far too many theologies, church programs, and sermons facilitate feel-good religious experiences. No wonder Christianity has such a low impact in "the real world."

Information Overload

Trust in the LORD with all your heart; do not depend on your own understanding. Seek His will in all you do, and He will show you which path to take.

— PROVERBS 3:5-6 NLT —

I was stunned when I recently read that approximately 4.4 million American children between the ages of four and seventeen have already been diagnosed with ADD (Attention Deficit Disorder) and that between 10-12 percent of boys between the ages of six and fourteen are victims of this disorder. In South Africa it is also on the increase. We live in a world where serious pressure is experienced from a very early age. Our bodies simply cannot keep up with the progress in our new world anymore. Tension, the drive for achievement, and especially information overload are literally making people ill.

Speaking of information overload, in 2006, 161 billion gigabytes of information was sent across the Internet. That is three million times more than all the accumulated book knowledge throughout history, within a mere one-year period! People yearn to find sense and meaning that would bring peace to the soul. Do you also yearn for peace amidst the chaos? Well, with the Lord, the waters of rest are still flowing. His way takes you to green pastures. Embrace this knowledge with your heart and with your hands and feet. Join God there.

Word Count

A gentle answer turns away wrath,
but a harsh word stirs up anger.
— PROVERBS 15:1 NIV —

A good friend of mine recently told me about someone who wrote the following in a letter: "Please excuse me for the fact that my letter is so long. Unfortunately, I didn't have the time to write a shorter one." True words indeed!

We are all victims of too many words. We sometimes talk, write, sing, and type too much. We don't necessarily need thick writing pads or a great number of words to utter true wisdom. Short messages are often those we reflect upon the longest. Very often we find that the more words we use, the smaller the impact. (Please convey this message to those long-drawn talkers who love to take over conversations!)

Consider how many short text messages are sent with great effect every day, where 160 characters triumph. Or on Twitter, with only 140 characters. Be a counter of words from now on.

Choose your words carefully. Talk less. Practice using fewer words. Remember the warning from Proverbs that our words can either be like knife stabs or the finest silver.

Hijacked by Grace

"Prove by the way you live that you have
repented of your sins and turned to God."

— MATTHEW 3:8 NLT —

The young Paul was like a man possessed when he heard the followers of Jesus claim that He was the resurrected Messiah. No one who died on a cross could be the Messiah. It was blasphemy! Paul persecuted the followers of Jesus with a vengeance everywhere he went.

Then, one day, he encountered the resurrected Jesus on the road to Damascus. This meeting altered his entire life. A true revolutionary was born that day when Jesus and Paul met face-to-face—a day that redefined religion and life for millions of people throughout history. Talk about impact!

After being "hijacked by grace," Paul's new purpose took him on dangerous yet highly adventurous journeys to the farthermost corners of the world. He travelled more than 11,000 miles on foot during his various missionary journeys across the Roman Empire. The new Paul who instantly turned into a loyal follower of Jesus had a new vision, one that provoked, disrupted, and challenged everyone and everything around him, but one that made a huge impact! Perhaps we should follow suit.

Leave Haste Behind

*A day is like a thousand years to the
Lord, and a thousand years is like a day.*

— 2 PETER 3:8 NLT —

Being hasty is a human characteristic, not a divine one. I refer to haste. God always has time. He is never in a hurry as He's going to His next appointment. Take a look at the life Jesus led on earth. He always had time, even in the face of death. When His friend Lazarus died (John 11), He was still on time! He wants us to exchange our hurried, high-octane hearts for tranquil hearts.

We should have the courage to spend time walking with God in His garden. We should once again bring His garden back to life outside the gates of Paradise. God still has so many secrets He wants to share with us here on earth; so many new joys. But then we have to take action against our hurried lives. How? Well, we have to receive medicine from the Lord for that "hurry sickness" we suffer from.

This is an illness that poisons our entire existence. Haste steals our joy. It robs us of our loved ones and of everyone that matters in our lives. What for? Only so that we can say we are the latest winners of the rat race?

Strange but True

*No prophecy in Scripture ever came from the prophet's own
understanding, or from human initiative. No, those prophets
were moved by the Holy Spirit, and they spoke from God.*

— 2 PETER 1:20-21 NLT —

Some believers like to define their roles in God's service in
terms of the prophets of the Old Testament. Strangely, they
usually only use the stories of the prophets. The real day-
to-day lives of the prophets never get much attention when
these believers begin to define their calling or the nature of
their ministries. However, to be a prophet in the tradition
of a Jeremiah, Micah, or Nahum is to live against the grain.
The true prophets of Israel lived on the fringes of society.
They weren't the religious favorites of the day. Prophets
never formed part of the mainstream religion.

To be a prophet is to see what others don't always see
and to hear what others don't usually hear. But God's prophets don't just see and hear His new future; they also make
known what they heard, saw, and experienced. Prophets
always communicate God's new day in the kingdom. They
reveal God's heart. They are figures of hope with a new
message of restoration. No wonder they vigorously challenge all systems, institutions, individuals, and groups that
stand in the way of God's plans.

Hope Floats

Guide me in Your truth and teach me, for You are
God my Savior, and my hope is in You all day long.
— PSALM 25:5 NIV —

Good Friday is not really an appropriate name for the day Jesus died. It is definitely not good news when someone who came to adorn the world with so much grace had to pay for this by death. And yet the last words of Jesus on the cross give the right perspective to this Friday. Do you remember His words from to the Gospel of John, "It is finished"? Without a doubt! The price has been fully paid. The account is completely settled. The ledger between God and each person who embraces the redemption of Jesus has been balanced.

Hope floats. Hope does not sink into the sea of despondency; anger does not constantly win. Grace is the new password for heaven's gates. God and people can once again be good neighbors. Strangers and lost people may again sit down at God's table. Death definitely does not have the final say. Neither does all the injustice, hurt, and suffering of the life you live. Because today there is an empty cross on Calvary!

Put your hand in the hand of the risen Christ and celebrate with Him at the festive table forever!

The World in His Hands

The LORD directs the steps of the godly. He delights
in every detail of their lives. Though they stumble,
they will never fall, for the LORD holds them by the hand.

— PSALM 37:23–24 NLT —

At this very moment earth is traveling through space at more than 65,000 miles per hour, while today it will complete approximately 1.4 million miles of its annual journey around the sun. At the same time earth is rotating around its own axis at an astonishing 994 miles per hour. Staggering, isn't it! It is amazing to think that God maintains everything perfectly day after day. He is the Creator of the universe but also the maintainer of the mighty and beautiful works of His hands. Therefore you can trust God with great things.

Nothing is ever too big for Him. He balances our world with everyone on it and everything in it. But nothing is ever too small for Him either. The details of your life are really of interest to Him.

Take all your needs to Him today in prayer. Do so in the name of Jesus. He hears you. He sees you. He cares so much about you. The God of power is also the God of the details of your life. Small is never too insignificant for Him, just as nothing is ever too big.

True Identity

*Therefore, there is now no condemnation
for those who are in Christ Jesus.*

— ROMANS 8:1 NIV —

The biggest freedom on earth is being able to take off your masks in God's presence. Ask the man in Luke 18 who could only mumble one short sentence, "Have mercy on me!" Immediately he walked away a man who had been set right with God. The gospel is about what God does for free to enable you to be one with Him again, not about what you have to do to be redeemed and reunited with Him.

Freedom starts when you realize that you no longer have to try and obtain the Lord's favor. Then a whole new life opens up for you. The true key to freedom is who you are in Christ, not what you have to do for Him! To find your identity in God's free grace is the big secret. Freedom means finding rest in the Lord, not in your spiritual attempts that keep you running around from early in the morning until late at night.

Please listen, you don't have to try and win over God's favor. He has decided to love you long ago based on who you already are in Christ.

One Step at a Time

God's way is perfect. All the LORD's promises prove true.
He is a shield to all who look to Him for protection.
— PSALM 18:30 NLT —

I admire people whose lives are so neatly organized. And those who pray and quickly receive an answer. But I have to add that I am astonished at the number of church members who think that prayer is an easy shortcut, an instant quick fix. For me, it is not that easy.

I associate myself with John Eldredge, who writes in his best-seller *Waking the Dead* that he experiences approximately 20 bright days per year when he knows exactly what God expects of him. The rest of the time, God's will seems to him like driving in dense fog. Maybe you know that feeling, too. Well, then you will appreciate the words of Oswald Chambers, the missionary giant who touched so many lives: "I never see my way. I never have far-reaching plans."

Maybe God does not specialize in five- and ten-year plans. He mostly does things one day at a time, like Exodus 16 and the Lord's Prayer teaches us. Let us find His way for today and live on course one day at a time!

Unstuff

*"Whoever becomes simple and elemental again,
like this child, will rank high in God's kingdom."*

— MATTHEW 18:4 THE MESSAGE —

Live more simply so that others can simply live. "How?" you may wonder, while considering the fact that you barely make ends meet yourself. Well, live more generously, like the Lord expects you to. You don't have to be wealthy or have "enough" before you start sharing what you have with others. If you are in the fortunate position of being able to buy something new, like a CD, garment, TV, cell phone, or treat, buy a cheaper item for a change and give the difference in the purchasing price to someone in need.

Decide when enough is really enough in your life. Ask the Lord to give you a generous heart, one that prefers giving to receiving. Also try doing a few practical things. You could, for instance, choose to have a simple meal with your friends once a month. Quietly give the money that a more expensive meal would have cost to someone who is in the Lord's service.

Live as simply as you can afford, even if you are not wealthy, so that others can at least live!

November

Carrying the Cross

Be completely humble and gentle;
be patient, bearing with one another in love.
— EPHESIANS 4:2 NIV —

In between all the reasons for complaining about how bad life is, you and I can choose to find our joy elsewhere. Following Jesus means having hope. Bearing His cross means being a living blessing to others.

Every day that we enjoy the privilege of living and breathing, we have the chance and honor to bear the cross of Jesus. And who knows, you and I may be the only "Bible" available to someone who finds themselves in a place of despondency. What about a gentle word of hope for them, or maybe a piece of bread to make their plight more bearable? How about a quiet prayer for a friend who is currently experiencing the sharp edge of life?

Let us carry the cross of Jesus that offers life and hope to those around us. When others start tasting and seeing life because the cross of Jesus is resting on our own shoulders, we eventually hardly even feel the weight of it anymore. The cross is only a burden when we get caught up in self-pity or when we are not a living blessing to others.

Normal

*Get insurance with G*OD *and do a good*
deed, settle down and stick to your last.
*Keep company with G*OD*, get in on the best.*
— PSALM 37:3–4 THE MESSAGE —

I love the words of the American actress Whoopi Goldberg, "Normal is just a cycle on a washing machine." Maybe normal is precisely that—a setting on a washing machine. If we all lived and behaved like the normal person on the street, we would be in serious trouble. If we should be exactly like the "reasonable person" the judicial system talks about, we would never be people who can dream "outside of the box."

The world, and especially the church, desperately needs "out of the box" people, who dance to a different beat. The ones whose lives have not fallen into a rut of predictable boredom but who joyfully redeem every bit of time at their disposal. They are the ones who discover new horizons and conquer new heights in the name of the Lord. They inspire and infuse others to progress further and higher and more courageously on the Lord's way.

Such people regard unfamiliar territory as a challenge. They thrive on courage and risks. Hopefully you too are part of this elite group of nonconformists. People like these turn the world upside down in the name of Jesus.

Desire

*For those who find me find life
and receive favor from the L*ORD.

— PROVERBS 8:35 NIV —

Robert Olsen is correct when he writes that people have a lifelong addiction to a never-ending desire for more! The popular term for this is "consumerism." According to him, it is part of human nature to constantly want more. Nobody will ever have enough. There are always more items and things to have, and we are miserable until we have it.

Many people try to find the meaning of life to escape this consumer mentality. Religion is one of the "crutches" many people try only to discover that "it doesn't work." Of course religion does not work, at least not if you want to use it as a quick solution. One thing I discovered recently is that Jesus is not in the "quick fix" business the way desire-driven people in the church see it.

On the contrary, you can only follow Him on His terms. And that requires sacrifice, going the extra mile, and even suffering. It requires a new you who decides to follow a new master. But it also brings a strange new peace that will completely baffle your mind.

Modern-Day Heroes

Prophecy resulted when the Holy Spirit
prompted men and women to speak God's Word.

— 2 PETER 1:21 THE MESSAGE —

The real heroes of God in biblical times were the prophets who challenged the existing political, religious, and social systems through speeches and symbolic actions. The reason: they saw and experienced God's vision for His people. The prophets just had to challenge the powers of the day to reform and rethink their present ways. No wonder God's prophets were often misunderstood, ridiculed, and dismissed as heretics. But they couldn't help themselves. They were instruments of God. They were in His service. His full-time calling on their lives surpassed their obedience to all others. They only played for an audience of one, whatever the cost.

Modern-day prophets are urgently called for. The ones who don't settle for the same old answers in the same old safe spiritual environments. They risk their own popularity and careers to explore God's new routes of hope. They make an impact where it really counts—amongst the poor, the downtrodden, the sick, and the lonely. They often opt to work amongst the poorest of the poor and sinners. Are you one of them?

Keep on Growing

Fear of the Lord is the foundation of true wisdom.
All who obey His commandments will grow in wisdom.

— PSALM 111:10 NLT —

Alvin Toffler writes, "The illiterate of the future are not those who cannot read or write, but those who cannot learn, unlearn, and relearn." What a challenge to remain inquisitive. Curiosity and inquisitiveness are precious qualities that God instilled in each one of us. Why is it that we lose it so quickly?

Why are our lives often so predictable, safe, and boring? Why don't we think for ourselves? Why do pastors and ministers constantly have to think on our behalf? Why do we hide behind a few Bible verses after having "received Scripture" that causes us to refrain from seeking deeper meaning from the Word and finding the actual truths locked in its pages?

When we daily discover old and new treasures, as Jesus teaches us in Matthew 13, our lives will be one lifelong adventure. Our hearts and minds will never grow old. And we will continually be surprised by God. When we continue to learn, we will keep on growing. Dare to grow a little more in your knowledge and understanding of God today, and see what happens!

Let's Go Fishing

"Come, follow me," Jesus said,
"and I will send you out to fish for people."
— MATTHEW 4:19 NIV —

I read about an American denomination that is busy raising millions of dollars to help 500 burnt-out pastors. When a clerical consultant asked their leaders why they didn't change their priorities to support the 500 most effective pastors in their denominations, the answer was rather damning: "We could never raise money for that!"

Yes, struggling congregations and clergymen need to be supported, but then it must be seen for what it is: temporary emergency assistance. When churches are artificially sustained with money rather than empowering the growing ministries of people who want to change the world in the name of the Lord, then we are missing the point. Effectiveness in the Lord's service is all about empowering believers to spread the kingdom of the Lord in a visible way. There are more than enough new champions of faith among us in whom we should invest our prayers, involvement, time, and money.

To notice them, help them, and support them is a challenge. Open your spiritual eyes for a change to see the new things that God is doing above and below the radar screens of the church. And be there!

Blessing Others

*Out of His fullness we have all received
grace in place of grace already given.*
— JOHN 1:16 NIV —

God favors His children with heavenly grace. But we may not keep it to ourselves. We are called to be a living blessing to others. The people Jesus cared for—the poor, the crippled, the blind, and the paralyzed of Luke 14, or the captives, strangers, naked, and hungry of Matthew 25—must be on our radar screens daily. They should share in our festivities.

Did you know that a mere forty-two out of every one hundred people in a country such as South Africa currently have jobs? Or that, according to a recent Markinor survey, only sixty-eight out of every one hundred households have running water in their houses? Of these, only thirty-one have a water heater. Sixty-nine households don't enjoy the luxury of a warm shower. Meanwhile, thirteen out of every one hundred people in South Africa are HIV positive. While 73 percent say that they are Christians.

Shouldn't we as Christians have a bigger impact? Aren't we supposed to be a living blessing to those around us? If God favors us, then we should share this with one another. Otherwise we are stealing from heaven by keeping all the blessings to ourselves!

Keeping Silent

*Joyful are those who have the God of Israel as
their helper, whose hope is in the Lord their God.*

— PSALM 146:5 NLT —

How can we look the other way when thirty-thousand
people die worldwide every day due to water pollution and
the serious illnesses related to it? How can we remain silent
when hundreds of people are dying in Zimbabwe due to
cholera? Doesn't it deeply affect us when global warming
is threatening the continued existence of our planet? Can
we turn a blind eye when poisonous gases are warming
our atmosphere beyond its limits? Can we remain deaf
when racist language dominates many of the conversations
around us? Dare we keep quiet when innocent blood is shed
due to senseless crimes?

Should we keep on praying when everyone around us
has thrown in the towel and started following their own
leads? Should we also surrender and give up hope? No, how
could we? The living Lord is with us, the one who says that
those who cry and grieve about all the suffering will soon
be comforted (Matt. 5). We can cry but also laugh at the
same time. Therefore, our hearts are heavily burdened, but
also light. Because the Lord is also present in the darkness
which sometimes threatens to overwhelm us.

How Far Is God?

*"My Presence will go with you,
and I will give you rest."*

— EXODUS 33:14 NIV —

"How far from us is God really, sir?" a little girl asked me recently. "Why do you want to know?" I asked. "Well, my mom and dad say I am wasting my time praying to God because He is too far to hear," she answered.

"No, He is not far. I had a conversation with Him a few minutes ago," I immediately responded. "In fact, God is always only one prayer away. All distance disappears in the exact place where you and I bow down before God and talk to Him in the name of Jesus. Then God is right there— a mere prayer away! We never have to shout, or use a loudspeaker to talk to Him, because He is not deaf. Neither do you have to use big and difficult words, or say long prayers. All God wants from us is sincerity. He is interested in the language of your heart. That is all."

"I agree, because I know that God is always close to me. It seems that my parents have become blind to His presence," the girl remarked with sadness in her voice, walking away.

Hard Work

Always give yourselves fully to the work of the Lord,
because you know that your labor in the Lord is not in vain.

— 1 CORINTHIANS 15:58 NIV —

Some people complain about how hard they work. Then I say something to the effect that hard work is not an Olympic sport that qualifies for medals. Sometimes I wonder whether some people think that hard work is somehow an achievement that earns them bonus points. Or something that others should admire you for.

I constantly remind myself of the story Jesus told in Luke 17:7-10 where He says if I have done everything for the Lord that I should have, then I don't deserve a standing ovation from Him or others. Hard work in His vineyard is a normal part of my calling. In the end, I am merely God's servant. Everything I do for God I should do diligently, without expecting any recognition. It is my life's commission to do God's will.

Hard work very often goes hand in hand with a life devoted to God. No, it is never about merit, as if the Lord should reward me if I do my share. On the contrary, it is all about gratitude on my part for the opportunity of being able to work for Him.

Investor or Consumer?

"Do not store up for yourselves treasures on earth, where moths and vermin destroy, and where thieves break in and steal. But store up for yourselves treasures in heaven."

— MATTHEW 6:19-20 NIV —

There are two types of people: consumers and investors. Consumers use up everything and everyone around them—people, friendship, money. You name it, and they use it and abuse it. Consumers can never get enough of anything. They are bottomless pits. No matter what you do for them, it is never enough. Somewhere in the future they are going to complain about the fact that you don't do enough for them. After all, they believe that you and life owes them!

Alternately, there is a small group of people who live from abundance, whom we'll call investors. They have enough, even though they have few material possessions. They are content. Investors have hope when the rest of the world is hopeless. After all, they live from the Lord's abundant treasure chambers of grace. How do you change from a consumer to an investor? Well, invest your life exclusively in God! Be content with Him. He is more than enough. God's heavenly treasure chambers overflow with grace, peace, freedom, and love. Become a daily partaker of His heavenly abundance. Then you will have more than enough. Then your cup will overflow!

Facts and Figures

"Let your light shine before others, that they may see your good deeds and glorify your Father in heaven."
— MATTHEW 5:16 NIV —

Facts and figures impress people. When thousands of people show up to listen to a well-known preacher, many call it a roaring success. I'm not against large crowds attending religious events, but when attendance becomes the definition for success in Christianity, we are in trouble. Far too many preachers are marketed nowadays as crowd-drawing celebrities. Did we get stuck in that infamous equation that bodies, budget, and buildings equals success? Why do we uncritically apply the rest of the world's definitions of success in church?

Perhaps I'm the only stranger in Jerusalem, but I'm convinced that Jesus focused more on reaching individuals, outcasts, marginalized people, and the poor than on getting people to fill revival meetings and worship events. Success to Jesus means sowing one mustard seed at a time. And mustard seeds multiply, as Jesus teaches us in Matthew 13. The real test for kingdom growth is discipleship. Crowds and audiences don't really change the world. Yes, they fill seats. They cheer, sing, celebrate, and rejoice. But the real agents of change are committed followers of Christ—the difference between fans and disciples.

Praying for Strangers

*When God's people are in need, be ready
to help them. Always be eager to practice
hospitality. Bless those who persecute you.
Don't curse them; pray that God will bless them.*

— ROMAN 12:13–14 NLT —

Do you also get dispirited when you see yet another beggar standing at the side of the road? Next time, do something better than just ignoring them. Pray for them! Yes, you read correctly. Pray for them. Dare to place that unknown beggar before the Lord's throne. And who knows, maybe you will be the only person who would do such an "unthinkable" thing as praying for them.

While you are being so reckless praying for people who "accidentally" cross your path, why don't you also dare to pray to God on behalf of the expressionless person in the car next to you. Or for the shop attendant or the lady at the cash register. Instead of constantly glaring at your watch and wishing it was your turn to be served, you can fill the time with short prayers for unknown people—people with real names and real faces. Who knows what God can do with such quiet prayers!

Darkness or Light?

*You are a chosen people, a royal priesthood, a holy nation,
God's special possession, that you may declare the praises of
Him who called you out of darkness into his wonderful light.*

— 1 PETER 2:9 NIV —

Somebody said to me that the future looks rather bleak.
"What future are you talking about?" I asked. "Do you
mean the future in three months' time? Or the one in five
years' time? We are now living the future we were so
worried about five years ago!" And yet those of us who are
living get by! Amazing! No, it is sheer grace! It is all thanks
to God! He is really faithful! God has ensured that we made
it to today! And, furthermore, He has brought the bread of
mercy right to our doorstep.

Are you without bread today? *No?* Do you have enough
blankets on your bed? *Yes?* Will you have enough bread to
eat for the next month? Definitely! Will your health make
it through today and maybe even tomorrow? Indeed! Then
why are you so worried? Why do you complain that there
is no future? This constitutes a motion of no confidence in
your heavenly Father. He guarantees that He will give you
bread for today. He, who takes care of the birds and the
flowers, will care for you. His grace will be enough for you
every day, yes, more than enough!

Bold Prayer

*So let us come boldly to the throne of our gracious
God. There we will receive His mercy, and we
will find grace to help us when we need it most.*

— HEBREWS 4:16 NLT —

John Maxwell once said that the most audacious prayer
the average person prays every day is that age-old prayer,
"Lord, bless the food that we are about to eat!" Or, like
many of us have adapted it, "Bless the hands that prepared
the food." If that has become your main prayer, then you
should say the following one as well: "Lord, help me for I
know not what I do!" Prayers are not formal recitations for
the sake of some or other tradition, or merely something I
do to soothe my conscience. Prayer is a momentous matter.
It involves personally talking to the living God who holds
heaven and earth in the palm of His hand.

Ecclesiastes 4 warns us to be careful with our words in
the presence of the Lord. We have to count and consider
our words very carefully because we are speaking to the
King of the universe every time. We should know our place
before Him. Every word that comes from our lips should be
sincere.

They must be chosen wisely! But it must also be bold—
meaning that they should be encompassed in faith. We
should trust God to uproot trees and plant them in the sea,
as Jesus teaches us in Luke 17.

"Mine, Mine!"

Don't forget to do good and to share with those in need. These are the sacrifices that please God.

— HEBREWS 13:16 NLT —

"Mine!" That is what little children say when you touch their toys. Some grown-ups still live like that. "Mine" is what they say to themselves when they see a new house, car, garment, or gadget. There is no rest to be found until that item becomes "mine." But then a strange thing happens—shortly after "mine" has been attained, the next item appears in the shop window that must also be "mine."

We live in a world that constantly creates new needs and desires in us. If we are not careful, we can become lifelong prisoners of this kind of lifestyle. That is precisely why the Bible warns us against an insatiable desire for the things that are displayed on the "must-have" shelves of life. When we become slaves of this, it later results in us only feeling good when we receive new things. The solution to this addiction? Be content with what you have—it's that simple! Find joy in the Lord and in good relationships with those you love.

Start appreciating the little or the abundance that the Lord has gracefully bestowed upon you. Thank Him from your heart for all you have.

Sleep

"I will refresh the weary and satisfy the faint."
— JEREMIAH 31:25 NIV —

Someone once told me how a pastor threw his Bible at someone who had fallen asleep in his church. "If you don't want to hear the Word at least you will feel it," he added. Maybe it was only a joke. Sleep, in fact, is a very important part of our lives. Do you sleep well? Or do your problems make you toss and turn at night? If so, the time has come for your faith in Christ to have a direct impact on your sleeping patterns.

Listen to what David says about this: "I lie down and sleep; I wake again, because the Lord sustains me" (Ps. 3:5). Rather gripping, isn't it? Trust in the Lord to deal with all your problems for a change. Then they will no longer keep you awake at night. Then you will fall asleep in the arms of the Almighty God every time.

You will no longer wake from fitful sleep in the morning; you will wake refreshed and invigorated.

Surrendering All

You, Lord, are our Father. We are the clay,
You are the potter; we are all the work of Your hand.

— ISAIAH 64:8 NIV —

One of my good friends told me of a very busy little boy who created havoc in a children's service. Later, he asked the little boy, "Who taught you to be so busy?" He answered as honestly as he could, "Sir, can I tell you a secret? I taught myself!" That was the most honest answer I've ever heard. Yes, it is indeed ourselves, and not always our circumstances, that make us behave the way we do. We teach ourselves every day to think, to talk, and to react in certain ways.

If we don't clamp down on negative things on a regular basis—like those small bits of bitterness, anger, or suspicion that all too easily find a nesting place in our hearts—we will become addicted to them before we know it.

It is not necessarily the big things that derail our lives but sometimes precisely those little things that unobtrusively get stuck in our heads. The solution? Well, we have to place our lives in God's hands today like soft clay so that He can renew us from the inside.

Auto-Pilot Mode

Live a life filled with love.
— EPHESIANS 5:2 NLT —

Much of our lives are spent in autopilot. We live detached lives. We constantly plan for tomorrow and save all our energy for that big somewhere on the other side of the rainbow. This autopilot lifestyle leads to a highly structured, "routinized" way of life. In churches you'll see this in the well-planned programs and religious events, lacking spontaneity or passion. Many people in church experience stagnation. They feel spiritually empty and numb as the world around them becomes more and more dull. They become bored, cynical, and skeptical. Nothing excites them any longer. Not even God can surprise them because they have already planned His next renewal, revival, and final return in the finest detail.

We need to attune to every moment God grants us with curiosity, openness, acceptance, and love. In this way, through our constant awareness of God's graceful presence, a deep sense of compassion can be nurtured inside us through His Spirit. It will begin to flow out of us to others. The distance between God and us, and the gap between ourselves and others, will be bridged as we become more aware of God's grace.

A Living Example

In everything set them an example by doing what is good.
In your teaching show integrity, seriousness and
soundness of speech that cannot be condemned.

— TITUS 2:7-8 NIV —

Very early on in life children learn from grown-ups that only winners really matter. First place is the most important to many parents and teachers. The academic achievers, the first team, the executive committee of learners—they usually receive most of the attention. It is really wonderful when children can develop their talents and abilities from an early age. But does the pursuit of first place create a happy life before God? Aren't grown-ups perhaps guilty of placing far too much pressure on children to be mini grown-ups?

Shouldn't children learn other crucial values in life besides winning, winning, winning? Do they often see how we as parents serve the Lord with commitment? Do they see every day that we have open hearts and open hands for people less fortunate? Are we living examples of forgiveness and love towards others? Who then gives us the sole right to endlessly complain about the "youth of today" or to refer to them as the "lost generation"? Maybe we deserve this title! The young ones merely learn from us how to do it the wrong way!

Divine Grace

Be kind and compassionate to one another,
forgiving each other, just as in Christ God forgave you.

— EPHESIANS 4:32 NIV —

The gracious heart of Jesus beats warmly for the losers of His day. Those who got a red card from the religious leaders were at the top of His gracious list.

Think about the prostitute in Luke 7. She wiped her tears from the feet of Jesus using her hair, after she burst in uninvited on a dinner where Jesus was the guest of honor. While the pious choked with indignation over the fact that Jesus forgave her sins, she heard the most beautiful words ever: "Your faith has saved you; go in peace." No wonder the religious leaders later had Him killed. They couldn't stand the fact that Jesus gave away God's kindness for free to people like her.

The grace Jesus offers isn't even cheap; it is completely free! But that is exactly what Jesus is like, even today! You are always welcome in His company, no matter how deep or far you have fallen. With Him there is always an extra portion of heavenly grace to be had! All you need to do is ask.

Into the Storm

*Grace and peace to you from God
our Father and the Lord Jesus Christ.*

— 1 CORINTHIANS 1:3 NIV —

When George Bush and Tony Blair, the two most influential leaders in the world at the time, were hot on the heels of Saddam Hussein, he was hiding in a sewer pipe in Bagdad.

When the pope and the emperor declared him to be enemy number one, Martin Luther translated the New Testament into German. That is what the heroes of the Lord do; they walk even deeper into the storm. The more fierce the battle, the more firmly they stand at their posts.

Martin Luther single-handedly faced the wandering church of his day and then chose the way of God. Contrary to everyone else, He submitted to the graceful words of the Bible. His love for God overruled his fear of people. That is why Luther nailed his 95 Theses to the church door in Wittenburg, Germany, in 1517, which finally catapulted the church in a new direction.

Henceforth, grace was once again present in the church. Divine grace again sparkled like the sun. Are you also living with God's grace? Is your faith built on Christ alone? And is the Word your only guide?

A Good Name

A good name is more desirable than great riches;
to be esteemed is better than silver or gold.

— PROVERBS 22:1 NIV —

The other day I ran into a former pastor who had been falsely accused in a scandal. Out of pure frustration he later resigned. When he asked one woman why she had participated in the gossip without ever talking to him first, she answered him, "Well, Pastor, it was such an enjoyable story to tell. It just had to be the truth!" Can you believe it? And these are the people who should have known better and lived according to the Word!

People are sometimes prepared to rip one another to shreds without batting an eyelid. The crystal-clear, biblical principle in Matthew 18—that one should talk to someone rather than about the person behind their back—is ignored in far too many religious circles.

May God keep you and me from this! May He use our words to defend the good name of other people when they are not around. May our words always frame the lives of others with honor.

The Easy Way

You must have the same attitude that Christ Jesus had.
— PHILIPPIANS 2:5 NLT —

We should have the same attitude as Christ. This is what Paul writes in Philippians. He says we should look at things with a different eye; listen with a different ear; feel with a different heart; and live from a different disposition. The attitude of Jesus Christ, which sacrifices all, should reign in our lives. Every choice we make, every breath we take, every footstep, and every heartbeat should be driven by self-denial and sacrifice.

The attitude of Christ is not just about questions regarding our career choice or our choice of friends. It's about matters relating to life and death. It's about radical cross bearing. You don't have the attitude of Christ merely when it comes to a few crossroad choices in your life. No, it is all about the question of whether your entire existence echoes the heartbeat of Christ every day.

Therefore, when you reach a crossroad with Christ's cross on your shoulders, the steep road is always your first choice. Because that is what Christ would have done. He would have gone deeper into the storm to find people who have gone astray.

Favor

*The Lord will withhold no good thing
from those who do what is right.*

— PSALM 84:11 NLT —

Let's be honest—it is wonderful to be the blue-eyed boy and to receive preferential treatment now and then. It makes you feel very special. Well, God treats all of us that way when we follow Jesus. He calls us His children. That is what Paul writes in Romans 8. We are no longer slaves who are afraid of our ill-tempered owner. We are children of the King who lives in the house of the Lord every day. He is our Father. He is close to us. In addition, He covers us with His kindness from head to toe.

God promises many times in the Bible that He will provide our daily needs. And yet most of us have cupboards overflowing with meat, vegetables, and other delicacies. Not even rising prices and high inflation have caused us to go without food or with only dry bread as a staple food. To top it all, there is more than enough food and clothing for many days to come in most of our houses.

It seems to me that the Lord is favoring us. Why then are we complaining while we enjoy so much abundance? Isn't that blatant ingratitude?

Always Near

*The Lord Himself goes before you and will be
with you; He will never leave you nor forsake you.*

— DEUTERONOMY 31:8 NIV —

There are times during your walk with the Lord that you may feel far from Him. Never forget during these "valleys" that God really is only a prayer away. Distance suddenly melts away when you call on His name. All it takes is just a little perseverance.

Isn't it remarkable to think that He has time for each one of us—for each Christian no matter who you are in the world? For Him, time is not a factor; instantly He is there to hear your prayer, no matter how big or small. Yes, our God is omnipotent and omnipresent!

Footprints

*All of you together are Christ's body,
and each of you is a part of it.*
— 1 CORINTHIANS 12:27 NLT —

Too many Christians' idea of a good life is merely the secular world view with a dash of goodness. It is just as measurable and translatable in terms of money, materialistic possessions, and comfort. "I" still comes first, even though it is covered in a Christian veneer.

World-renowned church researcher George Barna recently evaluated the general behavior of Christians and non-Christians and found there was no significant difference in lifestyle. Statistics confirm that church attendance doesn't necessarily motivate people to live more like Christ. It makes people more religious, but it does not automatically make them serve Christ better!

If only 7 percent of people in churches find the Lord, and a full 50 percent admit that they do not experience the presence of God in the church, then something must be seriously wrong! These statistics emphasize the fact that we must live radically differently if we really want to make an impact as followers of Jesus. People are the body of Christ (1 Cor. 12). You and I are the church. Church happens in any place where the followers of Jesus leave footprints.

Real and Relevant

Having hope will give you courage.
You will be protected and will rest in safety.
— JOB 11:18 NLT —

Recently I heard about a few residents at a retirement home whose only income was a meager government pension. They did not have proper food to eat. Consequently, our church committee decided in faith to pay for the meals of twenty of these pensioners for the next year. I was moved to tears that all those serving on the committee were personally prepared to help people they didn't even know.

A week or two later I received a precious note from a lady who had been one of my teachers years ago. She wrote to say that she was in her seventies and saw for the first time how real and relevant the church can be after hearing about our involvement with these elderly people who were suffering so much. And I know she is a very dedicated church member.

How can faith be practiced so sparsely in the church? We constantly hear the most beautiful sermons about faith, not to mention all the Bible studies on this topic. But where does the average Christian ever see faith in action? And even more importantly: where do they practice their faith? What story does your life tell today that will fill other people with hope?

Dignity

Give to everyone what you owe them: If you owe taxes, pay taxes; if revenue, then revenue; if respect, then respect; if honor, then honor.

— ROMAN 13:7 NIV —

Pastor Semenya and his wife's nursery school for poor children is one of our church's projects. These worthy servants of the Lord do wonderful work. But financially things were really bad at one stage. Then the Lord placed them on our radar. After the church opened the hearts and wallets of family members across the globe, the nursery school was renovated, food supplies bought, their daughter's studies paid for, and Pastor Semenya even received a second-hand car via a church member who felt it was a fitting way of serving the Lord.

When my wife and the management of our congregation recently attended church there, Pastor Semenya passed a remark that touched us deeply: "Now we feel like human beings again!"

Do you treat people in a way that makes them feel human? Do you treat them with dignity when they have been robbed due to poverty and suffering? That is what Christ expects of us. Every person who crosses your path today is God's work of art. Look carefully until you see it. Then treat them in such a way that they will realize they are special.

Never Too Busy

In repentance and rest is your salvation,
in quietness and trust is your strength.
— ISAIAH 30:15 NIV —

How many times have you phoned a call center and had to wait in a long queue? "Your call will be answered in approximately one minute and 30 seconds." Well, if you talk with the living God, you will never be told to wait your turn. You aren't told to hold because your request is being processed.

You never have to hammer on the doors of heaven to attract God's personal attention. You never have to shout to remind Him that you are there. God is never too busy to listen to any of His children. When His children wish to speak with Him, He is never busy with more important matters. The Lord does not avert His eyes when we are in a crisis.

Even though it may feel as if God isn't near, *He is*! Believe in His Word and not in your feelings and changing emotions. God hears and answers. Behind the scenes, things have already started happening because you are praying!

December

Radical Transformation

Guard your heart above all else, for
it determines the course of your life.
— PROVERBS 4:23 NLT —

Did you know that the dominant ideas in your head determine how you live? Your beliefs about other cultures, religions, your colleagues, church, and family determine your entire life. Do you really know what your own stories sound like? Take some time to consider this for a moment. But also think about the following sentence that will change your life forever if you believe it: You have to radically invite the Spirit of God into your life to transform the main stories of your life!

It doesn't help if you give your heart to the Lord but the ideas in your head remain your own. Millions of Christians have been caught in this trap. Their thoughts are controlled by stories other than those of the Lord. They still think selfish and loveless thoughts because they don't allow the Spirit to intervene. Far too few Christians live according to a brand-new story—the story of Jesus!

His story is always one in which humility, tenderness, sacrifice, and faith triumphs. The story of Jesus is radically different from the dominant themes that feature in the lives of most people. What about you? Which stories triumph in you—those you have written yourself or those of the Spirit?

God's Protection

The Lord protects all those who love Him.
— PSALM 145:20 NLT —

There are far more Scripture verses in the Bible that say God protects us *in* danger than *from* danger. The Lord does not necessarily safeguard us from all crises, but He does guarantee His presence in the midst of every storm. God doesn't allow us to take shelter in "safe harbors" all the time.

He does not automatically guarantee safety, good weather, and sunshine. He wants to teach us to walk with Christ in our storms. That is why the Bible often says that we should seek the Lord in times of affliction. He is our only rock when the storms are raging. He is our steady anchor when the winds are howling. He is present in the storm and always on duty!

When we find ourselves in a crisis, we have to use prayer as our first line of defense. We must call on the Lord, not our minister or some other prayer chain. It is always good if others pray for us during these times, but the Lord commands us to talk to Him during times of crisis. That is the ABCs of any storm survival strategy. Do it! God will give deliverance in His own way.

An Original

O Lᴏʀᴅ, You have examined my heart and know everything about me. You know when I sit down or stand up. You know my thoughts even when I'm far away.

— PSALM 139:1-3 NLT —

The Lord wants you to be yourself. He really doesn't want you to be someone else, because then you would have been that other person. As mentioned previously, a speaker recently said that when he asks people who they would like to be, more than 90 percent of them want to be someone else. If you spend your whole life trying to be someone else, then you are always going to be second best and not yourself.

Listen carefully: Until the day you die, you are going to be you! Make peace with that. The Lord deemed it fit to make you with your own unique personality, appearance, and thoughts. He artistically designed you in your mother's womb, as David describes in Psalm 139. He planned your life in great detail long before you were born. You are the grand result of a divine design session.

Thank God for being you! Live your God-given potential to the full in unique ways every single day. Serve Him with your gifts, talents, and personality like only you can. Only you can do that bit of work that the Lord created you for.

The Right to My Soul

Commit to the Lord whatever you do,
and He will establish your plans.

— PROVERBS 16:3 NIV —

"I put my soul into my work," someone told me the other day. Well, I don't think my place of work has any right to my soul. They do have the right to a share of my time, because they buy it from me. My work can also lay claim to my loyalty. But my work cannot demand all my time and my absolute loyalty. Neither can my work determine my entire identity. I am more than my profession. I have a life after hours. I am so much more than a worker at a particular place.

No matter how good my work is for me or how hard I work, the day that I leave or retire, I will simply be replaced by someone else! No one is indispensable. But with the Lord, it is the opposite. Each one of His children is indispensable in His eyes. We are all irreplaceable. That is why only the Lord has a right to our entire lives. His wish is our command!

His dreams determine our direction, and His choices are our whole lives. Therefore, we should follow Him wholeheartedly at work and also after hours.

World-Shakers

*Because of Christ and our faith in Him, we can now
come boldly and confidently into God's presence.*
— EPHESIANS 3:12 NLT —

Being mindful is not self indulgent. On the contrary, it is an inner awareness of God's amazing goodness that enhances our spiritual capacity for caring in our relationships with Him and others. We must escape our mindless routines. They often trap us in deadly habits and negative thought patterns that steal our passion and creativity. Only when we experience deep community with God through the work of His Holy Spirit does life become more gracious and enriching.

The more we realize that we are truly filled with God's closeness through the work of the Holy Spirit, the more we become aware of His extraordinary grace and the privilege of being alive in His presence right this very moment. The more we cultivate our awareness of God's grace, the more we succeed in breaking free from our prisons of negativity and cynicism. As we experience God's peace, we begin to treat ourselves and others with more grace and dignity.

As we become more aware of God's hand in changing our world through Christ, we join His band of world-shakers, who spread the good news of Christ everywhere they go.

The Naked Truth

"You will know the truth,
and the truth will set you free."
— JOHN 8:32 NLT —

Have you heard of "the naked truth"? Isn't it an interesting expression? Maybe because lies are always dressed up as something they're not. Or maybe because half-truths love walking around in disguise. And white lies are really actually pitch black. Besides, the truth is not dressed up. It never tries to hide anything. The truth is right out in the open, visible and transparent.

People who love the truth are people after God's own heart. These are people who don't need to constantly keep track of what they had said to whom, because they know they always speak the honest, candid truth. They go to sleep peacefully each night without feeling guilty about all the truths they twisted during the course of the day to suit their needs.

Loving the truth is a very precious part of our faith. To speak, think, and live the truth is the visible signature of a life of integrity before God and people. In Ephesians 6 Paul writes that the truth is the belt around our waists. It keeps our spiritual clothes in place. Is your belt properly secured today?

Friendship

*Two are better than one...If either of them
falls down, one can help the other up.*

— ECCLESIASTES 4:9–10 NIV —

Maybe you know the expression that you should write the bad things your friends do to you in sand but the good things they do should be engraved in stone. Wise words! The wind blows sand away so easily, but the wind cannot accomplish much against stone. Beware of not holding little things against your loved ones, or you may lose them. Take a back seat. Do as the Bible says: Forgive. Reach out and offer a helping hand. Be willing to start over.

When you lose a friend, you have really lost a lot. This kind of loss is immeasurable. Don't allow it to happen. A good friend is worth much more than gold. Every friend is a gift from the Lord to enrich and fulfill your life.

Never neglect your friends. Pray for them regularly and spend time with them. Make them aware that they are special and precious to you. Protect their good name and listen to their sound advice. Support and help them when they stumble and fall. Do everything in your power to be a one-of-a-kind friend.

Who Wins?

The Lord is my light and my salvation—
whom shall I fear? The Lord is the stronghold
of my life—of whom shall I be afraid?
— PSALM 27:1 NIV —

Who wins when darkness and light meet? Well, the Pharisees believed it was darkness. In biblical times, religious people were told to avoid sinners. Many churchgoers still believe this today. That is why they have so little impact for the Lord. They hide away in religious shelters and complain about the ever-increasing evil of our times.

Jesus differs radically from this fault-finding mentality. He wasn't scared of being with unclean people. Jesus wasn't afraid of sin or sickness. Learn from Jesus that light is stronger than darkness. Godliness is far more contagious than ungodliness. Paul teaches this in 1 Corinthians in terms of marriage when he says that believers should not get divorced if one's partner is not a believer. Those who should be wary are the ones who take cover in the darkness. They can only encounter God's grace when they come into contact with God's children.

The Final Score

*I have fought the good fight, I have finished
the race, and I have remained faithful.*
— 2 TIMOTHY 4:7 NLT —

How about a piece of truly good news for the hopeless? Here
it is: God has already sorted out the future in its entirety.
It is not classified information. The conclusion of world history is described quite clearly in different places throughout the Bible. Go and read about the final scoreboard in the
Word, and you will see: THE LORD TRIUMPHS! Nothing
and nobody can stop Him. Even as you read this, God is
busy establishing His new heaven and new earth.

If you do not realize every day that the Lord is winning,
then you will be lost in hopelessness. If you forget that
Christ is waiting for you at the end of your journey on earth
with a crown of righteousness in His hand (2 Tim. 4:7-8),
then you will live as pessimistically as the rest of the people
around you.

God's future is unfalteringly certain. It is described
in black and white in Scripture. Your here and now and
your tomorrow and the days thereafter are all in His hand.
Nothing and nobody can snatch you out of Christ's hand,
He assures us in John 10:28-30. Take this truth to heart and
truly believe it.

Pious Words

Show me Your ways, L<small>ORD</small>, teach me Your paths.
— PSALM 25:4–5 NIV —

Recently I watched a reality show about women competing for the hearts of a number of men. One lady, who wasn't chosen, said afterwards that everything happens for a reason. If Jesus wanted this guy to pick her, then He would ensure that it happened. Conversely, the woman who was chosen said that she had simply trusted in the Lord and that her dream had come true. It sounded to me like these women regarded themselves as passive victims of God's will. Had they perhaps forgotten that they had willingly entered into this show and actively taken part in it?

Paul says in 1 Corinthians 4 that we are joint managers of God's earthly household. Consequently we have to take joint responsibility for our choices. Maybe we too easily hide behind clichés like "there is a purpose to everything." Rash pronouncements about the will of God are dangerous. He is the Lord, and we are only ordinary people.

We should have more respect and reverence for Him. We have to learn to count our words carefully in His presence. Perhaps we should try to be more humble when we talk about God's will.

On His Terms—Part I

You can make many plans,
but the LORD's purpose will prevail.
— PROVERBS 19:21 NLT —

It's not all about you! I am referring to your faith. God does not work for you. Not even your prayers are opportunities to give Him instructions concerning what He ought to do for you and others.

Really consider this for a change, because many people walk around sulking about God. Apparently He did not help them when He was supposed to. He didn't take the illness away, or He didn't stop the crime. Neither did He put food on the table quick enough. Consequently they walk around bad-mouthing God, saying that He is not kind or that He doesn't care anymore. Well, that happens because many of us have the idea in our heads that the Lord really owes us something. We serve Him, and therefore He has to do something for us in return!

Listen, the only reason why we serve God is because He is God. He mercifully redeemed us when we were lost. He loved us while we were still His enemies. He made us His own while we were so far away from Him. That is why we serve Him. It's all about Him. We serve Him on His terms.

On His Terms—Part II

*Let us run with endurance
the race God has set before us.*

— HEBREWS 12:1 NLT —

God is not in our service; He does not work for us. We don't determine the conditions of the relationship. We should get to know God and serve Him as He reveals Himself to us in the Bible. Fortunately, our God is a merciful God. He abounds in grace and abundantly shares it with each one of us. He pours out bucketfuls of kindness over us. His rest, His peace, His joy—that is what we receive if we walk with Him.

The Lord is our only strength when we are weak. He is our resting place when we are weary. He is our hope when everything around us is hopeless. God is our shelter when we feel insecure. He is our only reason for living. He is our wealth and our rock.

The Lord is our oxygen, our breath, and our entire lives. The Lord is with us in every storm. He walks with us through every dark valley and every straight road. He remains at our side until well past the finishing line.

Use It or Lose It!

*Trust in the L*ORD *with all your heart; do not depend
on your own understanding. Seek His will in all
you do, and He will show you which path to take.*

— PROVERBS 3:5-6 NLT —

In a certain sense, faith works like the rule in rugby that states "use it or lose it." Yes, I know Christ has already given me eternal life. I believe with all my heart that He will carry me safely past the journey's end. But I also know that I can't keep clinging to last year's used-up faith. Faith is all about how I live for Him in the present.

My relationship with the Lord must have an impact on my life today. If not, it is merely "archive material." If all I have are just fond memories of how God used me somewhere in the past, I am heading for the "Museum of Deceased Believers"!

Faith means trusting Christ every day with my most precious possession—*my life*. I have to daily live with the realization that my faith is really only as alive and relevant as my latest step on God's path. Faith means holding on to Christ right now, all day long. It means looking to Him today for life, strength, provision, mercy, compassion, and His presence. It means expecting everything from Him.

Perfect Timing

For God says, "At just the right time, I heard you.
On the day of salvation, I helped you." Indeed, the
"right time" is now. Today is the day of salvation.

— 2 CORINTHIANS 6:2 NLT —

The Lord does two great things every day: He provides heavenly bread to all His loved ones (Exod. 16) and He also hands out brand-new life (2 Cor. 4).

God is on duty today. In fact, He reports on time for every day. Throughout the ages God has always appeared to help and assist everyone who calls Him by name. God is the God of today. God has many glorious yesterdays behind Him, and tomorrow there will be an enormous victory procession when Christ returns. But today is His day; it is His day for work, His day for caring, and His day for sharing His mercy.

Today is the day of salvation, as Paul writes in 2 Corinthians. He cannot wait for tomorrow, as it is too far into the future. Today God wants to share His bread with you and give away abundant life. Today He wants to change the world. Today He wants to adorn your life with His heavenly grace. Are you on time for His great plans? Or are you still lingering around, lost in yesterday?

Spiritual Traffic Jams

*The Lord has told you what is good, and this
is what He requires of you: to do what is right,
to love mercy, and to walk humbly with your God.*

— MICAH 6:8 NLT —

Nowadays you can hardly travel on a freeway without getting caught in a traffic jam, not to mention peak time, when you sit stuck behind hordes of cars. Some church members are also caught up in spiritual traffic jams. They spend their whole lives sitting at an imaginary red traffic light, waiting for the spiritual light to turn green so that they can get going for God.

Some think you have to wait for months and years for God to make His plans known to you. Until then, they sit around passively in spiritual traffic that isn't making any progress in the right direction. Such people simply talk of their intention to one day do something big for God. But they never get around to actually doing it!

Listen, God's will is a road with all green lights. You discover His plans while you are driving. You find God's will while you are living the right life for Him. It really doesn't help much if you are constantly stationary on the right road. Get going. Experience and do God's will today.

Making a Difference

*"Not by might nor by power, but by
My Spirit," says the LORD Almighty.*

— ZECHARIAH 4:6 NIV —

Recently I learned that six out of every ten people in Africa live under the breadline. And now, on top of that, the price of bread is going up due to the rise in wheat prices worldwide. Living under the breadline means those less fortunate than ourselves have to try and survive with less than $1 per day.

Jesus teaches me that I cannot look the other way when people around me are suffering. I cannot lessen the plight of the entire world, but I can ensure that at least one other person smiles due to the mercy of God flowing through me. I can pray for one person. I can visit or call one person. I can be a soft pillow for one other person. I can give one person's dignity back. I can make time to ask one person how they are doing and really listen to what they have to say.

While you trust the man from Nazareth with your life every day, He wants to entrust the needs of at least one other person to you. Are you ready? Can He trust you with one person? Or is your faith still a private matter?

Sharing Yourself

Don't forget to do good and to share with those
in need. These are the sacrifices that please God.
— HEBREWS 13:16 NLT —

Relationships require far more than just exchanging information with each other. Not too long ago I had to do strategic planning with a church council. I soon realized that few people, who had been serving on the council for more than ten years, knew very much about one another. They were actually still complete strangers who merely had meetings together. And then as a team they had to make important decisions about the Lord's work!

Relationships are not merely a case of knowing all the answers to questions like what job someone does, how many children they have, and where they spend their holidays. That is information. Real relationships mean sharing a part of your life with another person. No, it means sharing yourself. Real relationships happen when you and someone else start sharing the same heartbeat.

Relationships require you to be someone's tower of strength. It requires time, sacrifice, and honesty. And prayer on a regular basis. Real relationships always require a lot. You have to calculate the price of friendship well, because you put your life on the line for a friend. Just ask Jesus!

Moving Forward

Your own ears will hear Him. Right behind you a voice will say, "This is the way you should go," whether to the right or to the left.

— ISAIAH 30:21 NLT —

The other day somebody told me how a resident of a small town gave directions to his home. The route was complicated. The man asked whether there was a landmark to help him know if he was on the right road. "Yes," the person replied, "when you turn left at the last turnoff and go on another hundred feet, look in your rearview mirror. If you see a stop sign, then you know that you are on the right road." He was very serious. What a surprising way of looking at things but also an insightful way. Sometimes you really have to look back if you want to know whether the road ahead of you is indeed the right one.

Well, the hour glass of this year is slowly but surely running out. Which correct roads do you see when you look back over the past year? What stands out as the most significant landmarks of the Lord's love and kindness? Which spiritual lessons that you learned over the past year will be your signposts for the new road ahead? Which people served as outstanding role models for you? Whose directions are you going to follow in the future? What wisdom from God's Word is going to lead you forward?

In Their Midst

*As they sat down to eat, He took the bread
and blessed it. Then He broke it and gave it to
them. Suddenly, their eyes were opened, and they
recognized Him. And at that moment He disappeared!*

— LUKE 24:30–31 NLT —

Cleopas was upset when the women told him that they had found the grave of Jesus empty on that Sunday after the crucifixion (Luke 24:1-35). Angry and disappointed, he and another disciple started back on their seven-mile journey to their home town of Emmaus in the hot desert sun. But then a man joined them. They did not recognize Jesus at first. He should have been celebrating with His angels that day because He had finally broken the gates of death. He could have been among His disciples, rejoicing in His triumph. But on the greatest Sunday ever in world history, Jesus chose to walk with two doubting skeptics to their little village, eating a humble dinner with them that night.

Only once they sat at the table did their eyes open. Only after a day in His presence did Cleopas and the other disciple recognize the pierced hands that passed the bread to them! Jesus celebrates His triumph differently from how we do. He celebrates by lovingly walking beside people who doubt. He does this by breaking bread with them—and helping them to see.

New Humanity

For He Himself is our peace.
— EPHESIANS 2:14 NIV —

In Ephesians, Paul makes the point that a new form of humanity, a new Christian race, took shape at the cross. In His death, Christ united both Jews and non-Jews. Later Paul makes the statement that Christ reconciles people to one another and to God. According to the plan of the Father, God the Son became the Lord of peace by making a new way for people to have a relationship with God. Christ is the peacemaker between people of different cultures and races. The same Christ who brings peace between God and mankind (v. 16) also brings peace between man and their fellow man (vv. 14-15).

The blood of Christ is the sacrifice that made Jews and non-Jews into one new person. He brought those who are far and those who are near into a new body, a new humanity, a single new person! How did Jesus unite people of different backgrounds who lived in constant opposition to one another? Paul provides the answer in Ephesians 2:14. Here he states that Christ broke down the dividing wall, literally: the division between Jews and non-Jews. Why do we then constantly rebuild these fences, then?

A Sharp Tongue

The more talk, the less truth;
the wise measure their words.
— PROVERBS 10:19 THE MESSAGE —

There is the saying "From your mouth to God's ears." What this means is that what we say can become a self-fulfilling prophecy. Whether positive or negative, words are given life once they leave our mouths. "If you do not have anything positive to say, say nothing at all." These are wise words, ones we would do well to heed if we are to reflect Jesus in our own lives.

Do you remember when Isaiah told the Lord that his lips were unclean and that his words did not glorify God? A burning coal was taken from the heavenly altar and use to touch his mouth. His mouth was cleansed with heavenly fire.

After that he could openly share words of hope and life with others. Let your tongue also be touched by heavenly fire!

Begin Again

*"All who are victorious will inherit all these blessings,
and I will be their God, and they will be My children."*

— REVELATION 21:7 NLT —

Imagine you got the chance to start over; what would you do differently? According to research, most people would like to do something differently. What a pity that the story of our lives, of which we are the main authors, very often end up as failures. Sometimes our lives are so disordered and chaotic that we literally want to do everything over if only we had another chance.

Did you know that you really do have a chance of starting over on the Lord's terms? After all, you have the rest of the day ahead of you. It is crammed with unused hours, minutes, and seconds. You have a choice—whether you are going to seize it and make the best of it to glorify the Lord, or allow the rest of the day to slip through your fingers.

Don't let today be just another twenty-four hours of the week. Start by making a few small changes, then progress from there.

You and I don't have to change the whole world today. We simply have to be a living blessing in the name of Jesus to those who cross our paths. That is all.

Christ in Christmas

Glory to God in highest heaven, and peace
on earth to those with whom God is pleased.
— LUKE 2:14 NLT —

Christmas is nearly here. The same decorations in shops, the same types of music, gifts, lights, food, sentimental cards, and advertisements are seen all around the world. And, yes, also the same complaints about the abuse of Christmas.

Many people can't wait for Christmas so that they can either make money or complain about it. To celebrate or not to celebrate—that is not the question! Don't be like the rest—create your own kind of celebration this Christmas. Truly make Jesus the King! Let Him be the center and the Lord of the celebration that you and your loved ones celebrate together.

Bring gifts to Jesus this year, not the other way around. During these days, let your life be the most decorated gift that testifies to how wonderful and important He is. Let your relationships with others show how precious Christ is to you. Ensure that He is truly the substance of your days during this year. Let Him be the reason why you get up and go to sleep, why you care, why you love, and why you live. Celebrate a new feast, a feast of life. You have all the reasons in the world to do so!

Considering Others

For to us a child is born, to us a son is given,
and the government will be on His shoulders.
And He will be called Wonderful Counselor,
Mighty God, Everlasting Father, Prince of Peace.

— ISAIAH 9:6 NIV —

"Our menu for this year's Christmas lunch is bread," I was told. "That is all we have to eat!" When I shared this with someone else, the person said, "It breaks my heart!" But when I added that I have come up with a plan to provide something other than bread and asked whether he would be prepared to get involved, I got the following answer: "Oh dear, I first have to see to it that my own family has food on the table!" Without really thinking, I replied, "That shouldn't be necessary. I saw you in the restaurant the other day, having a meal."

Forgive me; maybe I was unnecessarily frank. Or maybe not, because Jesus taught me that when I notice real need with actual names and addresses, I cannot turn a blind eye. It is not enough to talk about the plight of others while sitting around a full table. All that matters are those small tokens of compassion—a plate of food here, a hug there. I know I cannot lighten the load of every suffering person but neither can I look the other way. If I do, I might not see the Lord either!

Heavenly Joy

She gave birth to her first child, a son. She wrapped
Him snugly in strips of cloth and laid Him in a manger,
because there was no lodging available for them.

— LUKE 2:7 NLT —

Merry Christmas! May these two words mean far more to you than the mere fact that they sound familiar or that it seems like the right thing to say today. May these two words also bestow upon us the peace that comes from the Lord, who came to honor us with His earthly presence.

I hope these words bring you to a halt in front of the crib, where the Christ Child first came to adorn the earth. And may this year's Christmas move you to rest at His feet. May you experience peace, even though strife is rampant all around you. May you enjoy happiness, although many people know only hatred and bitterness.

Today, tomorrow, and the day after, may you experience heavenly abundance, despite any earthly shortcoming you may suffer. May heaven and earth rejoice with you because you call the child of the crib and the cross your Lord and Master. May this be the main reason why this Christmas is a merry and blessed time for you.

Relationships Are Important

The Lord has done great things for us,
and we are filled with joy.

— PSALM 126:3 NIV —

Joy comes in small portions—like that cup of coffee you share with a friend. Or the unplanned visit with someone you meet. Life is all about relationships. Did you know that your mind was created to make decisions regarding people almost one tenth of a second faster than decisions about other things. A recent study found that when we are relaxed and not doing anything, our brain is most probably busy taking a closer look at our relationships.

The Lord created us to love. We are wired for relationships. We are designed to be able to experience deep feelings of compassion and love. Don't sacrifice your relationships in the new year for the sake of becoming a slave to full schedules, meetings, and activities. Your faith must be relationship-oriented, not task-oriented. Your faith is not all about the things that you do for the Lord but also about the relationships you build.

It is about the good things that you do for people with real names and addresses. Be there for the people close to you in the year ahead. But also be there for the strangers who may cross your path unexpectedly.

Taking Responsibility

*"Where your treasure is,
there your heart will be also."*
— MATTHEW 6:21 NIV —

I hear you say you have no other choice but to live the hurried life you are currently living. There must be food on the table; the next mortgage payment must be paid; groceries have to be bought; and the kids' school fees are due. Yes, that may be true, but in the meantime you may be missing God's purpose for your life because you don't allow any quality time for Him in your life. Your life is a deadly race to get everything done.

With feeble excuses to justify your flustered lifestyle, you drive yourself even further towards burnout and hope-lessness day after day. It looks like you still haven't noticed that your heavenly Father is looking after you. After all these years, do you still fail to realize that He knows exactly what you need (vv. 25-33)?

Start trusting in Him from now on to provide that which He knows you need. Take note not what you think you need, but on whatever He has decided! Find rest—the right kind of rest. Don't get stuck in the same old bad habits next year by living another year beyond your speed limit.

A Living Blessing

*"Give, and you will receive. Your gift will return to you
in full—pressed down, shaken together to make room
for more, running over, and poured into your lap.
The amount you give will determine the amount you get back."*

— LUKE 6:38 NLT —

The hourglass is almost empty. The fuel for this year is nearly depleted. Another successful earthly journey around the sun is almost over. Have you been a living blessing to someone during this past year? Have you conquered those damning statistics that say the average church member goes through life without ever having lead another person to Christ?

Can someone, at the end of this year, agree that your presence in their life opened up a new window to God for them? Has somebody discovered Christ as the Good Shepherd because you were walking with them in love? Well, then it has been a phenomenal year. Nothing else measures up against one lost sheep that has returned home, as Jesus tells us in Luke 15. Nothing! The return of lost items is always headline news in heaven. The safe return of every lost person is cause for a special feast in the presence of the Father. If you have given reason for joyous celebration in heaven due to just a single person, then this has been the year of your life!

Eternal Compass

The LORD makes firm the steps of the one who delights
in Him; though he may stumble, he will not fall,
for the LORD upholds him with His hand.

— PSALM 37:23-24 NIV —

New Year's resolutions are so fashionable at the moment! Everyone is turning over a new leaf. Excess weight acquired during the festive season is courageously tackled, and bad habits of the past year are discarded. What is your great resolution for the new year? How many of the previous year's good intentions did you honor? Tragically, most people don't stick to their New Year's resolutions much longer than the third week of January. Why? Well, because any decisions that don't come from your heart will not have any long-term effect.

Your convictions are like an internal compass that determines your direction in life. These convictions are the driving force that makes you get up every morning. What drives you to take on the challenges of life joyfully every day? Well, I know who gives me the strength and desire to get up every morning with hope in my heart. His name is Jesus Christ. He is the Lord. I want to make His priorities my priorities in the year to come. Whatever is important to Him will be the thing that matters most in my life during the coming year.

New Year's Plans

May He give you the desire of your
heart and make all your plans succeed.
— PSALM 20:4 NIV —

It is once again that time of the year when New Year's resolutions are made at every turn. Can you believe it! I have also made a few serious resolutions for the new year that is lurking just around the corner, such as setting aside more quiet time in my life. God doesn't compete with all the noise in and around me. I realize that I will have to hear Him on His terms in the year to come and not on mine. Consequently, I want to have more quiet time so that I may get to know the Lord better.

Another resolution: I don't want to send or answer any angry e-mails or text messages whatsoever. It is a waste of unnecessary energy to try and reason with smart alecks or those who think they are always right. Neither do I want to join the band of crazy drivers who are always speeding, only to win two minutes of time and two hours of high blood pressure as the "reward."

I want to live each day at "today speed"—one day at a time. I reckon that it is just about fast enough.

The Army of God

*If you keep yourself pure, you will be a special utensil
for honorable use. Your life will be clean, and you will
be ready for the Master to use you for every good work.*

— 2 TIMOTHY 2:21 NLT —

The new year is upon us. It didn't come down on us out of
the blue. Actually we have seen it coming—ever since last
year. Only last week we were counting down the days, then
the hours, then the minutes, and then the seconds. And now
the new year is upon us at last. Will it be a fresh, exciting
year for you? Are you going to be a living difference? Are
you going to report for duty as a *one (wo)man army* in the
name of the Lord?

It is up to you how you will live during the year that
lies ahead. Choose wisely. Every day has only twenty-four
hours. Nobody has ever succeeded in adding an hour to the
day. Buy out the available time in each day, as Paul suggests.

Opportunities sometimes cross your path in the most
unexpected ways. Ask the Lord to make you sensitive to
these opportunities so that you will recognize them and
seize each one. Pray that the Lord will give you the discernment to know in whose lives you should tarry a little
longer, for whom you should actively pray, and where you
should offer more assistance.